Peer Pedagogies on Digital Platforms

Learning with Minecraft Let's Play Videos

Michael Dezuanni

The MIT Press
Cambridge, Massachusetts
London, England

This book was set in ITC Stone Serif Std and ITC Stone Sans Std by New Best-set Typesetters Ltd. Printed and bound in the United States of America.

Library of Congress Cataloging-in-Publication Data

Names: Dezuanni, Michael, author.
Title: Peer pedagogies on digital platforms : learning with Minecraft Let's Play videos / Michael Dezuanni.
Description: Cambridge, Massachusetts : The MIT Press, [2020] | Series: Learning in large-scale environments | Includes bibliographical references and index.
Identifiers: LCCN 2019059144 | ISBN 9780262539722 (paperback)
Subjects: LCSH: YouTube (Electronic resource) | Minecraft (Game)—Social aspects. | Peer teaching. | Learning, Psychology of. | Media literacy. | Video games in education. | Computer-assisted instruction.
Classification: LCC GV1469.35.M535 D49 2020 | DDC 794.8—dc23
LC record available at https://lccn.loc.gov/2019059144

10 9 8 7 6 5 4 3 2 1

Contents

Series Foreword

Learning across the life span is more important than ever before, and with the wealth of resources and communities available online, there has never been a better time to be a learner. Learners of all ages—in formal and informal settings—are turning to online tools to help them develop new skills and knowledge, for work, school, and leisure. The field of large-scale learning engages in the study of networked environments with many, many learners and few experts to guide them.

Large-scale learning environments are incredibly diverse: massive open online courses (MOOCs), intelligent tutoring systems, open learning courseware, learning games, citizen science communities, collaborative programming communities, community tutorial systems, social learning networks, and countless informal communities of learners on platforms such as Reddit, YouTube, and fan fiction sites. These systems either depend on the direct participation of large numbers of learners in a single instance, or they are enriched by continuous improvement based on analyzing data generated by many learners over time. They share a common purpose—to increase human potential—and a common infrastructure of data and computation to enable learning at scale.

Technologies for large-scale learning are sometimes built deliberately, as in the case of MOOC platforms, and they are sometimes adapted from technologies originally developed for other purposes, as in the case of video-sharing sites. In some cases, they are used by individual learners around the world, and in other cases, large-scale learning environments are embedded within more traditional and small-scale educational systems such as classrooms and schools. They can be used to foster human capacity and create new opportunities, but they can also be used to teach and spread hateful ideologies. With a capacious enough definition of learning, large-scale learning technologies are implicated in nearly every part of the human experience in the networked world, from schooling to professional learning to politics to health care and beyond.

The Learning in Large-Scale Environments series from the MIT Press seeks to investigate, critique, and explain these large-scale environments and the various ways they are hybridized with residential learning space. Just as large-scale learning environments are diverse, our series includes books with a diverse set of methodological and theoretical perspectives, ranging from learning science to computer science to sociocultural research traditions. The series examines large-scale learning environments at multiple levels, including technological underpinnings, policy consequences, social contexts and relationships, learning frameworks, and the experiences of educators and learners who use them. Our hope is that researchers will find valuable contributions to the scholarly literature and that educators and policymakers will find useful insights as they consider how best to support the learning needs of students of all ages around the world.

Justin Reich
Nichole Pinkard

Series Editors, Learning in Large-Scale Environments

Acknowledgments

This project would not have been possible without the support of colleagues in the Digital Media Research Centre at Queensland University of Technology. At each stage of the project, I have been able to put forward ideas and receive robust feedback within a supportive community of brilliant and generous scholars. In particular, I thank Jean Burgess for encouraging me to take on a book project and for her support throughout its development. I also thank Stuart Cunningham and Jarrod Walczer for our conversations about YouTube and social media entertainment and their connections to young people's digital cultures. Special thanks go to Amber Marshall for her support in the early phases of data analysis and Edward Hurcombe for editing support in the final stages.

Several friends and colleagues have generously provided feedback on the ideas outlined in the book at various seminars and presentations, especially members of the Young, Creative and Connected research network. Special thanks go to Catherine Beavis and Stuart Poyntz, who inspired and supported me in more ways than I can count. Other scholars have also generously provided feedback on work associated with this project at various times, including at a workshop in Rovaniemi, Finland, which was hosted by Kristiina Kumpulainen, co-led by Julian Sefton-Green, and included Jackie Marsh, Ola Erstad, Barbara Comber, Rebekah Willett, John Potter, Jessica Pandya, Reijo Kupiainen, Satu Valkonen, Sara Sintonen, and Jenni Vartiainen. During the workshop sessions and through generous conversations with wonderful colleagues in Rovaniemi, I was able to bring together a number of the key elements that underpin the theoretical framing for this book.

I would like to thank the wonderful team at the MIT Press who have been supportive throughout, including Susan Buckley, Noah J. Springer, and Liz Agresta. Finally, I thank my family, both an inspiration and incredible support as I have completed this project. Together, we have had lots of fun watching Let's Play videos, playing Minecraft, and making Let's Play videos, but I have far too often had to "go to work" at my computer. Thank you for your understanding, love, and support.

1 Introduction: Learning with Minecraft and YouTube

Every day, millions of children around the world watch video game play on YouTube in the form of an entertainment genre known as Let's Play videos. How do I know this? In the past month, a popular family-friendly Let's Player called DanTDM has attracted 116 million views (Social Blade 2020a); a Let's Play channel, PopularMMOs, has had 59 million views (Social Blade 2020b); and a twelve-year-old Canadian Let's Player called KarinaOMG has attracted 47 million views (Social Blade 2020c). Although these Let's Players play a range of video games, Minecraft has been a mainstay for each of them and for dozens of other successful Let's Players. The Let's Play genre is a product of what Cunningham and Craig (2019) have called social media entertainment (SME), which is characterized by a shift in entertainment industry power from traditional media and entertainment companies to technology companies. Ofcom (2019a) shows that children in the United Kingdom now spend more time online than watching screen content on a television set, and YouTube dominates their online viewing time. In the United States, the PEW Research Center found that 81 percent of all parents of children eleven years and younger have let their children watch YouTube, and 34 percent of parents say their children regularly watch YouTube (Smith, Toor, and Van Kessel 2018). Meanwhile, what counts as entertainment on YouTube can sometimes seem baffling to adults who grew up on a diet of after-school television programming. Press reports about children and the media are replete with stories about parents who do not understand why their children want to watch other people play games (Vrabel 2017), unbox toys (Silcoff 2014), or make slime (Kois 2017). Popular children's content on YouTube is often distinctly different from children's television programming.

This book sets out to explain why Let's Play videos are so appealing to children and argues that a significant aspect of their popularity is that the videos provide opportunities for knowledge and skill exchange. I am interested in how children learn from others on digital platforms, with a particular focus on Minecraft and YouTube. This is principally a focus on the pleasures of gaming for fun, play, and experimentation and how YouTube has become a site for extending and sharing a passion for the game with others. While my previous work on Minecraft and learning has closely traced children's knowledge building with the game in classrooms and through informal learning (Dezuanni 2018, 2020), in this book, I take a broader view to gain insights into digital platforms, pedagogical practices, and the implications for learning. I focus on Let's Player practices, the videos themselves, and fans' responses to videos through commenting practices and their creative responses to Let's Play culture. The book is not about school-based learning or about how video games and video content are being used in formal education, although the book's findings have implications for how we might think about schooling in digital contexts. Rather, it is about the pedagogical relationships that are frequently central to interaction on digital platforms. Scholarship within the field of informal and connected learning (Gee and Hayes 2010; Erstad and Sefton-Green 2013; Kumpulainen and Sefton-Green 2014; Livingstone and Sefton-Green 2016; Ito et al. 2019) provides important frameworks for thinking about growing up and learning in digital times. Less attention has been paid, though, to the specifics of the peer pedagogical relationships that form on digital platforms, fueled by fandom and "impassioned learning" (Dezuanni and O'Mara 2017). In particular, there has been very little focus on how children are learning from and with "microcelebrities" (Senft 2008) on YouTube.

My goal in writing this book has been to pay attention to how children participate on digital platforms by forming close connections with other participants, including how they develop parasocial relationships with You-Tubers. As I will demonstrate, Let's Players aim to connect with fans on a much more personal level than television entertainers have done in the past. From this perspective, my focus is on the relationships that interaction with digital platforms enables among people, digital experiences, and other people in everyday life. I focus on family-friendly Let's Players in this book because I am particularly in interested in how children learn on digital platforms. While considerable scholarship has considered teens' learning with digital technologies in formal and informal settings, similar scholarship about children is still emerging. I set out to understand how digital games exist as part of broader digital ecosystems that enable children to learn from others in unique ways. I have aimed to understand something new about games, children, and learning that aligns with Papert's (1980) vision for the study of the cultures of learning that can form around computers in everyday life. Papert's argument was not that computers are inherently educational. His study, he claimed, was about how computer systems

> can be carriers of powerful ideas and of the seeds of cultural change, how they can help people form new relationships with knowledge that cuts across the traditional lines separating humanities from sciences and knowledge of the self from both of these. It is about using computers to challenge current beliefs about who can understand what and at what age. (Papert 1980, 4–5)

In this spirit, I am not really interested in asking if games or video-sharing sites are "educational" or good for learning. I have no doubt that if the right types of games and videos are used appropriately in the classroom, effective learning occurs, as demonstrated in a range of existing scholarship (Gee 2007a; Squire 2011; Whitton 2014; Beavis, Dezuanni, and O'Mara 2017; Cunningham et al. 2016). Rather, my focus is on how digital platforms become sites of knowledge and skill exchange via peer pedagogies and, in Papert's terms, how digital platforms help people form new relationships with knowledge that cuts across categories of knowledge constructed by formal schooling.

Use of the terms *platform* and *peer pedagogies* in the book's title requires some explanation. *Digital platform* is used as a metaphor to encapsulate digital services that provide much more than access to digital experiences and content, including a range of social, cultural, and economic practices. In the early 2000s, Montfort and Bogost (2009) defined the field of platform studies as a focus on the underlying architectures of technological experience, particularly the hardware systems and software that enable digital experiences. More recently, scholars such as Gillespie (2017) have placed greater emphasis on the social, political, and cultural aspects of digital platforms. I am calling Minecraft and YouTube "platforms" because they are technological systems that allow social and material participation. In addition, the affordances and structures of each individually and in concert together have implications for how people interact, form relationships, and exchange knowledge.

I use *pedagogy* in this book to describe a broad set of practices that occur in relationships between people where knowledge and skills are being shared. I draw on a history of pedagogy scholarship that refuses to reduce the concept to practices that occur only within formal schooling (Schön 1987; Lave and Wenger 1991; Papert 1980; Ellsworth 1997; Hartley 1999; Gee and Hayes 2010; Resnick 2017). I add the modifier *peer* to *pedagogies* to argue that pedagogical relationships on digital platforms often have different structures and power dynamics than do school-based pedagogical relationships. Of course, there are many nondigital out-of-school sites that aim to establish less hierarchical pedagogical relationships between young people and mentors or teachers (Sefton-Green 2013; Ito et al. 2019). My argument, though, is that digital platforms increase the number and variety of opportunities children have to learn in less hierarchical ways. Furthermore, *peer* is a useful term because it highlights how the pedagogical relationships that form on digital platforms are based not on age but on shared passions and interests. "Peerness" is actively fostered by the Let's Players I discuss and may be a construct rather than an accurate reflection of the nature of the relationship between YouTubers and their fans. Nonetheless, like the concept of authenticity discussed in chapter 3, "peerness" is highly useful for thinking about how Let's Players and their fans relate to one another.

The Minecraft "Supersystem"

Minecraft is a fascinating game, digital system, and platform to consider regarding peer pedagogies for many reasons, but I have chosen to focus on it is because it is difficult to separate Minecraft's popularity as a game from its popularity as YouTube video content. The two platforms, owned by Tech giants Google (YouTube) and Microsoft (Minecraft), have a symbiotic relationship that comes together through Let's Play videos (Arnroth 2014). Minecraft is the second most successful game in history (behind *Tetris*), having sold over 176 million copies, with 112 million active monthly players (Gilbert 2019). Meanwhile, to date, the almost 1.2 million videos tagged with "Minecraft" uploaded to over 24,000 channels have been viewed over 202 billion times (Let's Play Index 2019), easily making it the most watched game on YouTube. To place Let's Play videos in the context of Minecraft's broader digital ecosystem, or what Kinder (1991) would refer to as the Minecraft "supersystem," it is useful to consider the various ways the game potentially exists in children's and Let's Players' lives as represented in table 1.1.

Minecraft is a highly successful franchise and plays a significant role in children's everyday lives and popular culture. Available industry metrics suggest that Minecraft has been among the top brands that children have recognized in recent years (Ranking the Brands 2018). Major retail chains such as Walmart in the United States carry a significant amount of Minecraft merchandise, including everything from bedding sheets, to plush toys, to backpacks. A search for "Minecraft" on Amazon.com produces over 10,000 product results. To date, Lego has produced nine separate Lego sets and several mini figures. Minecraft-themed books have been given prominent shelf space in the children's section of major bookstores, including a range of official publications from Mojang, the Microsoft-owned company that makes Minecraft, but also by independent authors, including Let's Players like StacyPlays, who have created story worlds in Minecraft.

Although Minecraft is prominent in many children's lives, their experiences of the game and its spinoffs may be highly varied. At its most basic level, Minecraft is a digital making platform based on block construction. I provide further explanation about how it functions in this way in chapter 2. For now, I note that despite Minecraft's fundamental simplicity, or perhaps because of it, there is no definitive version of Minecraft. Even its most basic forms provide a choice of several play modes, including "survival," "creative," "adventure," "hardcore," and "spectator" modes, and levels of difficulty including "peaceful," "easy," "normal," and "hard," although not all of these choices are available on all Minecraft systems. Furthermore, Minecraft is regularly updated. In its earliest years, 2009 and 2010, the playing community provided a great deal of input into the design and development of the game (Arnroth 2014). Although fan input became less possible as the game became more popular, there is a sense that Minecraft is in perpetual beta mode, with a new update always around the corner. The game has also been modifiable since almost the beginning of its existence, and players have been able to download community-created game resources to change their play experience. More recently, Microsoft has attempted to formalize and monetize this process through the Minecraft Marketplace, but the community continues to create and distribute a huge number of

Table 1.1
Major Components of the Minecraft Supersystem, 2020

Game editions	Minecraft is available for Windows, Mac, Linux, Windows 10, Xbox One, Xbox 360, PlayStation Vita, PlayStation 3, PlayStation 4, Wii U, Nintendo Switch, New 3Ds, and devices running iOS, Android, Windows Phone, Kindle Fire, Gear VR, Apple TV, Fire TV. (Mojang 2020)
Marketplace	The Minecraft Marketplace is the official online store that sells community-made Minecraft resources for Minecraft "bedrock" edition versions, including game modifications, skins, textures, minigames, and "worlds." Players use "Minecoins" to purchase these resources to modify their game experience.
Community resources	Community sites distribute unofficial community-produced game resources for many versions of the game. Resources are freely available, although sites typically carry advertising. A popular example is the Skindex (Minecraft Skins 2020).
MineCon Earth	An annual live online event accompanied by physical meet-up events around the world and often featuring Let's Players (MINECON 2019)
Minecraft story mode	Described by its producers as a "playable television show based on your favorite game." One of the episodes features several Let's Players, including Stampylonghead, StacyPlays, LDShodowLady, and DanTDM (Telltale 2019)
Minecraft Dungeons	A separate Minecraft game produced by Mojang, built on the Minecraft platform but with its own objectives and challenges (Minecraft Dungeons 2019).
Official publications	Mojang partners with Egmont publishing to publish the *Minecraft: Official Magazine* (Egmont 2019) and a range of other official Minecraft books, such as *Minecraft Annuals* (Minecraft 2019a)
YouTube content	In addition to Let's Play videos, a large range of video content is produced on the Minecraft platform and distributed on YouTube, including machinima, animations, and "how-to" tutorials.
Feature film	A live-action film inspired by Minecraft is under production by Mojang and Vertigo productions, scheduled for release by Warner Brothers in 2022 (Minecraft 2019b)
Lego sets	Several Minecraft sets and minifigures have been produced by Lego.
Merchandise and toys	A range of officially sanctioned Minecraft merchandise and toys is available in the Minecraft shop and through other retailers (Minecraft Shop 2020).
Fiction	Numerous novels set in Minecraft have been published, including the Wild Rescuers series by Let's Player StacyPlays.
Fan fiction	A search for Minecraft on the fan fiction site Wattpad produces over 50,000 results.
Internet ephemera	Minecraft memes proliferate on the Internet.

assets for others to use. Minecraft is a product of the Internet. Its success has always been fueled by the participation of fans in its development and online sharing of resources and knowledge about the game.

Experiencing Minecraft in diverse ways is not just a consequence of how it exists as a "game." Equally important is how the game is experienced socially and materially. Today, children play games and view content using a range of digital devices and systems that make digital experiences available in a variety of ways. Mobile devices such as smartphones and tablet computers with the ability to host apps, including both the Minecraft and YouTube apps, can be used anywhere in the home, the car, shopping centers, and restaurants. "Smart" or digital televisions typically include the YouTube app, and mobile device content can be mirrored on large television screens, allowing anything viewed on a mobile device to be projected onto the larger screen. Gaming consoles like the Xbox and PlayStation, both of which allow Minecraft play, have become entertainment centers that can host the YouTube app. In this sense, the material integration of opportunities to play Minecraft and watch YouTube is extensive and varied, producing what Jenkins (2006) calls a "convergence culture." Jenkins argues this culture is not centered on a "black box" technology that integrates all entertainment forms, but is a system of opportunities on a range of digital devices and platforms that enable choice and promote a diffusion of media experiences. This means that while very large numbers of children may play Minecraft and watch Minecraft Let's Plays, there is a proliferation of choice in gameplay modes, Let's Play content, and device experience. The consequence is that children are less likely to have universally common media experiences and are more likely to be members of communities of online peer-based interest. While their friends at school may never have heard of their favorite Let's Player, they know that thousands, if not millions, of other children around the world are also fans.

The Family-Friendly Minecraft Let's Play Microindustry

Minecraft Let's Players are pivotal actors connecting the Minecraft and YouTube platforms, and given the vast range of ways the game can be experienced, they play a crucial role in defining how Minecraft may be experienced. This book's central thesis is that Let's Players are hugely popular because they provide models for Minecraft play and that they do this in entertaining and authentic ways. Let's Players are fun and rewarding to "hang out" with on a daily basis. The invitation to play ("let's play") is an invitation to share in someone else's entertainment experience and to learn alongside them as they try out new things. At its simplest, a Let's Play is a recorded gameplay session where the on-screen action is recorded as a video file and the player's commentary is recorded as a soundtrack. Most Minecraft Let's Plays are between twenty and thirty minutes long and feature designs and builds, adventures and fighting monsters, or playing minigames. Using this formula, a group of family-friendly Minecraft You-Tubers has developed what might be described as a loose microindustry on YouTube. The principal way Let's Players earn income is through attracting large numbers of subscribers and viewers who watch the advertising attached to the videos, and this rewards Let's Players through the Google AdSense system. Table 1.2 provides an overview of some of the most popular family-friendly Minecraft Let's Players.

Table 1.2
The Most Popular Family-Friendly Minecraft Let's Players

Let's Player	Number of Subscriptions	Number of Views
DanTDM	22.4 million	16.1 billion
PopularMMOs	16.9 million	13.6 billion
Stampylonghead	**9.2 million**	**7.2 billion**
iHasCupquake	6.6 million	2.7 billion
Mumbo Jumbo	5 million	1,4 billion
LDShadowLady	4.8 million	2.1 billion
Grian	4.4 million	986 million
iBallisticSquid	4.1 million	2.7 billion
KarinaOMG	**3.9 million**	**1.5 billion**
Big B St4tz2	2.2 million	544 million
StacyPlays	**2.0 million**	**813 million**
Smallish Beans	1.7 million	477 million
Amylee 33	1 million	363 million
Squaishy Quack	966,000	349 million

Note: Numbers represent YouTube channel subscriptions and overall video views at the time of writing; not all views are of Let's Play videos. The three Let's Players discussed in this book's case studies are in bold. Source: Social Blade (2020e).

Although this group of Let's Players might be described as constituting a microindustry, their impact on children's entertainment is not small, as indicated by the number of views they attract. "Micro" is used to describe how contained the industry is in comparison to traditional media industries. The YouTube creators behind these channels work in relative isolation, mostly recording in their homes; only a few have the support of a production crew. Let's Players typically record, edit, upload, and promote their own videos. Members of the microindustry have collaborated on some Let's Play series together, they sometimes appear together at conventions, and they frequently cross-promote each other's achievements. Overall, though, the industry differs significantly from the traditional media industries (Cunningham and Craig 2019). As production and distribution platforms, Minecraft and YouTube represent new dimensions in how media may be arranged to generate significant income. From their own home and more or less in isolation, successful Let's Players can generate millions of dollars of income per year (Clark 2018). The term *microcelebrity* (Senft 2008; Abidin 2018) may also be applied to this group. In addition to their large numbers of YouTube and other social media followers, many of the Let's Players listed in table 1.2 have large fan bases and are the subjects of a significant amount of attention in online sites dedicated to fan practices. As I discuss throughout the book, there is an inevitable tension between Let's Players' attempts to remain authentic and available to their viewers—to undertake what Baym (2018) refers to as "relational labor"—and the pressure to build a subscriber base, and this has implications for peer pedagogies.

Learning with Minecraft Let's Players

The obvious question to ask about Minecraft Let's Players and peer pedagogies is what kinds of learning opportunities they make available and how they make them available to their viewers. Throughout the book, I propose that the following types of learning occur when children interact with Let's Players: learning about the game and gameplay itself; learning how to act and socially interact in and around the game; learning how to make connections across various types of information about Minecraft and about Let's Players; and learning how to participate in popular culture. These are all aspects of skill acquisition that Jenkins (2006, 185) identified when he asked, "What skills do children need to become full participants in convergence culture?" As Jenkins argues, these are not trivial abilities, despite the fact that children may be applying them to a digital game. Many of the skills children develop as they participate in and around Minecraft are precisely the aptitudes they need to be successful in digital times (Resnick 2017). Furthermore, they are motivated to learn them through passionate interest, which is frequently missing from children's formal schooling experiences (Gee 2007b).

On a fundamental level, digital platforms rely on peer pedagogies for their success. No system of formal teaching or training has the ability to promote the uptake of digital platforms at the scale that Minecraft and YouTube do. Minecraft does not come with a user guide or manual, at least not in the traditional sense. New players learn to participate by acquiring knowledge about everything from how to place a block on the ground through how to build complex "electrical" circuits using "redstone." Along the way, they may learn how to play different versions of the game, how to download modifications to change their play experience, and how to keep abreast of Minecraft's updates. If they are playing with others, children negotiate social interactions, collaboration, rules of play, and decision making. Minecraft knowledge also has exchange value, which may take the form of personal reciprocity and friendship, recognition, status, and reputation (Dezuanni, Beavis, and O'Mara 2015).

To learn to participate within and around Minecraft, children do not need to watch Let's Players on YouTube, but it helps if they do. In addition, interacting with Let's Players promotes opportunities for learning as children participate in popular culture. For instance, a search for the name "DanTDM" on the fan fiction site Wattpad returns over 17,400 results, meaning thousands of young people have written stories about the YouTuber and tens of thousands of fans have read them. While DanTDM is particularly popular, similar examples can be found across the Internet of children sharing art and stories about their favorite Let's Players. Examples like this are significant because they point to the connection among fandom, peer pedagogies, and learning not just in relation to Minecraft play but as it applies to paratextual practices beyond the game. These practices also point to the forms of learning that children take part in through participatory culture on and around digital platforms. As Ito et al. (2010) explain in their discussion of "genres of participation" in new media contexts, "people learn in all contexts of activity, not because they are internalizing knowledge, culture, and expertise as isolated individuals, but because they are part of shared cultural systems and are engaged in collective social action. (Ito et al. 2010, 14). The idea of participatory culture (Jenkins 2006) contrasts with older notions of passive spectatorship and the separation of producers and consumers into discrete roles. Let's Play culture and peer pedagogies are characterized by the direct interactions and relationships formed between YouTubers and their fans. As I explore in detail in the coming chapters, other scholars have illustrated the various ways young people participate and learn with digital media in a host of remarkable and complex ways (Kinder 1991; Gee and Hayes 2010; Steinkuehler and Oh 2012; Erstad and Sefton-Green 2013; Ito et al. 2019). I aim to contribute to this important and ongoing scholarship by illuminating in detail the participatory practices that take place around Let's Play culture.

Chapters 2, 3, and 4 aim to answer the question of how Let's Players make learning opportunities available to viewers. It does this by exploring digital literacies, the Let's Play genre, and peer pedagogies in detail. Chapter 2 on literacy maintains that to understand how peer pedagogies operate on digital platforms, it is necessary to discuss the sociomaterial literacies required to participate within and around Minecraft. It also outlines the platform literacies that are relevant to the production and consumption of Let's Play videos. The chapter's final section focuses on critical media literacies and ways that Let's Players may promote critical engagement with Minecraft content. Chapter 3 on genre provides details about Let's Play conventions and Minecraft video content and how it is arranged to appeal to children. In particular, the chapter focuses on how Let's Players in the family-friendly category aim to develop authenticity through the promotion of friendship in an effort to remain recognizable to fans (Marwick 2013; Abidin 2018). The chapter argues that remaining authentic becomes a challenge as Let's Players begin to monetize their content and establish themselves as social media entertainers and as they try to vary their content. Chapter 4 locates pedagogy within the scholarly tradition that recognizes the pedagogies of everyday life and media pedagogies. It notes that understanding peer interactions helps to explain how pedagogies function on digital platforms even where audience members do not identify as members of particular communities. It suggests that friendship, trust, and emotional investment are fundamental to peer interactions and pedagogical practices, even where individuals have not met "in real life." It also argues that the continual work on the part of Let's Players to reduce social distance between themselves and their fans is an effort to remain peer-like.

Stampylonghead, StacyPlays, and KarinaOMG

The book next provides case studies of three family-friendly Let's Players: Stampylonghead (Stampy), StacyPlays, and KarinaOMG. Chapter 5 provides an overview of how case studies of the Let's Players were undertaken. It puts forward an outline of the textual analysis I conducted on the Let's Players' videos, including a selection of viewer comments. I explain how I used industry information and metrics to conduct an analysis of the family-friendly microindustry and how I analyzed selected audience and fan practices to gain further insight into Let's Players' popularity. Chapter 6 presents Stampy as the most successful of the three I look at and as one of the earliest Let's Players to gain wider attention in mainstream media, particularly in the United Kingdom. The chapter presents him as a Peter Pan–like figure whose authenticity relies on how consistently fun he is and how knowledgeable he is about Minecraft play. It draws attention to how his authenticity was challenged when he crossed over into making straight educational content in his Wonder Quest series. In chapter 7, I focus on StacyPlays, a successful Minecraft Let's Player and author of novels inspired by her Let's Play world. The chapter explores how Stacy's authenticity is based on her love of pets and animals and how her Minecraft world includes versions of her actual pets. Chapter 8 provides a case study of twelve-year-old KarinaOMG, whose family has created a successful business making content for YouTube. In addition to Karina's own Let's Play channel, she and her brother have a highly successful channel where they undertake challenges together and vlog about their lives. Her brother and father also have their own channels. I argue that KarinaOMG is the most rounded of the three Let's Players as a social media entertainer and that her authenticity relies on balancing her ordinariness as the "kid next door" and the promotion of her family's accumulation of wealth. Through exploring each of these Let's Players, I aim to provide insights into how they create opportunities for peer pedagogies to emerge.

2   Minecraft's Digital Media Literacies and Learning

To understand how peer pedagogies operate on digital platforms, it is essential to discuss the literacy practices that underpin participation on and around Minecraft. This chapter connects literacy practices with peer pedagogies and suggests participants' repertoires of literacy practice expand in and around a platform like Minecraft via peer pedagogies. It discusses the digital media literacy practices required for Minecraft digital making and other activities associated with the game, including Let's Play production, distribution, and consumption. This requires a consideration of Minecraft literacy practices on several levels, not just within the game itself; literacy is socially and materially produced both on and among digital platforms, and also through discursive and material practices surrounding the use of the platforms. Children's Minecraft literacy practices include digital making, but they also include talking about the game (Dezuanni, Beavis, and O'Mara 2015), reading about it (Stone 2018), watching Minecraft videos on YouTube (Newman 2016), and taking part in fan practices (Arnroth 2014). They may also assemble knowledge about the production of the game, its histories, controversies about the game, and issues associated with it—for instance, on the Planet Minecraft forum (Planet Minecraft 2019), potentially forming "critical" media literacies. I apply a sociomaterial literacies lens to thinking about Minecraft and digital media literacies because participation with the game involves material, as much as social practices.

The approach to understanding sociomaterial literacy practices underpinning this book is based on a model for analyzing digital media literacies across four nodes: digital materials, digital production, digital reading, and critical and conceptual understanding. I have outlined versions of this model to try to understand the relationship between social and material aspects of literacy through a digital media literacies lens (Dezuanni 2015, 2018). This work has some similarities to scholarship undertaken by Steinkuehler and Oh (2012), with a specific focus on apprenticeship in massively multiplayer online games (MMOs). They draw on Gee's work on language, activities, and identities to focus on textual, material, and contextual factors relevant to analyzing MMOs:

- Semiotics: the available symbol systems and their constructions of the world
- The material world—the relevant objects, places, times, and people involved
- Sociocultural reality—existing relationships, identities, presumed audiences, and affects, status, solidarity and shared or disparate values and knowledge
- Activities—the specific social activities being engaged in
- Politics—the social goods at stake and how they ought to be distributed
- Coherence—past and future interactions relevant to the current communication

This approach argues it is necessary to recognize both the material and conceptual aspects of digital literacy participation in order to understand how knowledge is developed and exchanged in digital contexts. If we consider the use of digital blocks in Minecraft as digital materials, for instance, we may better understand not just how they are an essential aspect of meaning making, but also the physical labor that goes into acquiring and manipulating these blocks and the value that children place on them. If we think of mining and crafting in these terms, it is less surprising when children are upset when they somehow lose their work or if another player "griefs" them—that is, purposely destroys their creations. Exploring digital production as digital making recognizes it as a material practice that occurs at a specific time and place. Digital reading has both material and social dimensions, including the reception, consumption, and circulation of digital media and associated dialogue, commentary, and analysis. Critical and conceptual understandings are assembled through digital production and reading, using framings and categorizations that become contested and normalized within particular fan communities or audiences.

Digital Making

At the most fundamental level, meaning making on Minecraft centers on *digital making*. Participation within the game itself relies on the game's features, including how participants are invited to interact with the platform's "digital materials"; its affordances, including what the platform enables and constrains; and its structures, including the game's logics, purpose, and potential. It is impossible to undertake digital making on Minecraft without interacting both physically and discursively with the game's foundational design feature, the digital block (Cisneros and Dikkers 2015, Dezuanni 2018). Depending on the computer or device that a player is using, manipulating an on-screen avatar to interact with a block requires different kinds of physical manipulation of controls: tapping, pressing, and swiping on a tablet; manipulation of a mouse or trackpad and keyboard on a desktop or laptop computer; or use of a games controller on a console system. Manipulating an avatar to achieve actions in the game, then, requires physical interaction with a technological system. All of this occurs in physical space "in real life"—at home in a bedroom, living room, or media room; in a car, bus, or train on the way to school; in a classroom or the school library at lunchtime; or at a table in a restaurant while adults are talking over dinner. The physicality of manipulating blocks and moving them around in space is a significant aspect of a player's Minecraft experience and the literacies they deploy in playing the game (Keogh 2018).

Discursive interaction on Minecraft requires knowledge of how different kinds of blocks, the foundational design or elemental "grammatical" resource within the game, are imbued with particular characteristics. Different block types can be gathered (mined) and then deployed for various purposes (crafted) in Minecraft. The dirt block is the most basic block type and can be used to build basic structures, including shelters. It can be combined with more dirt to reach higher structures; it can be used to build a fence; seeds can be planted in it to grow food; and many more things besides. Wood blocks can be mined by cutting down trees, stone blocks can be gathered by digging stone, iron blocks can be mined by digging deep into the earth or by exploring caves, and so on. Most of these blocks can then be combined with other blocks to craft implements like axes, shovels, picks, and swords. The mechanism for combining and manipulating these blocks, the crafting table, enables the player to change the meaning and purpose of blocks. Crafting blocks transforms their affordances and the ways in which they can be combined and deployed.

At the most basic level, then, playing Minecraft requires an understanding of how to gather, edit, deploy, and communicate with Minecraft blocks, the digital materials central to the platform's communicational logics. As participants become more proficient on the platform, their repertoires of practice become more sophisticated and complex. Their involvement becomes structured around particular in-game objectives or tasks, such as building a shelter to survive the night when monsters appear in the game in "survival mode." As I will discuss in greater detail, these Minecraft practices often occur alongside other players either within the game itself on a shared server, through single-player experiences where friends may share their screens with each other to show what they have been building, or to illustrate a technique. Throughout the book, I argue that Let's Play video production is an extension of this sharing practice, although on a very large scale.

Platform Literacies

I refer to Minecraft as a platform as much as I refer to it as a game because it is used as more than a technological system for individual or multiplayer gaming. It may also be thought of as a platform for the development of other players' gaming experiences. This occurs most straightforwardly as a function of the game's sandbox genre gameplay as players literally build their own and other players' in-world experiences. It also occurs on a much more organized level as independent developers create gameplay "maps" that can be downloaded and played. On another level, Minecraft is used as a media production platform for video content creation, and a larger amount of Let's Play animation and Machinima content has been produced on Minecraft for YouTube than on any other gaming platform to date (Hale 2018). Finally, the Minecraft system has always invited modification as a key attribute of its co-creation philosophy, and the "modding" community's development of the game's Mod Coder Pack (MCP) has enabled the creation of a vast number of Minecraft modifications (Minecraft Wiki 2019). Even relatively inexperienced players can benefit from unofficial modifications to change their play experience. For many children, then, interacting with Minecraft's features, affordances, and structures includes going beyond interaction with "the game" to include interaction with online repositories of game maps, modifications, and video-based storytelling. It is useful to think of this as a set of platform literacies because they involve overlapping and often interdependent repertoires of practice:

1. *Gameplay*—interacting with the Minecraft system as a game

2. *Video production*—recording one's own gameplay or using the game to create new content, for instance, Minecraft Let's Plays

3. *Gameplay design*—using the Minecraft system to design one's own and other players' experiences of the game

4. *Modification*—changing the gameplay experience by using other people's maps, textures, or other mods or by creating one's own mods.

Platform literacies, as they apply to Minecraft, involve sociomaterial practices across both hardware and software. The theorization of platforms has tended to privilege the material aspects of computer technologies over user experience, and there is a legacy within some strands of scholarship that continues to consider platforms as the nuts and bolts of technological experience. The field of platform studies as established by scholars such as Montfort and Bogost (2009) focuses on the underlying architectures of technological experience. For instance, in their book about the Atari video computer system, they argue:

> The Atari Video Computer System (or VCS, a system also known by its product number, 2600) is a well-defined example of a platform. A platform in its purest form is an abstraction, a particular standard or specification before any particular implementation of it. To be used by people and to take part in our culture directly, a platform must take material form, as the Atari VCS certainly did. This can be done by means of the chips, boards, peripherals, controllers, and other components that make up the hardware of a physical computer system. The platforms that are most clearly encapsulated are those that are sold as a complete hardware system in a packaged form, ready to accept media such as cartridges. The Atari VCS is a very simple, elegant, and influential platform of this sort. (2)

Montfort and Bogost (2009) go on to explain that it is also useful to consider the operating system and programming languages sitting on top of a platform, software, and aspects such as controllers and video cards. They acknowledge that digital media studies have addressed the cultural relevance of software that runs on platforms and that platform studies may be undertaken from a cultural perspective, but they argue that "only the serious investigation of computing systems as specific machines can reveal the relationships between these systems and creativity, design, expression, and culture" (3–4).

This focus on technological architectures has partially given way to a focus on the sociocultural implications of technologies. For instance, the use of the term *platform* within social media—by social media companies themselves and by scholars—has placed greater emphasis on the social, political, and cultural aspects of the use of media technologies (Gillespie 2017). In this book, I draw on Hartley's (2009) theorization of Web 2.0 services as "enabling social technologies" to explore the technological and social aspects of digital platforms, particularly Minecraft and YouTube, and to consider them in an expanded sense. Hartley theorized that YouTube and similar Internet technologies are "enabling social technologies" for generating and sharing knowledge. He compares Internet-based technologies with older broadcast systems characterized by established expertise, control, regulation and one-way communication and says:

> It is now possible to look for an *enabling social technology*, with near ubiquitous, and near universal access, where individual agents can navigate large-scale networks for their own purposes, while simultaneously contributing to the growth of knowledge and the archive of the possible. (Hartley 2009, 133, emphasis in original)

When viewed as enabling social technologies, Minecraft and YouTube can be considered as platforms that involve a range of sociomaterial literacy practices and function as sites of knowledge building and exchange. In this context, platform literacies entail the ability to work within and across platforms to assemble resources for oneself but also for others. There is a significant benefit to thinking beyond Minecraft as "a game" or primarily as a technological platform. An account of the ways the platform is used on its own, or in combination with other platforms, in many aspects of young people's social and community-based lives has the potential to reveal the richness of children's engagements with it. A socially inclusive approach enables a consideration of children's Minecraft involvement across various aspects of their lives as gamers, designers, builders, content consumers, content creators, readers, and critics. Such an approach decenters Minecraft "the game" from being the exclusive object of analysis to allow consideration of a range of social and community-specific activities and practices mediated by platforms.

Minecraft's Everyday Digital Literacies

Although the platform metaphor provides important insights into the locations of children's complex Minecraft literacy practices, it is necessary to outline a more complete introduction to the various ways Minecraft is available as popular culture and through meta-narratives in children's everyday lives. Complex children's entertainment ecologies have emerged as new media forms. In 1991, Kinder recognized the sophisticated relationship forming among "Saturday morning television," movies, and platforms like the Nintendo Entertainment system as becoming "primary models for the child's discursive repertoire" for consumption and story-based play:

> Television and video games teach children to recognise and recombine popular narrative genres and thereby facilitate intertextual reenvoicement. We can only speculate on what kinds of narratives will be generated by such reenvoicements; but already metanarratives like *The Arabian Nights* and *À la recherche du temps perdu* are being succeeded by proliferating supersystems such as *Super Mario Brothers*, *Back to the Future*, and *Teenage Mutant Ninja Turtles*—with all of their protean sequels, adaptations, and marketing spinoffs. (Kinder 1991, 23)

Using Kinder's term, Minecraft may be thought of as a "supersystem" and a primary model within children's discursive repertoires in everyday life. Minecraft has enjoyed a highly visible presence in children's lives since the mid-2010s, at least in societies where the Internet and digital devices are widely available. It is not too far-fetched to suggest Minecraft play has had a greater impact on children's social and cultural experiences than most other popular cultural practices in recent years. Playing with Minecraft's digital blocks has become a shared experience for millions of children and represents perhaps the first time in history so many children have had the means to create and share on a digital platform on such a massive scale. I am not suggesting digital making has become children's only activity on digital platforms; however, it is a significant activity in children's culture. In addition to Minecraft, digital making is now common across a range of other digital games and experiences, including Roblox (Roblox Entertainment 2005), Terraria (Re-Logic 2011), aspects of Fortnite (Epic Games 2017), and of course Lego (both physical and digital blocks). Furthermore, the circulation of content created on these platforms on YouTube has emerged as a major alternative to television as an entertainment source.

Children's opportunities to participate in the Minecraft supersystem are indicative of their broader opportunities to take part in digital culture in a variety of ways in daily life. Research has established that children living in postindustrial societies engage with digital media every day for significant amounts of time (Livingstone 2002) and in a variety of ways (Marsh 2004; Erstad 2011); that their associated literacy practices are often sophisticated (Ito et al. 2010; Lankshear and Knobel 2011); and that digital media provide a range of opportunities for learning (Gee 2010; Ito et al. 2019). Underlying these strands of scholarship on children and young people's digital lives is recognition of a great deal of variety in participation with digital media. There is a justified suspicion of the notion of the "digital native" (Selwyn 2009; Brown and Czerniewicz 2010) who has an inherent or "hardwired" affinity with technology and acknowledgment that children and young people invest time in participating with digital media in a variety of ways for a variety of purposes. In the US context in the 2000s, Ito and colleagues (2010) established that young people take part in "genres of participation" with digital media, committing various amounts of attention to different types of activity. Young people, they argued, often "hang out" in digital spaces in casual ways; they "mess around" when they get a little more serious about their digital activities and "geek out" when they develop a specific passion and commit to pursuing a particular digital activity. Researchers have also argued that while children's digital entertainment sometimes seems trivial to adults, there is significant complexity in the engagements that take place with digital media. As Lange (2014) suggests, "while some parents and educators see what happens on YouTube as frivolity, in fact, kids are exhibiting an awareness that they must have the skills to use new technical tools in order to self-actualize and achieve visible personhood among heterogeneous, networked publics."

The literacies associated with digital participation are multilayered. As I have already suggested, on one level, digital participation involves interactions with various digital materials. Lankshear and Knobel (2011) argue, for instance, that "new literacy" theories recognize "the production and exchange of multimodal forms of texts that can arrive via digital code as sound, text, images, video, animations and any combination of these" (28). Digital materials are applied in specific social and cultural contexts for a variety of purposes and often as an aspect of participation in a specific community (Ito et al. 2019). The codes and conventions of participation in particular online or digitally based communities matter a great deal as to what counts as knowledge in the community; the kinds of spoken, written, and visual languages that become circulated; and the ways in which participation is rewarded, ignored, or refused (Baym 2010, 77).

Digital technologies have also become central to children's lives as they are used across what Edwards (2013) refers to as "converged play," or the merging of play across digital and nondigital environments. As already noted, Minecraft play may take place in nondigital as well as digital ways. Children's literacy practices with Minecraft across the converged experience of online and offline boundaries may be considered an extension of their literacy practices in everyday life. In his theorization of "media life," Deuze (2012) suggests individuals are constantly constructing their online and offline lived experiences and that separating online or media experience from "real life" makes little sense:

> Media life, in this context, can be seen as a perspectival attempt to bridge the gap between the supposed nowhere of media and somewhere of life. The places we inhabit, both physical and virtual, are not just temporary assemblies of people and things in a specific place, nor should they be considered to be exclusively disembodied practices existing somewhere in cyberspace. (42)

One way to consider "media life" and "converged play" in more detail is via Klastrup's (2009) concept of "worldness." According to Klastrup (2009), "worldness is the feeling of presence in a world, immersion but also membership in a community, and the ability to manipulate and navigate the world." In her discussion of the game Everquest (Verant Interactive 989 Studios, 1999), she suggests it is necessary to study social interaction and engagement with other instances of the game beyond the online world:

> If I am to define the "worldness" of this particular game world, it includes both the experiences of being *in-the-world* (immersion and presence), but also the experience of the malfunctions *of* the world; and the shared experience of juggling both the reality and un-reality of the world, as well as the experience of the world as it is presented in all the many websites on and stories *about* the world. (Klastrup 2009, emphasis in original)

In this context, "Worldness" provides a framework for thinking about the porous boundaries between online and offline media experiences. While Klastrup's analysis relates specifically to virtual game environments, the implication of her approach is that all digital platforms provide opportunities for online and offline lived experience. An online environment can be experienced as both a fiction and a lived reality of shared practice, including a wide range of offline activities associated with this online participation, including talk, negotiation, sharing, and physical play. Separating online and offline activities makes little sense as participants often experience activities across digital and nondigital boundaries. Klastrup (2009) suggests, "In computer-mediated universes like these with all the options of interaction presented to us, we can no longer distinguish between fiction and reality, and it is the constant challenge of this boundary that makes these worlds such fascinating places to live in and talk about."

Squire (2011, 8) suggests that effective games are "possibility spaces": "games are fun because they provide new problems to solve. We stop playing them when we get bored—when all the learning is done." In addition, Squire (2011) writes that as "possibility spaces," games are deeply social and collaborative and that mentoring is a crucial aspect for being successful in many games, particularly in massively multiplayer games, which leads to shared problem solving. Squire's study of Apolyton University shows how complex and formalized knowledge sharing and collaborative problem solving in games can become (Squire 2012). Apolyton University was developed by heavily invested Civilization (MicroProse 1991) players, complete with course listings (2012, 15). He says, "Apolyton University is inquiry- and interest-driven, seeking to transform game-playing practices, generate new knowledge, and . . . transform the game itself" (2012, 14).

Gee (2007a) has also convincingly argued that digital games have particular implications for literacy and learning. Gee's central thesis is that "good" games are structured in ways that promote effective learning and that if a game cannot be learned well, it will not be successful (Gee 2007b). By this, he means game structures and the ways they present goals and challenges reward players in sophisticated ways that resemble good learning principles. Gee also argues that the literacies of gaming and gameplay expose the dynamism of literacies related to digital games because players contribute to the production of meaning in "productive" ways (135). He writes, "At some level, to play a game successfully, gamers must think like game designers; they must at least think about how elements of game design work to help or hinder their goals as players" (2007, 135).

Gee also argues that digital games are particularly rich sites for the development of "affinity spaces," which become rich and supportive spaces for learning centered on shared passions or sets of practices (Gee 2007a;

Gee and Hayes 2012). Building on the theory of communities of practice (Wenger 1998), Gee and Hayes (2012) outline eleven elements that tend to be common within affinity spaces:

1. A common endeavor, typically a passion, brings people together. This is more important in the community than other identity markers such as race, class, age, gender, or disability.
2. They are not segregated by age.
3. People of all ability levels share a common space.
4. Everyone is able to produce materials, not just consume.
5. Content is transformed by interaction—for instance, through people making new things.
6. The development of both specialist and broad, general knowledge is encouraged, and specialist knowledge is pooled.
7. Both individual and distributed knowledge are encouraged.
8. The use of dispersed knowledge is facilitated.
9. Tacit knowledge is honored and explicit knowledge encouraged.
10. There are many different forms of participation and different ways to participate.
11. There are many different routes to status.

It is not difficult to map Minecraft practices onto these affinity space traits, and in many respects, this book is a discussion of how playing in and around Minecraft takes place in affinity spaces. However, the book also challenges some of the underlying assumptions about affinity as it explores the pedagogical processes that play out around Minecraft play and the consumption of Minecraft content on YouTube.

Performative Literacies

From a literacy theory perspective, the considerations of Minecraft I have outlined exemplify the need for an expanded account of literacy practices in digital contexts. This becomes even more evident through a consideration of the material literacies of digital making and associated activities. Digital literacy practices are material because they require physical interaction with a device, devices are used in real time and space, and digital materials are not trivial simulations but have social and economic value "in real life" (Dezuanni 2015, 2018). Fundamental to teasing this out in more detail is the notion that the "text" has limitations as an explanation for meaning production and how participation occurs in and around digital platforms. It is virtually impossible to analyze Minecraft as a text and consider its use as textual engagement.

The so-called material turn in cultural scholarship is underpinned by posthumanist accounts of the status of individuals in relation the material world around them. These accounts draw attention to the limits of humanist scholarship on the basis that it insists on the primacy of humans in the production of meaning and agency (Latour 2007; Barad 2003; Bennett 2010). From a sociomaterialist perspective, texts are not produced and circulated by human actors, but are assembled in concert with technologies. N. Katherine Hayles, for instance, maintains that the idea of the "text" is fundamentally limiting, suggesting the alternative "work as assemblage" (Hayles 2003, 279). Hayles arrives at this position through an interrogation of the sociomaterial practice of what she refers to as human-computer coauthorship. She writes that digital reading and writing are no less material than the processes associated with paper-based literacies; the practices merely involve different material processes. Karen Barad (2007) draws on Judith Butler's work on performativity to maintain that where meaning is understood in humanist sociolinguistic terms, through representationalism, it fails to account for materiality. She says "the move toward performative alternatives to representationalism shifts the focus from questions of correspondence between descriptions and reality (e.g. do they mirror nature or culture?) to matters of practices, doings and actions" (2007, 135).

A sociomaterial, performative approach makes a lot of sense when exploring Minecraft literacy practices because so much of what is exchanged includes practices, doings, and actions, not just representational processes. Learning to play Minecraft involves much more than learning Minecraft's features, affordances, or the game's particular design practices. Being a Minecraft player requires physically moving through space, creating structures, and interacting with others within the constraints of what is possible on the platform in terms of what the software allows and what is possible on the device or computer in use. It also includes social and material practice through converged play, and this has implications for becoming a "Minecrafter" in more general terms. In this sense, for children heavily invested in Minecraft, acquiring and deploying Minecraft literacies and knowledge may become central to how they present themselves to the world, particularly to their real and imagined peers.

Critical Media Literacies

The final literacy layer I consider in this chapter focuses on the conceptual resources children assemble to respond to Minecraft and associated YouTube content through critical thinking. As they take part in peer pedagogies, children potentially learn about Minecraft and YouTube in abstract, conceptual, and creative ways. Buckingham and Sefton-Green (1994) argue that children develop critical dispositions toward popular culture as they discuss their media experiences in less familiar and more abstract ways. Drawing on Vygotsky's (1986) work, they make a distinction between "spontaneous," or everyday, media and popular culture knowledge, which may be developed tacitly through general engagement, and more "scientific" or abstract knowledge. Buckingham and Sefton-Green's argument is that media literacy education provides opportunities for the development of abstract knowledge, because it allows individuals to develop critical distance from their own media consumption and to apply more formal language to analysis to assist the process of making critical discussion more abstract and generalizable.

For Buckingham and Sefton-Green and other media education advocates, critical media literacies are essential for a conceptualization of literacy because they enable a response to the ways in which communication occurs within contexts imbued with sociomaterial power relations. In their discussion of literacies in new technologies in schooling, Durrant and Green (2000, 98–99) argue for a three-dimensional consideration of literacy: the operational, cultural, and critical dimensions of literacy. The critical, they note, "draws in explicit consideration of context and history, and also of power" (99). They suggest students need "not only to be able to use such resources and to participate effectively and creatively in their associated cultures, but also to critique them, to read and use them against the grain, to appropriate and even re-design them" (100). One strand of this book, then, considers if peer pedagogies promote scientific knowledge about Minecraft, in addition to spontaneous knowledge about the game. More abstract or conceptual knowledge about Minecraft might include knowledge about platform affordances (technological knowledge); institutional knowledge about who owns the platforms and how they generate revenue from them, including through merchandising; knowledge about audience and for whom particular kinds of content are produced; or what it means to be a fan within a particular community. Attention may also be paid to how things are portrayed and controversies associated with particular content, and it may include developing genre knowledge—for instance, of what a Let's Play video typically includes.

Children may make their way to abstract knowledge about Minecraft in several ways. There are different avenues for thinking about the industrial context in which Minecraft is made. Official Minecraft books establish a narrative about the game's parent company, Mojang, and Minecraft's development history, including its "mission" as a company (Mojang 2019). A host of YouTube videos made for children focus on Minecraft's development history, including commentary about why particular changes have been made to the game (Kwebbelkop 2019; Minecraft 2011; AntVenom 2019), providing models for how to talk about the game in a critical way. The game's broader production context may also be the topic of conversation among children. Willett's (2018) study of children's responses to commercial games industries suggests that families are an important mediator for games industry knowledge, leading to various levels of knowledge about commercial practices and games. At the more abstract end of the continuum of knowledge among Willett's participants, one nine-year-old expressed concern for the future of Minecraft following Microsoft's purchase of parent company Mojang. He is able to articulate sophisticated ideas about the threat to Minecraft in terms of his perceptions about what Microsoft might do to Minecraft, what platforms the game might be available on, and the diminishing role of the game's original creators (Willett 2018). Let's Players also sometimes provide models for reflective and critical commentary about Minecraft. For instance, when popular Let's Player Stampy (chapter 6) decided to curtail production of videos for his Lovely World series, he posted a video (stampylongnose 2018c) explaining that changes to Minecraft made it difficult for him to produce videos on his Xbox 360. Suggesting "Minecraft for me isn't the same as what it used to be," he goes on to discuss technical details about changes to Minecraft due to Microsoft's focus on the "bedrock" edition of the game, leading to less support for other versions. (Chapter 10 expands this discussion of Stampy's critical disposition in the context of a discussion of media literacy and digital platforms.)

As Buckingham and others have pointed out (Buckingham, Graham and Sefton-Green 1995; Gauntlett 2015), creative practice in itself may lead to critical and conceptual understandings. For instance, players who see how others have used Minecraft in a range of creative ways realize the potential to develop abstract understandings of Minecraft's capabilities and limitations. Creative practice also enables individuals to experiment with various representations that may provide opportunities to develop a critical orientation toward media production (Gauntlett 2015). In this regard, it is interesting to consider the role that "skins" play in Minecraft. An avatar's skin provides an opportunity for players to introduce a version of themselves into the game, and within games studies, there has been substantial focus on the relationship between the construction of avatars, player identity, and performativity (Walkerdine 2006; Keogh 2018).

The problem of Minecraft's "Steve" illustrates how players have an opportunity to confront the game's underlying limits and to play around with new identities, with at least some potential for developing a critical orientation toward the game. In early versions of Minecraft, the only avatar available was the male-gendered "Steve." The game's original designer, Notch (Markus Persson), created controversy in a 2012 blog post, "Gender in Minecraft," when he argued, "The human model is intended to represent a Human Being. Not a male Human Being or a female Human Being, but simply a Human Being" (Persson 2012). He clarified his position saying that although the mesh model is called "Steve," this name stuck only after he jokingly gave the model that name as an alternative to "Minecraft guy." It was not until 2015 that players were provided an alternative to play as the more gender-neutral "Alex" in the game. The problem of having to play as the generic Steve was quickly overcome in the game's modding community where a vast range of new skins became available, for instance, in "The Skindex" (Minecraft Skins 2019), an online site where hundreds of thousands of alternative skins for "Steve" are freely available. This unofficial site is example of one of hundreds of modification sites that quickly popped up around the platform. It is possible for players to create their own skin on the site using the online editor and to upload and share these, which enables creative input into the game in a way not possible in the game itself.

From a media education perspective, the ability to modify a skin provides the potential for players to question Steve's appearance and intervene to provide alternatives. On one level, this seems to provide the opportunity for a critical and creative response to the game that potentially develops knowledge around issues of gender and representation. Jenkins (2006) suggests, for instance, that participating in media culture through modification and remixing may lead to a more active relationship with media culture. There are limits to the extent to which it is possible to modify an avatar, though, depending on the technological system being used because modification is easier on a computer than on a touch screen device. Player knowledge and skill also matter because less experienced players are unlikely to know how to upload new skins. Furthermore, as Buckingham (1998) writes, it is difficult to know the extent to which modification, or even parody and satire related to media culture, leads to in-depth or analytical knowledge without explicit dialogue around these activities. One of the objectives of this book, then, is to explore the extent to which Let's Players introduce reflective accounts into their gameplay narration. As I will show, a particularly interesting aspect of Let's Play production is that recorded commentary is sometimes explicitly self-reflexive, and this sometimes leads to the introduction of language that frames Minecraft play in abstractly "critical" terms.

In this chapter, I have argued that understanding Minecraft Let's Play videos and peer pedagogies requires an understanding of the game's features, structures, platform affordances, and the ways these are taken up as sociomaterial literacy practices in everyday life. At the most fundamental level, this includes an understanding of digital making as block construction play and how this occurs on different devices. However, it is not enough to focus on the game's textual and interactional elements, because playing in and around Minecraft involves performative practices, doings, and actions, not just representational practices. Understanding sociomaterial performative practices provides insight into how Let's Players appeal to viewers to reduce social distance between themselves and their fans. In addition, it is not sufficient to focus on Minecraft as a game. It is necessary to think about the platform literacies associated with the game that involve overlapping and often interdependent repertoires of literacy practices—for example, gameplay, gameplay design, in-game video production, and modification.

It is also necessary to understand how Minecraft and Let's Play videos fit within children's everyday media lives as they participate in the production and consumption of Minecraft. Finally, the opportunities children have to develop critical digital media literacies as they play Minecraft and watch Let's Play videos is of interest because they draw attention to how children are placed within sociomaterial power relations. As I outline in more detail about Let's Play videos and peer pedagogies in the following chapters, I will return to these various aspects of literacy to provide insight into the relationship between Let's Players and the communities that develop around them.

3 The Let's Play Genre, Microcelebrity, and Learning

YouTube's rise as a children's entertainment platform has included the development of several new genres of entertainment, including Let's Play videos. In the past few years, it has become as likely for children to watch Let's Plays or other new genres such as unboxing videos or Machinima on YouTube as it is for them to watch television (Ofcom 2019b. As Burgess and Green (2018) show, YouTube has become the primary source of video-based entertainment and information. This chapter discusses Let's Play video's unique characteristics and argues that the genre appeals to children at least partly because of its promotion of peer pedagogies. The call to play, literally "let's play" together, is both an invitation to hang out and have fun and to learn how to play in new ways. Chapter 4 discusses the pedagogical processes at work in Let's Play videos in detail, but for now, it is important to note that Let's Play videos are a unique form of entertainment that allows children to connect to knowledge in new ways, and this has implications for learning. The Let's Play genre provides children with opportunities to interact with video game content as they watch and listen to other players' interactions with video games. It also allows them to interact with video gamers as celebrities who seek to reduce the social distance between themselves and their fans in an attempt to remain authentic. This creates opportunities for peer pedagogies because knowledge is potentially shared in Let's Plays with a flatter pedagogical structure than children often experience when engaging with new knowledge. This process is reinforced by the genre's conventions and the ways in which Let's Players invite fans to interact with them.

Let's Plays as Entertainment

Let's Plays have become one of YouTube's most successful genres, and the production of Minecraft videos has proved to be lucrative for some You-Tubers. Industry metrics suggest a group of family-friendly Minecraft Let's Players have had a significant impact on YouTube. These Let's Players record themselves playing Minecraft (and other games) and have developed what might be considered a YouTube-centered microindustry whose main audience consists of children from about four to twelve years of age. The *New York Times* reported in 2015 that eight to ten Let's Players were earning over $1 million a year creating Minecraft content for YouTube (Wingfield, 2015), and in the years since, a significant number of Minecraft Let's Players have launched successful careers across both family-friendly and more mature content. Many of the Social Blade top fifty YouTube games channels have at some stage featured Minecraft Let's Play content.

The Let's Play genre was not the first example of the successful adaptation of digital game content for YouTube. Machinima, animation created using video games engines, has also been a highly successful YouTube genre, created at least in part as a form of "fanvid" production (Ito 2011). Before appearing on YouTube, video game "walkthroughs" or "strategy guides," showing players how to complete games, emerged in the 1990s in magazines, and later on fan-created websites (Consalvo 2003). In contrast to walkthroughs, which can be highly didactic (Niemeyer and Gerber 2015), Let's Play videos are typically less focused on directly providing how-to information and are more focused on immersion and gameplay fun. Nor are Let's Plays principally a venue for the creation of narrative content. Glas (2015) argues that unlike Machinima, which uses digital gameplay as a mode of production for storytelling, Let's Plays do not aim to create stories per se. A significant part of the appeal of Let's Plays is that the recorded commentary is often humorous and potentially informative and, according to Glas (2015), an experience of vicarious play through ludic immersion. Therefore, watching a Let's Play video is more like watching over a friend's shoulder as he or she plays a game and having fun in a social setting in which a friend's gameplay fun is your own fun. In this sense, Let's Plays reflect the social nature of most videogame play. As research suggests (Provenzo 1991; Gee 2007a; Steinkuehler and Oh 2012), video gameplay has always included a deep social dimension and has therefore been a peer-based activity. Generations of children and young people have taught each other how to play video games, just as they have taught each other how to play games in nondigital spaces.

The symbiotic relationship between Minecraft play and the consumption of Minecraft Let's Play videos means children frequently both play Minecraft and watch Minecraft play. In this sense, Let's Plays are deeply paratextual to the games in which they are produced (de Rijk 2016); they are a key part of the Minecraft supersystem discussed in chapter 2. However, the appeal of Let's Play videos goes beyond the audience's desire to consume the original game concept in new ways. As de Rijk argues, they also rely on the performance characteristics and the unique style of the Let's Player presenting the video. Let's Players aim to develop a relationship with their viewers that opens up opportunities for peer-based pedagogies. Gilman (2014) argues that Let's Play videos constitute a form of remediation, removing interactivity from gameplay. That is, they allow viewers to enjoy gameplay without having to interact with the game themselves. This is an important observation because it draws attention to the significance of the work Let's Players undertake to repurpose video games to create a new form of entertainment. Much of the pleasure of watching Let's Plays is listening to the Let's Player's commentary, including that person's constructions of unique narratives, comments about the game, and disclosure of personal information while playing.

Let's Play Conventions

As a relatively recent genre, there is little research to draw on about Let's Play conventions, so in this section, I combine the small amount of available literature with my own descriptions of the typical features of the genre. In the most straightforward sense, Let's Plays are video recordings of digital gameplay as it occurs, created by the Let's Player herself. Burwell and Miller (2016) suggest, "As a hybrid of digital gaming and video, [Let's Plays] feature gameplay footage accompanied by simultaneous commentary recorded by the player." They suggest that in addition to merely recording gameplay, the player may also aim to promote, review, critique, or satirize a game. Often the recordings are of single-player gameplay, but it is also common for Let's Players to collaborate with other players to record their shared play experience. Recktenwald (2014) argues that Let's Play videos are part of a tripartite relationship between the Let's Player, the game, and the YouTube audience. He draws on Goffman's participation framework to demonstrate how Let's Player commentary aims to establish a connection to the audience as an interactional practice (2014, 40). The main appeal of watching Let's Play videos is attraction to the Let's Player's personality, which is established through commentary. In the case of Minecraft gameplay, commentary typically displays at least some elements of gameplay expertise.

Minecraft Let's Plays are typically episodic or contribute to a series of thematically aligned videos. Popular Let's Players often develop more than one series at a time, with each series focused on a particular narrative, task, theme, or game. The most common forms of Minecraft Let's Play content are "builds," involving the design and creation of new buildings and structures; "adventures," which often involve travel to a new part of the world, a new "biome," or exploring caves for resources; "challenges," which may be set by the Let's Player as a personal challenge or the Let's Player's fans; and "minigames" created in-world by the Let's Player for others to play or created by the fan community for the Let's Player to play. Other content typically produced by Let's Players, but that doesn't necessarily conform to Let's Play conventions, includes reviews or explanations of new game features, explanations of game modifications or hacks, and vlog content in which Let's Players speak directly to the camera to share aspects of their personal lives, including their experiences at events where they are featured as microcelebrities, such as VidCon.

Although Let's Play videos vary in length, the creators discussed in this book typically produce videos that are twenty to thirty minutes long. To produce a Let's Play, video is captured during play using screen capture software, and the video game vision, in-game sound, and a separate voiceover commentary are recorded simultaneously. Sometimes an image of the Let's Player is also recorded, typically a small picture-in-picture image of the player at the top left or right-hand corner of the screen. The videos may feature the player alone or in multiplayer mode, with friends whose voices may or may not be recorded. Video footage is recorded from the first-person perspective of the main player's avatar, although it is common for the player to switch to a third-person perspective at key moments of play—for instance, at the start and end of the video—to directly address the audience. Let's Play videos are typically lightly edited. Occasionally gameplay errors or longer passages of time are edited out or sped up to increase the pace of the video, but this is mostly avoided. The relatively small amount of postproduction makes producing and sharing the videos a relatively quick process and contributes to a sense of immediacy. Let's Plays are frequently uploaded several times a week, if not daily. Between 2012 and 2017, for instance, Stampylonghead produced and uploaded a thirty-minute Minecraft video daily, resulting in an archive of over two thousand videos in five years, to build his following of 9 million subscribers.

In terms of the scenarios presented in the videos, it is common for well-established Minecraft Let's Players like Stampylonghead (chapter 6) to prebuild environments or download "maps" (prebuilt Minecraft worlds) provided by fans to use as the basis for play. A great deal of work often goes into the preparation of the game environment before a recording is made. Some Let's Plays are highly orchestrated, with clear goals and planned moments of gameplay. For instance, StacyPlays (chapter 7) always visits her Dalmatian Plantation to acknowledge her fans. Other Let's Plays are more loosely planned and play out as more casual gameplay sessions, as is often the case for KarinaOMG (chapter 8).

The main goal of the family-friendly Let's Players discussed in this book is to produce videos that provide a fun and informative experience for their fans. The videos often include humorous, witty, or friendly commentary and appeal to a wide range of tastes. Comedy styles include Minecraft in-joke humor, punch-line jokes, jocularity, slapstick, and situational comedy. A key feature of the genre is the promotion of friendship either between the Let's Player and the person's friends or between the Let's Player and the audience as a whole. Speaking about his interactions with fans at the MIPTV television industry conference in Cannes in 2015, Stampy's creator, Joseph Garrett, suggests he becomes "involved in their life more, for me, than a kids' television presenter would be: they're messaging me, they're sending me pictures. You become more of a friend to them" (Dredge 2014). Sometimes the appeal of the Let's Play content itself is the friendly competition and drama that is created between Let's Players and their in-world friends. For Garrett, this includes the friendship he has developed with his real-life partner, Bethany Bates, the creator of Sqaishey Quack. As Stampy and Sqaishey, Garrett and Bates have created whole series of videos featuring their online interactions in Minecraft. A key feature of StacyPlays videos is her focus on pets, some of which are virtual representations of her actual pets. And KarinaOMG often collaborates with her brother, RonaldOMG. In this sense, Let's Plays provide the opportunity for vicarious play, not just of general gameplay experience but also of the friendship and social interaction that exists within and around gameplay.

Let's Players and Authenticity

An explanation for the popularity of Let's Players and the communities that form around them is that they provide both entertainment and forms of companionship centered on a shared passion or interest. For instance, Oosterloo (2017, 1) suggests that the Let's Player ShadyPenguinn constructs a playful identity and "creatively mixes his roles of entertainer, player and community leader to engage his audience." Let's Players often post every day, providing children with a routine interpersonal experience. They frequently reveal personal details about themselves and invite viewers into their worlds in ways that are rarely a feature of children's interactions with television celebrities. They regularly play with other players in their videos, whom they typically refer to as their friends, to share their friendship. As they develop their fan base, Let's Players often respond directly to their fans on social media or in the video comments on YouTube. During play, they use language that is recognizable to children, including terminology from the game and common expressions and phrases from popular culture. These are all attributes of developing an authentic persona as a Minecraft player and as an accessible and "everyday" person who could be a friend.

Cunningham and Craig (2017) argue that authenticity is one of social media entertainment's (SME) key attributes and results from intense degrees of interactivity between creators and fan communities, which define distinctive modes of address within SME. They suggest, "Every SME creator is subject to a level of fan and subscriber response and feedback that, in its almost real-time intensity and transparency, is almost without parallel in screen entertainment" (74). Authenticity within SME, they claim, is established through a dialogic relationship between the fan base and the creator through "affective" and "relational" labor. Papacharissi (2015) argues that the networked architectures of online media support structures of feeling and social experiences that are potentially deeply affective in both discursive and material ways. Applied to Let's Play practices, the affective labor undertaken by both Let's Players and fans helps to form authentic relationships. Baym (2018) maintains that "relational labor" is required between creators and fans and that the closer these relationships resemble friend-ships, the more relational labor may be demanded "both to craft relation-ships with audiences that feel close and to differentiate those relationships from more personal ones (174).

The relationships that exist between creators and fans on digital plat-forms tap into deep-seated beliefs, feelings, and emotions that become central to fandom and the connections fans have to microcelebrities. In her discussion of brand culture, Banet-Wiser (2012) notes that authenticity results from powerful cultural processes linking the stories we tell about ourselves related to self-identity, creativity, politics, and religion:

> Even if we discard as false a simple opposition between the authentic and the inauthentic, we still must reckon with the power of authenticity—of the self, of experience, of relationships. It is a symbolic construct that, even in a cynical age, continues to have cultural value in how we understand our moral frameworks and ourselves, and more generally how we make decisions about how to live our lives. We want to believe—indeed, I argue that we *need* to believe—that there are spaces in our lives driven by genuine affect and emotions, something outside of mere consumer culture, something above the reductiveness of profit margins, the crassness of capital exchange. (5)

The question of how social media celebrities establish and maintain authenticity has also emerged as key concern for Marwick (2013). Maintain-ing authenticity has several layers, according to Marwick, but is centered on consistency of actions over time. That is, fans judge authenticity by com-paring current actions with past actions for consistency. She suggests:

> Authenticity is not an absolute quality, but a social judgement that is always made in distinction to something else. Because authenticity takes many forms, there is not a universal understanding of what makes something "authentic." Rather, authenticity is judged over time, in that people's authenticity is deter-mined by comparing their current actions against their past for consistency. (120)

She suggests as well that authenticity may relate to uniformity of presenta-tion across platforms, the display of hidden inner life and revealing intimate information, and the ideals of personal integrity and honesty. Authentic-ity, she writes, is central to maintaining status as a microcelebrity, whether celebrity is sought or bestowed by others.

Several scholars have discussed Let's Players in terms of the types of personae they aim to project, which has implications for how they attempt to maintain authenticity. Kerttula (2016) notes that Let's Play videos' defining characteristic is that they tell the story of the player rather than the game and that it is the player's experience of the video game that attracts audiences rather than the game itself. In this sense, the story that Let's Players construct about themselves is central to their popularity. Nguyen (2016), takes this idea further, suggesting that Let's Play videos are an opportunity to perform as gamers and that "creating, sharing, and discussing Let's Plays can render visible a wider diversity of game-playing identities, experiences, and styles" (1). He notes that the commentary accompanying gameplay is an opportunity to construct and perform game-playing personalities. This approach decenters the game and places the player at the center of analysis. Zariko (2016), however, blends the focus on game and player to show that Let's Play videos' popularity relates to the creation of idiosyncratic play stories, which are the embodied and performative creation of the Let's Player. That is, play stories are performative gameplay instances where both the game and the Let's Player are simultaneously brought into being in particular ways that appeal to the audience.

The relationship between Let's Player popularity and performativity that Zariko introduced provides a productive means to consider the question of how Let's Players maintain authenticity through becoming and remaining recognizable to their community. For instance, the concept of the performative repetition of social and cultural norms for social intelligibility (Butler 1990, 2004) provides useful insight into how Let's Players develop and maintain authenticity. Beers Fägersten (2017), for instance, holds that successful Let's Players are typically recognizable to sections of the gaming community as a peer. She uses the example of how the world's most successful YouTuber, PewDiePie, uses swearing within his performance of an "online persona, one that is both in line with the context of video gaming and conducive to a para-social relationship, allowing PewDiePie to achieve the overall goals of communicating with his viewers as peers and reducing the social distance between them" (1). She suggests that swearing "not only simulates casual conversation between friends, but actively reduces social distance, creates the illusion of intimacy, and contributes to his unprecedented success on YouTube" (2). Put this way, authenticity is connected to Let's Players' ability to reduce social distance between themselves and their fans.

A Let's Player's ability to become recognizable to a community through repeating the kinds of social norms and activities that are familiar to the community is likely to be a key to success. In part, this requires Let's Players to constantly respond to their audience and involve their fans in various forms of content creation. Smith, Obrist, and Wright (2013) outline how Let's Players frequently invite viewers to create content to share with the Let's Player, which the Let's Player then incorporates into subsequent productions. This form of co-creation of content (Banks 2013) is central to the process, enabling fans to feel a deeper connection to Let's Players than they do to other media celebrities.

The paradox for Let's Players is that the more successful they become, the more difficult it may be to maintain a sense of authenticity, or a sense of "peerness." Interacting with fans in authentic ways is more difficult when they have hundreds of thousands or millions of viewers rather than a few hundred. The appeal of the "everydayness" and immediacy of Let's Play content may be threatened as production processes become more formalized or systematic. This relates not just to the amount of attention Let's Players can give to individual fans but also to the style of their content. Major (2015, 68) suggests that Let's Players need to meet a sweet spot between their videos looking too polished or too amateurish and that many actively cultivate a sense of familiarity for their audience. The style of a Let's Player's play may also relate to an audience's expectations for authenticity. In discussing livestream gameplay on the platform Twitch, Scully-Blaker et al. (2017) make a distinction between "playing along"—a kind of tandem play—and "playing for" as two poles along a continuum of gameplayer interaction with an audience. Following an analysis of exit interviews from live Twitch events with fans, they suggest that the "'ceiling' of tandem play is reached when a streamer is so focused on entertaining the largest number of people possible that they are no longer playing along with their spectators, but only playing for them" (2017, 2026). Although livestream gameplay is a different genre from Let's Play videos, the genres share a focus on the immediacy of gameplay and the need for authenticity. There is a similar threat for Let's Players who step outside authentic gameplay, or shift from tandem play, toward pure entertainment. In this sense, peerness is potentially threatened by an overemphasis on celebrity or if content is contrived or staged.

Social Media Entertainment

A mutually reinforcing relationship exists between Minecraft and YouTube, with Minecraft providing a platform for digital making and YouTube providing a distribution platform that enables producers to share video content beyond their networks of family and friends. This relationship has allowed some Minecraft YouTubers to become highly popular, and YouTube's AdSense system has enabled successful YouTubers to monetize their content, providing financial reward. Cunningham and Craig's (2019) SME framework is useful for understanding aspects of YouTube's economic structure and the construction of new audiences on digital platforms, including children's consumption of Let's Play videos. They demonstrate how new industries have emerged on YouTube and other digital platforms as creators have moved from sharing videos for personal reasons or as a hobby to turning their practice into a business. For Cunningham and Craig, the SME framework exists within the context of broader changes in the media industries, particularly what they identify as Silicon Valley's challenge to Hollywood. The shift in media entertainment power from Southern California to Northern California, they argue, reflects changes in entertainment industry business models as digital platforms have challenged the established media industries (2019, 22). Hollywood, the established music industry, and the publishing industry monopolized the production of media content throughout the twentieth century and into the early twenty-first century because they had control over the means of production and distribution and established control over intellectual property (2017). In the new SME model, Cunningham and Craig argue, almost anyone with access to a computer, and an Internet connection can potentially earn an income as a media producer if they can produce content that appeals to an audience. Therefore, monetization of Minecraft Let's Play content follows a significantly different model to how content was monetized using predigital media forms.

This new scenario is partly enabled by flexible attitudes to intellectual property in the new media industries. Many games companies have invited fans to repurpose their content and to produce and circulate modifications online (Banks 2013). Mojang, the company that produces Minecraft, has been particularly nonlitigious, allowing a wide range of unofficial Minecraft content, including Let's Plays, to circulate online. Unlike predigital media forms, gaming companies like Mojang have recognized the value in allowing "the community" to use their platform to produce and monetize content across other platforms, which adds value to their own product (Arnroth 2014). Fjællingsdal (2014) writes that Let's Plays are now central to the overall experience of video gaming, to the extent that "the Let's Play phenomenon, and the communities contained within it, holds potential for the future development of videogame industry as a whole" (4). Indeed, Mojang has relied on the development of user-generated content across digital platforms for Minecraft's ongoing success.

Meanwhile, YouTube has enabled users to circulate remixed or repurposed video content that traditional media companies argue violates intellectual property rights (Burgess and Green 2018). Google (YouTube's parent company) has systematized income generation through AdSense as an "easy way to earn money from your online content" (Google 2018). In this context, view counts and subscriptions are the drivers of YouTube's economic model, and as Minecraft Let's Players move from amateur content creation to embrace a more professional model, they are faced with choices about how to attract and keep viewers and how this relates to remaining authentic to fans.

Maintaining authenticity is deeply related to Let's Players' efforts to remain recognizable to their fans as they begin to monetize their content and establish themselves as social media entertainers. Building a subscriber base on YouTube and attracting more views for each video rely on the ability to be entertaining and "sharable" either on other social media platforms or by word of mouth. The YouTube platform provides content creators with a range of metrics to identify how each of their videos is tracking, including at what point each video attracts the most viewers and the precise moment that viewers stop watching. Creators can see a clear relationship between particular narration, topics, and activities and how popular a video is down to the second viewers turn off. Although YouTube's algorithm remains opaque to even experienced YouTubers (Cunningham and Craig 2019), the system encourages content manipulation at the microlevel. Therefore, the "spreadability" and "clickability" of content that are features of a great deal of economically successful SME are potential distractions for Let's Players who may be balancing the desire to build their subscriber base while simultaneously creating content that they enjoy making and remains authentic. Let's Play producers, particularly children's content producers, are also potentially vulnerable to Google's conditions. It is less easy to take sponsorship commissions for Let's Play content because it is more difficult to authentically place products within gameplay than it has been for other types of social media entertainment such as unboxing videos. For

Let's Players, the game and gameplay is the "product" they are selling, and AdSense may be their only source of income.

Whether Let's Players are motivated by financial reward, they are challenged by the contradiction that the more successful they become, the more difficult it is for them to maintain a close relationship with their audience. They seek to cultivate peer relationship with viewers through their commentary and supplementary activities, and a significant component of the work of producing successful Let's Plays is interacting with fans. However, peerness is challenged by the difficulties of remaining authentic and familiar as a fan base grows. Successful Let's Players are the new pop stars with millions of followers. In comparison to music, television, or film stars, though, their popularity relies heavily on their accessibility as much as it does the content they produce.

Let's Player Celebrity and Fandom

From a children's audience perspective, SME provides a compelling alternative to predigital media entertainment forms, particularly television, producing its own celebrities, fandoms, and exchange value. This is most visible at large-scale live events like VidCon, which are significant opportunities for fans, providing a rare chance for them to see their favorite YouTubers in real life and perhaps to meet them. These conventions take place in large arenas in front of thousands of enthusiastic fans, often resembling popular music concerts. The 2017 US VidCon event attracted over thirty thousand attendees (VidCon 2019). The 2018 VidCon US website promoted the "Community Track" as an opportunity to "meet the biggest online video stars IRL [in real life], make new friends, and don't forget to be awesome!" YouTube's most successful family-friendly Minecraft Let's Player, DanTDM, toured his own show to ninety-seven events around the world in 2017 (Kelsey 2017). His Sydney Opera House show was the theater's second fastest ever selling event (Kelsey 2017). In 2017, Dan TDM was also YouTube's highest-paid star, earning over $US16.5 million (Berg 2017). The most successful YouTube Let's Players have a popular culture presence that extends well past their online play, including publishing deals for fiction and nonfiction books and licensing general merchandise.

Let's Play fandom takes a range of forms. For instance, there are over 10,000 KarinaOMG fans on an unofficial club page for the game Roblox, for which Karina Kurzawa produces Let's Plays (Roblox 2020). The site describes KarinaOMG as "the sweetest, adorable and most loving youtuber, minecraft player and robloxian namely karina." A fan fiction writer, "Kristy," publishes fan fiction on the social writing platform Wattpad about StacyPlays, which to date has had almost 120,000 views, and a search for "Stampy" on Wattpad provides 19,100 results, suggesting there have been hundreds, if not thousands, of individual fan fiction stories written about him. There are hundreds of StacyPlays fan art images on the DeviantArt online art gallery, and the Stampylongnose page on the FanPop site includes over one thousand fan-produced images. High-profile Minecraft Let's Players also have a significant social media presence (table 3.1).

Let's Play fandom and audience interaction is clearest on YouTube itself, where fans post comments on videos. For instance, a Minecraft video created by DanTDM in early 2019, "THIS is the NEW Minecraft," had over 2.7 million views and over ten thousand comments at the time of writing. In particular, fan comments on YouTube videos become an integral aspect of fan practice and community creation on YouTube. YouTube comments enable fans to respond directly to the latest video uploads and interact with other Let's Play fans on a regular basis. Fans often make suggestions for future Let's Player activity in the comments, sometimes in response to a question posed by the Let's Player in the video. The comments also provide an opportunity for fans to say what they like and dislike about the current video.

One of this book's central questions addresses what Minecraft Let's Players have to offer fans and audience members more broadly. That is, what do audience members receive in return for dedicating time and effort to

Table 3.1
Social Media Following of Selected Minecraft Let's Players

	DanTDM	Stampy	StacyPlays	KarinaOMG	LDShadowLady
Facebook	898,000	711,000	31,000	27,000 (Sis versus Bro)	84,000
Instagram	3.0 million	820,000	410,000	451,000 (Karina Kurzawa)	1.2 million
Twitter	1.6 million	674,000	740,000	5,500	670,800

viewing Let's Plays and interacting with Let's Players? One answer is that Let's Players provide forms of entertainment, escape, and viewing pleasure. After all, most children play games and watch Let's Players playing games in their leisure time, as a break away from school and formal after-school activities, such as sports and music lessons, and household responsibilities, at least as far as children's lives are described in middle-class discourses. However, a significant body of literature argues that gameplay (and, by extension, Let's Plays) offers audiences much more than escapism. Livingstone (2002) writes, "For many young people, fandom is the 'glue' which connects personal identity, social and peer relations, and taste preferences within a media-rich environment" (115). In *The Ambiguity of Play* (2001), Sutton-Smith summarizes a wide range of play theories, or "rhetorics of play," that suggests play is attached to concepts such progress, fate and chance, identity, power, the imaginary, self-satisfaction, and frivolity. Play thus has a broad range of social, cultural, and material purposes. Dovey and Kennedy (2006) challenge the idea that a dichotomy should exist between play and work when we think about video games, suggesting, "It is more true to assert that play, through its function under the sign of consumerism, has itself become a form of work" (2006, 19). Furthermore, theorists like Gee (2007) have comprehensively argued that video gameplay is rewarding *because* it involves the hard work of learning.

The approach taken in this book is that audiences are attracted to Let's Players because they circulate forms of "capital" that are both interesting and useful to audience members, which in turn leads to forms of learning. Let's Players offer scripts or designs for how to become a Minecrafter, including the kinds of work that are required to participate on the platform in interesting ways for making digital artifacts and socially interacting with others in and around the game. As celebrities, Let's Players offer different kinds of resources for Minecraft play. Abidin (2018) draws on Bourdieu's theory of capital to argue that Internet celebrity has four overlapping features. These are worth quoting in detail because they provide a useful framework for thinking about what Minecraft Let's Players offer to audiences. Abidin suggests, "The qualities of exclusivity, exoticism, exceptionalism, and everydayness, each corresponds to a specific form of capital that arouse interest and attention, whether positive (i.e., out of admiration or love) or negative (i.e., out of disgust or judgment)" (19). She writes:

- Internet celebrity that is "exclusive" is the glamorization and celebration of practices and possessions so elite in access or rare in occurrence that it would be unusual for ordinary people to experience them without high "economic capital." (20)
- Internet celebrity that is "exotic" is perceived as distancing, far removed from one's comfort zone, or so novel or foreign that it piques the interest of audiences who hold contrasting or different forms of "cultural capital." (22)
- Internet celebrity that is "exceptional" highlights the unusual abilities, astounding qualities, or expert skills of a person that can be elite or mundane in nature but are spectacular and admired for their "technical capital" all the same. (28)
- Internet celebrity that is "everyday" curates the usually mundane and ordinary aspects of daily life with such candor and insight (as well as with much regularity and consistency) that a sustained social relationship based on a sense of community and trust is fostered as "social capital." (32–33)

Throughout this book, and particularly in chapters 6, 7, and 8, I argue that family-friendly Minecraft Let's Players who appeal to children share "everydayness" as a key feature of their celebrity, but each Let's Player also displays other microcelebrity qualities that make them appealing to children. For instance, StacyPlays offers forms of exoticism because she uses a modded version of Minecraft that is not readily available to many children; KarinaOMG offers forms of exclusiveness when she posts blog posts of herself and her family traveling the world in business class; and a principal aspect of Stampy's appeal is that he often displays exceptional skill in his builds and thus has significant "technical capital." These features of celebrity provide a means to think about the appeal of specific Let's Players and to understand how peerness, authenticity, and other attributes work together to enable learning.

Let's Plays and Impassioned Learning

I have aimed to establish that the Let's Play genre relies on the development of authentic relationships between Let's Players and their audiences and that this includes reducing social distance between themselves and their fans. However, I have not yet grappled with the question of why learning is central to viewers' engagement with Let's Play videos. This final section of this chapter introduces the concept of "impassioned learning" (Dezuanni and O'Mara 2017)—that learning is a key reward for viewing Let's Play videos. My reasoning hinges on accepting that we are always learning, whether explicitly or tacitly. This contrasts with the normative discourse that education and learning have come to represent activity that occurs when learners have a specific purpose for the acquisition of new knowledge or skills in formal settings.

A great deal of research demonstrates that children are motivated to learn for many reasons, including to have fun and to interact with like-minded people in communities of activity. Building on Vygotsky's social development theory, Wenger (1998) suggests that learning occurs through situated practice in both formal and informal contexts and is deeply social. As discussed in chapter 2, Gee's and Hayes's affinity spaces theory holds that individuals are rewarded for joining others with similar interests and from whom they might learn (2010). Ito and her colleagues refer to "interest-driven" learning to identify how young people come to learn socially in digital media contexts, stating "youth invested in specific media practices often describe a period in which they first began looking around online for some area of interest and eventually discovered a broader palette of resources to experiment with, or an interest-driven online group" (Ito et al. 2008, 22).

The idea of *impassioned learning* recognizes that learning may be compelled by a desire to engage deeply with specific subject matter and practices for a meaningful purpose, including for play. The term *passion curriculum* has previously been applied to examples of learning motivated by students' deep interests in particular kinds of activities in formal schooling contexts (Collins, Joseph, and Bielaczyc 2004). Extending the concept beyond the school, "impassioned learning" recognizes children's desire to participate more fully in an activity or community in any aspect of life that motivates them to acquire knowledge and skills. It produces peer pedagogies because the value of engaging in learning with and from a peer relies on a shared passion.

As they engage with Minecraft and its associated supersystem, children potentially encounter a plethora of learning opportunities. Of course, many children engage with Minecraft in a relatively casual way for general entertainment and to the extent that their Minecraft and Let's Player knowledge enables them to go to school and enter popular conversations and play scenarios about Minecraft (Willett et al. 2013, Dezuanni, Beavis, and O'Mara 2015). These children may still become involved in peer pedagogical relationships, but perhaps in a less committed way. Other children are willing to invest a great deal of time and work in exchange for new opportunities to participate on the Minecraft platform, including time spent watching Let's Play videos. Minecraft presents multiple layers of activity across a range of platforms that provide children with multiple opportunities for engagement and learning, including great complexity and depth for those who wish to take it up. The next chapter extends the argument that a principal reward for children for watching Let's Play videos is learning and that this leads to peer pedagogical practices on the part of both Let's Players and their fans. A central aspect of my argument is that Let's Players aim to retain authenticity within fan communities substantially through promoting peer pedagogies.

4 Peer Pedagogies and Digital Platforms

Remarkably little has been written about peer pedagogies in either digital or nondigital contexts. Peer learning has been used extensively, particularly in formal educational settings, to describe students' teaching and learning with each other (King 1999; Hogan and Tudge 1999; Topping 2005; Cohen and Sampson 2013). These accounts tend to focus on how peer learning supplements teacher-led classroom learning. Much less has been written about the specific pedagogic relationships that exist between children and children or between children and adults who have the potential to be peers, particularly in informal and digital settings. This chapter establishes how digital platforms mobilize peer pedagogies by exploring how Minecraft and YouTube provide children and young people with unique and compelling learning opportunities that rely on networked relationships. The networking of peer pedagogies within Minecraft and YouTube is particularly interesting because it represents pedagogical practice on a massive scale and through very different exchange and reward relationships to those that typically structure learning in formal settings or structured media pedagogies in the predigital era.

Introducing Peer Pedagogies

Peer pedagogies between Let's Players and audience members are relationships in which a flat structure emerges between "teachers" and "learners," arranged through a producer's attempts to reduce social distance and their ability to meet a viewer's need for knowledge. Audiences learn from Let's Players because they feel intimately connected to them, they feel respected by Let's Players as fans, and they value what Let's Players are sharing.

Pedagogy is not a straightforward concept, and adding the modifier "peer" to it adds a layer of complexity that requires clear justification. Typical definitions of pedagogy describe it as "the method and practice of teaching, especially as an academic subject or theoretical concept" (Oxford Living Dictionaries 2019). Pedagogy has been deployed politically with regard to teacher practice to the extent that it is difficult to disassociate the term from its common use in descriptions of the teaching process—for instance, in its use in descriptions of classroom interrelations and the teacher as "pedagogue" (Gore 1993). This perspective on pedagogy became formalized through the professionalization of teacher education in university courses and the development of national educational policies in English-speaking countries in the 1960s and 1970s (Simon 1983; Murphy 1996).

Within educational theory, pedagogy has also come to be used as a term to describe how teachers teach. Shulman's (1987) concept of pedagogical content knowledge, for instance, aims to theorize the relationship of teacher expertise, curriculum content, and student learning. He suggests that effective teachers develop expert knowledge of both the content of their subject areas and the arrangement of subject knowledge to optimize student learning (Shulman 1987). As Alexander (2000, 540) notes, though, definitions of pedagogy that focus on professional practice tend to refer to the act of teaching and teacher practice rather than learning and context. Alexander argues that pedagogy is different from teaching and suggests that it "connects the apparently self-contained act of teaching with culture, structure and mechanisms of social control." Thinking about pedagogy as a process that connects with broader social, cultural, and political processes expands how we might think about it as a practice that cannot be uncoupled from the social processes of learning more generally.

As teacher classroom activity has been theorized in more specific ways, the term *pedagogy* has been partially liberated to be applied more diversely. Murphy (1996) points to the introduction of didactics as a concept in educational theory that has been used to distinguish between teacher practice and broader concerns about learning in context. She explains didactics as the act of teaching a subject in a specialized way through a process of presentation. Didactics can be thought of as a formalized process that can be planned for and recorded as a deliberate set of strategies. Murphy suggests that the introduction of didactics frees up pedagogy to be a less scientific term that encompasses a teacher's intuitive and in-the-moment responses to student needs. From this perspective, pedagogy is less a scientific practice and more an art form or a socially responsive process encompassing emotional investment and interpersonal relations, along with the framing of learning.

Broader conceptualizations of pedagogy have been informed by a theoretical turn toward social understandings of learning that recognize it as less scientific and, arguably, more social, situated, messy, and artful. For instance, Schön's (1987) argument that learning often occurs through reflection in practice, his "epistemology of practice," aimed to turn thinking about the acquisition of professional knowledge away from technical rationality to recognize that knowledge is often embedded in reflective practice. Lave and Wenger's (1991) theory of situated practice suggests that learning occurs in the same situation in which it is applied. They contrast situated learning with classroom learning by suggesting that the latter often decontextualizes knowledge from the applications that make it meaningful. Steinkuehler and Oh (2012) draw on Lave and Wenger's work to argue that situated learning within communities of practice counters the notion of learning as cognition, and pedagogy as a process of instruction. They suggest "accounts of how an individual interacts with his or her material and social contexts and how these interactions change over time replace accounts of individual knowledge construction occurring 'in the head'" (157).

Recognizing learning as a process of social interaction, located in a specific time and place, contrasts it with more instrumentalist accounts that emphasize knowledge development as a directed activity centered on teacher expertise, formalized curricula, and rationalist cognition. By implication, if learning can occur anywhere, through a range of socially situated practices, then classroom teachers do not own pedagogy. Pedagogy can be thought of as social interaction in a social context that leads to the development of new knowledge and practices. From this perspective, accounts of socially situated and material learning practices (Papert 1993; Murphy 1996; Ellsworth 1997; Hartley 1999; Alexander 2001; Gee and Hayes 2010) say that knowledge is developed as much in everyday life—in homes, workplaces, via media experiences, and in the community—as it is in formal educational contexts. Lave and Wenger (1991) discuss how learning occurs in apprenticeship models where newcomers are initially involved in "legitimate peripheral participation" and over time develop knowledge and skills that locate them at the center of a "community of practice"— essentially a community of peers, where peer relations are established through shared knowledge and mastery of skill. Those on the periphery are not excluded from authentic practice pending the acquisition of knowledge; they too are invited to participate and to be engaged with practice. In this sense, a community of practice is less hierarchical than the somewhat artificial structure of most traditional classrooms. Later in the chapter, I explore the characteristics of peer pedagogies in greater detail. For now, I note that peer pedagogies contrast to many formal teacher/student pedagogical relationships because they occur between people where there is less social distance and where learning typically occurs in socially situated practice. In particular, being a peer is based not on age but on shared interest, shared abilities, or comparable social standing (Cambridge English Dictionary 2020). When discussing peers in *Lifelong Kindergarten*, Resnick (2017) suggests that the key feature of peer-based learning is that it promotes people working and learning together in supportive learning communities. This occurs in unique ways on digital platforms like Minecraft and YouTube. A theory of peer pedagogies recognizes the rewards Minecraft provides to children as an example of what Papert (1993) describes as a "transitional object to mediate relationships that are ultimately between person and person', for the development of what he described as 'powerful ideas'" (185).

Pedagogies and Identities beyond the Classroom

Uncoupling pedagogy from the constraints of formal classroom contexts frees the term to be deployed in efforts to understand how learning occurs in social and material relations in any aspect of life. Perhaps unsurprisingly, thinking about pedagogy in this expanded way requires a consideration of theories of identity, as learning is ultimately about the construction of self though the acquisition of knowledge and skills within normative social-material relations. This was recognized by the "critical pedagogy" movement that drew on feminist and Marxist scholarship to argue that undesirable social and cultural structures and norms are reproduced through learning. Freire's (1972) work on the role of dialogue, praxis, lived experience, and "conscientization" in popular and informal learning inspired a movement within educational scholarship and practice focused on the transformational attributes of education for social change. His challenge to structure and formality is in many respects a challenge to the notion of formal education and its pedagogical structures, which, he argued, reinforce disadvantage. Drawing directly on Freire, Giroux's concepts of public and critical pedagogies (1992, 1994, 1997, 2011) contend that it is necessary to recognize the pedagogies of everyday life. He suggests:

> I no longer believe that pedagogy is a discipline. On the contrary, I have argued for the last few years that pedagogy is about the creation of a public sphere, one that brings people together in a variety of sites to talk, exchange information, listen, feel their desires, and expand their capacities for joy, love, solidarity, and struggle. (1994, x).

In some respects, this approach to public pedagogy informs the approach taken in this book: it recognizes that pedagogies are present in the networked communities children participate in as they play in and around Minecraft. However, Giroux's underlying objective to liberate young people of their critical "unconsciousness" is more problematic because it fails to recognize young people's existing critical capacities (Buckingham 1998; Luke 1998). A further argument against critical pedagogy is the poststructuralist perspective that critical pedagogy is informed by a version of Marxist/feminist humanism that insists on essentialist identities that become relatively stable (Luke 1998). Liberation through pedagogy, according to the critical pedagogy movement, relies on the liberation of essentialist identities, which can be achieved through revealing unrecognized oppression. This book recognizes identity work as an ongoing and continually contested task. Rather than being somehow duped by a popular culture example such as Minecraft, for instance, young people draw on popular culture as one aspect of their experience of daily life in the ongoing construction of self.

A consideration of poststructuralist theories of subjectivity, performativity, and sociomaterialist accounts of meaning making provides a productive alternative to critical pedagogy. Foucault's (1988) concept of the "techniques of the self" argues that the development of subjectivity is an ongoing process of becoming intelligible to oneself and others, as required by social and cultural practices and norms. From this perspective, everyday life is pedagogic, although Foucault doesn't use this term. In the interrelations of everyday life, people aim to reduce social distance, to be intelligible to each other, through practicing life "ethically"—that is, in ways that others will understand as being truthful according to the social system at work. Butler (1990, 2004) builds on "techniques of the self" and Althusser's concept of "hailing"—the social process of being invited to act in particular ways—to suggest we performatively bring ourselves into being to become recognizable to others. Butler holds that it is risky to vary from a community's accepted norms of practice because becoming unrecognizable is likely to invite symbolic or actual violence. In this context, "performative variation" occurs within interpersonal relations in a particular community that tends toward normativity, and discourages difference. Performativity is not merely discursive but bodily and material. Barad (2007) suggests "Performativity, properly construed, is not an invitation to turn everything (including material bodies) into words; on the contrary, performativity is precisely a contestation of the excessive power granted to language to determine what is real" (2007, 133). From this perspective, pedagogy is not merely a process of knowledge transfer, but an invitation to undertake discursive and material performative acts that both repeat established disciplinary and social norms and potentially vary them to begin to establish new norms.

The learning that occurs in the consumption of a Let's Play video may be thought of as an exchange of normative practice in which the viewer is invited to repeat linguistic and material practices in order to become recognizable within a community of practice. Pedagogy is an intimate and interrelation process and may be conceived as performative repetition and variation of sociomaterial norms on the part of both the Let's Player and viewers. For instance, the popularity of KarinaOMG among children, discussed in chapter 8, is aligned to her sociomaterial mode of address that marks her as an authentic presence within children's culture. The way she addresses her audience as peers, acting in recognizably "preteen" ways through her actions and behaviors, the ways she dresses, and how she speaks create familiarity. Therefore, this is as much about her physicality as a "performer" in real life and the language she uses within her commentary as it is about her in-game play.

Minecraft Let's Play viewers have opportunities for performative repetition and variation as they participate on both Minecraft and YouTube, but also beyond these platforms. As chapters 6 to 8 illustrate, many children interact with YouTube videos by leaving comments for Let's Players and for other viewers, and these comments and responses are sometimes rewarded by Let's Players themselves. Stampy invites his fans to submit comments and fan art and may reward them by acknowledging them on a sign in his

Love Garden (part of his "lovely world"). Of course, the community also rewards and punishes YouTube commentary. In extreme examples, this can lead to hate comments—the kinds of excesses Butler refers to as symbolic violence.

Children's Minecraft play may aim to replicate what they have viewed on a Let's Player's channel, and they may play-act being a Let's Player as they play the game, narrating their own play in the style of a Let's Player. Some children take this a step further to record their own videos and post these to their own YouTube channels (Dredge 2016a; Meehan 2014). Outside the digital platforms, children may play-act being a Let's Player within general play, alone or with friends, at home, at school, or in other locations. These sociomaterial, nondigital embodiments of Let's Play activity become part of the process of children bringing themselves into being, recognizable to themselves and others through the repetition of normative practice with the potential to push the boundaries of acceptance through variation. In this sense, peer pedagogies are likely to reinforce social norms, but they also offer the opportunity for acts of variation.

As media culture and play, Let's Play activity is perhaps more permissive of variation than some sociomaterial sites. The relational aspects of peer pedagogies recognize that there is less social distance between "teacher" and "student" through a particular interrelationship of practice than may be the case in a formal educational environment. This does not mean that peer pedagogies are devoid of hierarchy or structure. Let's Play videos in fact present modes of address that may be more or less didactic or socially and culturally normative. Bernstein's (2000) theory of pedagogical classification and framing may be usefully applied to better illustrate how open or closed an invitation to knowledge exchange may be. I am not suggesting, then, that peer pedagogies have an entirely democratic structure, merely that they offer opportunities for children's participation in knowledge development that are inviting and often rewarding.

The Media's Pedagogical Functions

There is a significant history of scholarship about the media's pedagogical functions: concerns about the influence of movies on children's morals (Jowett, Jarvie, and Fuller 1996); consideration of the culturally corrosive influence of "cheap entertainments," including movies, advertising, and the popular press (Leavis and Thompson 1933); the Frankfurt School's focus on the dehumanizing consequences of mass production and the culture industries (Adorno 1991; Marcuse 1964); the Institute for Propaganda Analysis's development of materials to help children understand propaganda in the 1930s in the United States (Hobbs and McGee, 2014); and British culturalism's expansion of the concept of culture to include media culture (Hoggart 1957; Williams 1958). Not all of these ideologically diverse examples explicitly refer to pedagogy or learning, but they all describe the role of media in ways that might be considered pedagogical. As the expanded view of pedagogy outlined in the previous section suggests, the relationship between children and sociomaterial culture is at least partly a relationship of knowledge exchange and learning. Giroux puts it this way:

> Though I do not wish to romanticize popular culture, it is precisely in its diverse spaces and spheres that most of the education that matters today is taking place on a Global scale. Electronic media, the vastly proliferating network of images that inscribe themselves on us every day, and the hybridized sounds of new technologies, cultures and ways of life have drastically altered how identities are shaped, desires constricted, and dreams realized. (1994, x)

He also argues that the lack of an adequate conceptualization of critical pedagogical practice is responsible for the absence of an adequate politics of popular culture (1992). Giroux was particularly scathing of radical intellectuals who failed to treat popular culture seriously.

Popular culture's pedagogical functions are taken seriously by Hartley, although not in ways that would accord with Giroux's Marxist critical orientation. In "The Uses of Television" (1999) and "The Uses of Digital Literacy" (2011), Hartley argues from a culturalist perspective that recognizes active audience participation in the reception, construction, and circulation of knowledge and ideas. He holds that television *is* teaching (1999), suggesting that it has replaced the functions of the church as educator. He states that while the family continues to perform the main socializing role and is responsible for the systematic teaching of selfhood and the family belief system, television (but also other media) complements this process. In addition, while schools have focused on print literacy, the family and television continue a "nonliterate" pedagogical tradition, "using song, story, sight and talk rather than 'book-learning'" (1999, 43). Hartley goes further to suggest that the antagonism between rival belief systems of papists and protestants competing for souls during the Renaissance continues in the antagonism between print/school learning and more oral traditions of learning, including television (1999). He concludes that deep suspicions about television as teaching fail to recognize television's educational role in everyday life.

Hartley draws attention to the concept of "permanent education," introduced by Williams (1968), in which Williams wanted to consider the educational force "of our whole social and cultural experience" (14). Williams was interested not only in "continuing education of a formal or informal kind," but how "the whole environment, its institutions and relationships, actively and profoundly teaches" (1968). He asks, "Who can doubt, looking at television or newspapers, or reading the women's magazines, that here, centrally, is teaching, and teaching financed and distributed in a much larger way than is formal education?" (14). Hartley is not so concerned with Williams's warnings about the ways in which government, education, and media seem to be becoming integrated with potentially negative consequences or with his argument for a version of television that will provide intellectually desirable forms of education. Rather, Hartley is concerned with how audiences might use resources at hand, including television, to teach themselves. He turns to Eco for a more satisfactory version of "permanent education":

> Television is the school book of modern adults, as much as it is the only authoritative school book for our children. Education, real education, doesn't mean teaching young people to trust school. On the contrary, it consists of training young people to criticise school books *and write their own school books*. (Eco, 1979, 22, emphasis in original)

Hartley (2011) takes up this focus on the interrelationship of education and the ability to actively participate in the development of new knowledge through multimodal communication in his discussion of digital literacy:

> Now that every user is a publisher, consumption needs to be rethought as action, not behaviour, and media consumption as a mode of literacy: that is, an autonomous means of communication in which "writing" is as widespread as "reading"; something that was never possible during the era of broadcast, one-to-many, passively received "mass" communication. (13–14).

YouTube, Hartley suggests, is at the center of young people's DIY (do-it-yourself) and DIWO (do-it-with-others) creative content production practices that provide unprecedented opportunities for them to publish (2011). "The internet," he writes, "has rapidly evolved into a new 'enabling social technology *for knowledge'*" (2011, 109, emphasis in original). In this context, "permanent education" may be considered an aspect of everyday participation on digital platforms.

The other key contribution Hartley makes to a theorization of the pedagogic role of television and, by extension, YouTube is his discussion of how television teaches through appealing to an addressee (1999, 155). He asks, "What 'addressee' does the teaching discourse of television call into being?" His answer is that television's addressees are invited to engage along a continuum that extends from something similar to traditional teaching, which calls into being the student addressee, and advertising, which calls into being the consumer (156). Television addresses its audience, he notes, by promoting reconsumption through engagement with genres and by using semiotic devices "at every level from dialogue to plot, characterization to casting, language to location, that might carry viewers through" (156).

Ellsworth (1997) also recognizes a similarity between how media address viewers and pedagogical practice. Like Hartley, she identifies cinematic devices such as "plot, character, subtext, genre, causal links, [and] points of view" as elements that aim to "hail viewers and subjectively position them" (25). For Ellsworth, there are strong parallels between "mode of address" in film studies and teachers' pedagogical practices. She sets up a provocative discussion that seeks to reflect on how educational practice might be better understood through a consideration of how individuals interact with films. For Ellsworth, mode of address is a useful theoretical device because it reveals the distance between the intended addressee and the actual addressee, and she considers this volatile space to be productively pedagogical, calling it the "paradoxical power of address" (37). It is paradoxical, she writes, because there is no exact fit between address and viewer response, and it is powerful because it opens up opportunities for the addressee to contribute to meaning making and cultural production.

Ellsworth (1997) draws on Phelan (1993) and Butler (1990, 1993) to argue that teaching is performative rather than representational. In alignment with the discussion of performativity presented earlier in this chapter, she contends that teaching does not produce representations of knowledge that are easily replicated or exactly repeated because every attempt to repeat or represent occurs in a context of each individual's social meanings, associations, and contingent histories. According to Ellsworth (1997), performative pedagogy is productive because imperfect fits and slippages in meaning allow individuals to expand what counts as valued and valuable. As I suggest later in the chapter, drawing on Bernstein's work, pedagogy aims to classify and frame knowledge and practice in ways that are more and less formal and informal, and defined and undefined (Bernstein 2000). A consideration of performativity along the lines that Ellsworth suggested helps to illustrate how framing and classification in peer pedagogical interactions are always imperfect but potentially productive if considered through the lens of performativity.

Discussion of the media's pedagogical functions outlined in this section is directly relevant to a conceptualization of peer pedagogies on digital platforms because it provides a productive theoretical framework to think about how peers address each other as teachers and learners in digital contexts—but also how pedagogic interactions between peers are productive and generative. Let's Play videos use many of the cinematic and television techniques mentioned by Hartley and Ellsworth to address their assumed audience. However, Let's Play viewers interpret the videos in their own ways and produce a host of activity around Let's Plays and Minecraft that involve the production of new materials and knowledge. The affordances of digital technologies and platforms make it possible for children to "write their own knowledge" in the ways Eco and Hartley asserted. As discussed in chapter 3, Let's Play videos differ from most film and television genres because the Let's Player's commentary directly addresses the viewer as a peer and is more intimate because it aims to reduce the social distance between the Let's Player and the viewer. The possibility of direct interaction between participants on digital platforms also highlights the significance of interpersonal relations. Children may post comments on YouTube in response to Let's Play videos, and other commenters may respond directly to these comments. Finally, digital platforms provide opportunities for children to performatively bring themselves into being in ways that may tend toward normativity but produce opportunities for variation and newly valued knowledge and practice.

The Characteristics of Peer Pedagogies

An understanding of the characteristics of peer pedagogies is essential for considering how pedagogies function on digital platforms. My theorization of peer pedagogies is based on complementary processes of theorization and analysis. First, I have drawn on poststructuralist theory to consider how "work upon the self" relies on social and cultural norms and that peer relations produce particular norms of practice. Second, my analysis of Let's Player practices outlined in chapters 6, 7, and 8 has helped me to understand how peer relationships are constructed in and around Let's Play videos. Three points underpin my argument:

1. An understanding of peer interactions helps to explain how pedagogies function on digital platforms even when audience members do not identify as members of particular communities.

2. Friendship, trust, and emotional investment are fundamental to peer interactions and pedagogical practices, even where individuals have not met "in real life."

3. The continuing work on the part of Let's Players to reduce social distance between themselves and their fans is an effort to remain peer-like.

The first of these points raises a question about the extent to which community is central to the kinds of learning that occur on digital platforms. Gee and Hayes's theory of affinity spaces (2012), Kumpulainen and Sefton-Green's outline of "Connected Learning" (2014; see also Ito et al. 2019), and Jenkins's theory of participatory culture (2006) all focus in various ways on community as a key component of learning in digital contexts. Participatory culture, Jenkins suggests, includes a strong emphasis on social interaction, "with some type of informal mentorship whereby what is known by the most experienced is passed along to novices" and where members feel some degree of social connection with one another, at least to the extent that they care about others' responses to their creations (7). According to Gee and Hayes, affinity groups include "well-designed spaces that resource and mentor learners, old and new, beginners and masters alike, they are the 'learning system' built around a popular culture practice" (2010, 188). Kumpulainen and Sefton-Green (2014) write "connected learning is realized when the learner is able to pursue a personal interest or passion with the support of friends, caring adults, and/or expert communities and is in turn able to link this learning and interest to academic achievement, career success, or civic engagement" (10).

These theories provide convincing and vital theorizations of learning that might be productively applied to learning in and around Minecraft, and the concept of peer pedagogies in many ways aims to apply these theories to Let's Play participation. As a concept, however, peer pedagogies also aims to account for pedagogical relationships that are personal and individualized rather than necessarily being public. As a child watches a Let's Play video on a device or uses the YouTube app on a television, they do not necessarily identify themselves as a community member and do not necessarily benefit from an online community structure. Their relationship to a Let's Player and their pedagogical experience may be based on a perceived personal relationship. To put it another way, placing community at the center of analysis places emphasis on "the public" when intimate, personal, and emotional relationships may be just as important for pedagogy and learning.

Second, peer pedagogies rely on friendship and emotional engagement or the vicarious experience of friendship in ways that are not always recognized within other theorizations of learning in digital contexts. Although Let's Players are often older and may have more knowledge and skills than their young fans, these points of difference do not detract from the sense that the Let's Player is a friend of sorts. While friendship with fans may be a constructed illusion (Marwick 2013), the parasocial relationships that develop between Let's Players and fans often become emotionally gratifying to fans who identify microcelebrities as "friends" (Marwick 2013, 119). Rojek (2015) asserts that a central condition of media and celebrity culture, made more intense through digital media, is the role that mediation plays in connecting celebrity to everyday emotional investment. He draws on Simmel's theory of the nearness and farness of strangers in social relations to identify mediation as

> the vein between first-order (face-to-face relations with family, peer groups, communities) and second-order (media) constructions of social reality. It is at the heart of presumed intimacy since it translates characteristics that are remote, in Simmel's sense of the term, into emotions that are recognized as near. Crucially, it describes a mutually referring, conversational process. Embodied habitus ceases to be a matter of narrow materiality—the family, the home, the community. (Rojek 2015, 87, 88)

From this perspective, peer pedagogies on digital platforms become part of the process of connecting familial relations to the broader social world, and celebrities are a key aspect of the mediation process as they enable intimate parasocial relationships. Let's Players are accepted as conduits between the known and unknown because they are sometimes accepted in intimate rather than remote terms.

The third point to make about the relational characteristics of peer pedagogies refers to the specific performative work Let's Players undertake upon the self to remain recognizable as peers to their young fans. This work entails the "techniques of the self" (Foucault 1988) designed to remain approachable and accessible to fans in "real life." As well as building and playing in Minecraft, they use distinctive vocal expressions to commentate their play; use technical and everyday language that is familiar to their audience; reveal information about their everyday lives; invite their fans to participate in their videos by adding comments on YouTube; reward fans in their videos by personally mentioning them; act in positive and supportive ways toward other players on their worlds; and aim to remain approachable and accessible to fans in "real life." They also actively foster their network of fans across multiple digital platforms. In these ways, they build a sense of intimacy that is not available to children in many of their other media experiences. This closeness, and the authenticity invested within it, locates the Let's Player as being highly recognizable as both a fellow Minecrafter and an everyday person. Abidin (2018) reinforces these perspectives by outlining how online microcelebrities differ from more traditional celebrities:

> Where traditional celebrities practice a sense of separation and distance from their audiences, microcelebrities have their popularity premised on feelings of connection and interactive responsiveness with their audiences; where traditional celebrities may be known for their performance craft and skills, microcelebrities are expected to display themselves unedited as "real" people with "real" issues; and where traditional celebrities may have extensive fame among a large global audience, microcelebrities exercise popularity that while narrower in breadth is far deeper. (12)

The Minecraft Let's Player, then, is attractive as a celebrity, but this is balanced with a sense that this is a "real" person, an image that the Let's Player cultivates.

In summary, a theory of peer pedagogies recognizes that knowledge may be exchanged in intimate relations as well as more public or community-based relations; it recognizes that a sense of friendship is developed via parasocial relations, involving emotional investment; and it recognizes that peer pedagogies are activity constructed by microcelebrities to reduce social distance between themselves and their fans.

Available Designs and Pedagogical Framing

The outcome of Let's Players' pedagogical practices is that they provide young Minecraft players with available designs for their own Minecraft participation, including designs for playing, embodying, discussing, and displaying Minecraft. Within multiliteracies theory, "available designs" are part of a semiotic system that involves interactional practices between "available designs," "designing," and "the redesigned" (New London Group 1996, 74). This framework sees "semiotic activity as a creative application and combination of conventions (resources—Available Designs) that, in the process of Design, transforms at the same time it reproduces these conventions" (New London Group 1996, 74). Applying multiliteracies to digital media, Sheridan and Rowsell (2010, 5) maintain that "Design Literacies seeks to understand the emerging logics and dispositions of those designing innovative digital environments where many students learn to be problem-solvers in their everyday out-of-school literate activities." In this sense, Let's Players design new ways to engage with Minecraft. As Burwell and Miller (2016, 116) suggest, Let's Plays include processes of meaning making within games and mobilize literacies associated with remix and appropriation. Separately, Burwell (2017) suggests that Let's Play videos provide young people with models for media production. Within multiliteracies theory, the kinds of activities that take place in and around Minecraft Let's Players may be thought of as occurring within "orders of discourse":

> An *order of discourse* is the structured set of conventions associated with semiotic activity (including use of language) in a given social space—a particular society, or a particular institution such as a school or a workplace, or more loosely structured spaces of ordinary life encapsulated in the notion of different life worlds. An order of discourse is a socially produced array of discourses, intermeshing and dynamically interacting. It is a particular configuration of Design elements. (New London Group 1996, 74, emphasis in original)

From this perspective, Let's Plays establish orders of discourse about what it means to be a Minecrafter and a Let's Player. Minecraft's "existing designs" include not just the builds that Let's Players share on YouTube, but the embodied practice of being an authentic Minecraft participant. In Let's

Play videos, the existing design is not just discursive; it is material and performative in the form of peer modeling and in the form of the Let's Player herself.

Let's Players present their gameplay in a variety of ways as a reflection of the content they are interested in producing and according to how they aim to relate to their fans. Some Let's Players are more casual and unstructured in their play, while others are more purposeful. Some set out to entertain, while others are more intentional in their aim to instruct or pass on gameplay knowledge. Furthermore, across the hundreds of videos produced by a single Let's Player, there is movement from more or less "casualness" and more or less intentionality. Drawing on pedagogy theory, one way to think about this is through the concepts of classification and framing (Bernstein 1973), which provide a way to consider how Let's Players arrange and frame Minecraft knowledge and skills.

The selection of Minecraft content for Let's Play production—what to focus on in play—requires the classification of Minecraft knowledge and makes assumptions about what is important, fun, challenging, or potentially interesting for the audience. Assumptions are made about what counts as Minecraft play and what does not, and because Minecraft is such an open world, the choices made by Let's Players help to establish the most appropriate forms of play for particular player communities or audience members. For instance, some player communities may focus more on using the game's building and design features, while other communities may focus more on the opportunities provided by the game for combat with either "mobs" (nonplaying characters) or other "live" players. Alongside these processes of classification, this content can be framed in various ways to suggest varying degrees of formality and normativity, and knowledge about particular forms of Minecraft play may be more or less formalized. Within a particular Minecraft community, there may be set ways to undertake particular kinds of activity, or the "rules" of play may be very casual and relaxed. For instance, within the family-friendly practices of the Minecraft Let's Players discussed in this book, there is a distinctive lack of swearing and very few examples of players intentionally ruining other players' work, which is more frequent in Let's Plays made for older audiences.

Atkinson, Singh and Ladwig (1997, 121) suggests that "classification (power) and framing (control) structure the symbolic insulations between and within categories of discourse, agents and sites in the classroom." The principles of classification and framing may be either strongly or weakly regulated, "depending on the negotiating power of teachers and students" (121). Classification and framing may be used as a way to consider performativity, pedagogical norms, and opportunities for variation present in Let's Play videos. Using this theoretical framing, along with cinematic and television techniques for modes of address discussed earlier in the chapter, forms the basis for a substantial part of the analysis in chapters 6, 7, and 8.

5   Exploring YouTube Let's Plays and Peer Pedagogies

This chapter outlines my approach to exploring the peer pedagogies at work in children's interactions with Minecraft Let's Play videos. The approach aims to identify how Let's Players foster authentic selves to create a sense of intimacy with their viewers, developing the conditions for peer pedagogies to emerge. To tease apart how Let's Players establish authenticity and peer pedagogical relationships in the following chapters, I address six questions.

1. How do Minecraft Let's Players establish authenticity in the context of social media entertainment?
2. What kind of microindustry has formed around Minecraft Let's Play production?
3. What assumptions do Let's Players make about their viewers, and what performative practices allow them to be recognizable to their viewers?
4. What modes of address do Let's Players establish through their use of voice for commentary, including intonation and modulation, and through use of stylistic features such as camera shot, editing, and movement?
5. What insights can we gain into peer pedagogies by considering fan practices?
6. How are Minecraft knowledge and practice classified and framed in various ways by Let's Players, and what is the relationship of this to peer pedagogies?

To answer these questions, I watched hundreds of videos from three Minecraft Let's Players—Stampylonghead (Stampy), StacyPlays, and KarinaOMG—and selected between ten and fifteen videos from each for closer analysis. I chose these three Minecrafters for a range of reasons.

Stampy was one of the original and most successful family-friendly Minecraft Let's Players, and he has been interviewed numerous times, providing insights into his perspectives and decision making. He also maintains a vlog (stampylongnose) in which he directly answers fans' questions and provides background insights into his life and motivations for Let's Play production. Stampy also moved into the production of directly educational material for the Wonder Quest series (stampylonghead 2019), funded directly by YouTube, which provides a revealing contrast with his more entertainment-based content.

Like Stampy, StacyPlays maintains a vlog (stacyvlogs 2019) where she provides insights about her personal life and motivations, and she has been interviewed numerous times at conventions about her production practices. She has also produced educational content for her Field Trips series (stacyplays 2017b), providing a contrast with both her entertainment content and with Stampy's Wonder Quest videos. Stacy's content is also interesting because it is developed around a themed narrative, focusing on pets, pet rescue, and animal welfare.

Finally, I chose to focus on KarinaOMG as a successful Let's Player who is close in age to her fans. While Stampy is in his twenties and Stacy is in her thirties, Karina is not yet a teenager. She also presents an interesting case study because she is a more rounded social media entertainer than either Stampy or Stacy. Minecraft play is just one of her online activities, which includes producing a diverse range of content for her family's highly successful social media business.

These three are family-friendly Minecrafters in the sense that their content is highly self-regulated and intended for an audience of children. The videos contain no coarse language, no references to adult concepts, and very few examples where the Let's Players purposefully set out to harm other players unless it is part of the fun of an episode. As noted in chapter 1, similar Minecraft YouTubers include DanTDM, BigBStatz, Sqaishey Quack, LDShadowLady, PopularMMOs, iBallisticSquid, Grian, Amylee 33, Smallish Beans, iHasCupquake, and Mumbo Jumbo. Together, these Minecrafters and YouTubers form a loose microindustry based around the development of Minecraft content intended for children and early teens. Members of this group sometimes collaborate with each other to produce videos or have other relationships with each other; for instance, Stampy and Sqaishey met through Minecraft and eventually married each other. Several members of the group have appeared together at events such as MineFaire, a fan convention based in the United States, and several were featured in the *Minecraft: Story Mode* (Telltale 2019).

The videos I selected for closer analysis reflect the number of views they had garnered (examples of each Let's Player's most popular videos were chosen) and to represent the Let's Player's typical style. These videos were viewed and notated under several categories:

- Mode of address
- Video style, structure, and production values
- Voice tone and intonation
- Explicitness of "teaching"
- The video's likely appeal to children
- Common devices, such as catchphrases and patterns of activity
- Community building through directly addressing fans
- Fan comments
- Cross-platform presence

I have not aimed to complete a scientific or overly systematic analysis of the videos. Rather, I have developed a narrative about how each of the three Let's Players establishes authenticity with fans in different ways and how this enables peer pedagogies to flourish. The account is necessarily incomplete. Each of the three Let's Players has uploaded hundreds of videos, often experimenting across styles and genres. My account asserts that in general terms, Stampy's persona is that of the caring big brother with Peter Pan qualities; Stacy establishes herself as a fun family member who loves pets and animals; and KarinaOMG is the kid next door with "gamer" and "YouTuber" cred, who has made it big. Each of these personae invites peer pedagogies in different ways, but they all deeply rely on the establishment of friendship and authenticity because it is not possible to fake these roles and establish and maintain a large following.

A further restriction of my analysis is that the selection of the three main YouTubers discussed in the book reflects a broader lack of diversity in the YouTube family-friendly Minecraft video production community, which is relatively small; centered on the United Kingdom, Canada, and United States; and largely white. Burgess and Green maintain that YouTube's participatory culture has allowed a greater diversity of individuals to become cultural producers but that the platform's affordances and logics may discourage diverse perspectives. They suggest, "YouTube remains a potential enabler and amplifier of cosmopolitan cultural citizenship—a space in which individuals can represent their identities and perspectives, engage with the self-representations of others, and encounter cultural difference" (Burgess and Green 2018, 100). At the same time, they suggest that the platform's cultural logics and affordances shape opportunities for participation and audience engagement with diverse voices. There could be numerous reasons that the Minecraft Let's Players who have become visible on the platform represent such a narrow range of voices, including the logics of YouTube's algorithm and the take-up of Minecraft within Anglo-centric sociomaterial practice.

The Family-Friendly Minecraft Let's Player Microindustry

On one level, my analysis aims to describe the microindustry that has developed on YouTube around a small group of Minecraft Let's Players who make content for children aged from about four to twelve years of age. While I describe this as a microindustry because of the limited number of Let's Players producing content for this genre, the number of views gained by these producers makes it a multimillion-dollar network, producing content viewed by a very large number of children. To gain insights into this microindustry, I have drawn on available metrics from sources such as Socialblade.com to better understand the popularity of each of the creators on YouTube itself and on other platforms, including Facebook, Twitter, and Instagram. I have conducted extensive online searches to find as much information as I can about each of the YouTubers. These searches have provided a combination of industry information, journalistic accounts, and fan-produced materials. My research has also provided access to interviews with StacyPlays creator Stacy Hinojosa and Stampy creator Joseph Garrett. I could not locate similar interviews with Karina Kurzawa, KarinaOMG's creator, most likely due to her age. Interviews with YouTubers are typically recorded at industry conventions, which include panel discussions with YouTubers about their production processes and insights about the industry. Both Stacy and Stampy have also been interviewed by mainstream media, sometimes discussing their views on being a Minecraft YouTuber. The two older Minecrafters create separate vlog videos, in which they regularly discuss their production processes and sometimes YouTube and Minecraft as industry platforms. A final source of information about the popular cultural impact of the microindustry is the reach of Let's Player merchandise such as books, T-shirts, toys, and other licensed materials, which I have traced through searches of online retailers.

There are two reasons for analyzing the microindustry. The first is to provide background context to each of the YouTubers' production practices and to locate them appropriately in the industry in terms of the relative size and scale of their impact over time. This is not intended as a systematic account of audience reach, but rather to offer a general sense of each YouTuber's story of cultural production. Stampy, for instance, was one of the top ten most watched YouTubers in 2014, but his audience has not grown to the same extent as other YouTubers such as DanTDM. KarinaOMG is the youngest YouTuber of the three discussed in the book, but at the time of writing, the growth of her channel has rapidly outpaced both Stampy's and Stacy's channels. Gaining a sense of audience reach provides insight into the current state of the microindustry and the volatility of an industry that relies on high levels of personal commitment from the YouTubers as they strive to remain authentic and entertaining for their fans. That is, it provides insights into the digital labor required to maintain a sense of authenticity with fans.

The second reason to analyze the microindustry is to discuss how each Minecrafter helps to shape the industry through his or her various commercial activities. Each of the three Minecrafters monetizes his or her popularity in ways that extend beyond the production of Minecraft videos. Both Stampy and Stacy have published successful books—Stampy a children's book of activities associated with his Lovely World (Garrett 2016), and Hinojosa novels extending the narrative world she has established through her videos (StacyPlays 2018, 2019). Kurzawa produces highly popular videos with her brother, some of them directly monetized through sponsorships. All three YouTubers have merchandise available through online stores. Tracing examples of Let's Player content across various platforms, including traditional media forms, provides insight into how pedagogies may become both public and personal as fans engage with the story worlds created by the Let's Players across a range of platforms.

Addressing the Viewer through Entertainment and Play

At the heart of Let's Play production is entertainment, and one of the objectives of my analysis is to establish how Let's Players construct their personalities as children's entertainers. I aim to identify how Let's Players address viewers to gain and keep children's attention and loyalty. In a digital landscape of ever-increasing entertainment choice and abundance, the competition for children's attention is fierce. It is informative to identify the kinds of entertainment conventions that have emerged within what remains a relatively new entertainment genre. I aim to understand what makes Minecraft Let's Plays entertaining or fun to watch, although I am aware that video gameplay involves more than fun (Hung 2011). The payoff for investing time in gameplay may be understanding a new process, solving a problem, or persisting to achieve a new level (Gee 2007b). Therefore, a great deal of the pleasure of watching Let's Play videos is likely to be the vicarious experience of watching a Let's Player overcoming a challenge, learning how to complete a complex task, or being exposed to a new way to use the game as a platform for creativity. However, despite the rewards of video-gaming "hard fun" (Papert 2002), the popularity of Let's Plays is also likely due to how entertaining they are to watch. Because Let's Plays are not walkthroughs, as established in chapter 3, the fun of watching is centered on the stories Let's Players create as they play. Let's Players may create humor through comedic techniques and joke telling (including in-jokes), use surprise or suspense, play minigames, and provide viewers with new experiences. A focus of my analysis is to outline the kinds of narrative techniques the three Let's Players use to entertain their fans. One of the main outcomes of the analysis is to identify how Let's Players balance fun with Minecraft's challenges and how children learn from this.

One of the reasons children watch Minecraft Let's Plays is that they provide them with ideas about what can be done in the game. It is not always easy to know what to do in the game as it was intentionally produced, without tutorials or instructions, because it is an open-ended sandbox game (Arnroth 2014). To a great extent, Minecraft requires players to develop their own challenges and storylines because it does not include levels in the way that many digital games do. The level of increasing challenge in Minecraft gameplay is self-imposed in the sense that it is possible to play at a particular level without "advancing"; the game does not have obstacles that need to be overcome to enable ongoing play. One of Minecraft's main pleasures is sharing achievements with another player because it is difficult to measure achievement without an audience. Minecraft does not provide obvious feedback in the form of points, achievements, or other explicit rewards. This was borne out by a surprising finding from research I conducted with ten- and eleven-year-olds playing Minecraft at school in 2014 in which they said they preferred playing the game at school rather than at home because of the social interaction this afforded them (Dezuanni, Beavis, and O'Mara 2015). Most were not allowed to play on multiplayer servers at home and had to rely on play with siblings and the occasional visit from a friend to be able to share their builds and generate play together. When they were allowed to play the game at school, for many it was the first time they had experienced the game with their friends and they were excited to be able to visit their classmates' builds. From this perspective, Minecraft Let's Play videos fill a need for a social experience of the game for children interacting with it in relative isolation at home. The videos allow children to share someone else's play and achievements, and they are entertaining because they provide examples of what to do and how to play in Minecraft.

Stylistic Features and Mode of Address

A consideration of Let's Play videos' stylistic features provides an opportunity to further understand how performativity is manifested in material, as well as discursive, ways in the videos. It is not just what Let's Players say and what they build in their videos to construct a narrative that matters. Their appeal is also related to how they speak, how they present themselves through physical appearance and bodily gestures, and how they visually design their worlds. Voice intonation and modulation establishes a Let's Player's sonic presence within children's physical space and allows them to construct their personality through commentary. The style and quality of a Let's Player's voice is central to how they establish a mode of address to appeal to their audience. The three Let's Players discussed in the book have three distinctive voices, which are central to how they create entertaining characters. The use of catchphrases and taglines is particularly important to the personalities Let's Players develop because they become part of the Let's Player's brand or "presentational self" (Marshall 2010). Characterization is also established through commentary that reveals the Let's Player's inner thoughts about the game and life beyond the game, their attitudes to particular issues or challenges, and their reactions to other players or events in the game. Through their commentary, Let's Players may simultaneously present what Marshall refers to as a "public self," which is an official version of the self as a celebrity; the "public private self," in which more personal details are shared with the audience; and the "transgressive intimate self," where celebrities potentially "overshare" details about themselves and their views about the world (Marshall 2010). Minecraft Let's Play characterization thus becomes a complex blend of the creation of a persona and self-presentation as a celebrity.

Self-presentation in Let's Play videos occurs through physical appearance and bodily gesture though a complex combination of the "real-world" player and the player's avatar. Stampy presents himself as a cat in Minecraft, with a distinctive orange and white "skin"; Stacy's character always appears wearing a distinctive blue and white top; and Karina's Minecraft skin has a pink top with red hearts on it. My analysis aims to tease out how these Let's Players' online appearances relate to their real-world image and their fandom. For instance, many of Stacy's YouTube videos attract fan comments about her personal appearance, presumably directed toward her real-world appearance, rather than her avatar, even when she does not appear as herself in her Let's Play videos. This has implications for normative expectations of gender performance, peer relationships, and fandom, but as Keogh (2018) argues, it also raises questions about how audience members identify with Let's Players as both players and in-game avatars.

Although Minecraft avatars are very blocky in construction, it is possible for Let's Players to visually construct their characters through bodily gesture and through the manner in which they record their videos. Particular avatar actions serve to reinforce Let's Player commentary. For instance, the equivalent of the camera shot in the videos is the Let's Player's point-of-view perspective. That is, the viewer sees what the Let's Player "sees" in general play. In Minecraft, this is from the first-person perspective, and character-specific techniques are often used at key moments to emphasize achievements, surprises, or threats. Some Let's Players also use tropes at key moments. It is generic, for instance, for Let's Players to shift to a third-person image of their avatar at the beginning and end of the video, so the avatar visually "addresses" viewers.

The visual design of Minecraft worlds is the most direct way for Let's Players to appeal to viewers. The in-game sets or recording sites for the videos are usually carefully chosen or constructed to allow trouble-free and interesting narratives to emerge. Stacy, Stampy, and Karina have quite different approaches to visual design. Stampy's "lovely world" is highly designed and uses lots of primary colors to create a bright, positive space. Stacy's "Dogcraft" uses a "shaders" modification to change the appearance of the Minecraft world; and Karina usually plays in a relatively straight-forward version of Minecraft that is similar to the world her fans play; she also unpredictably mixes things up by introducing modifications for specific episodes. My analysis discusses these visual elements in more detail to explore how they are used as part of the overall construction of a world that appeals to children and becomes part of the reason for their loyalty to particular Let's Players.

Audience Practices

To gain an understanding of audience practices around Let's Play videos I analyzed the comments posted by fans on a select number of YouTube videos produced by each of the Let's Players. Successful Let's Play videos frequently attract several thousand comments, and commenting has been a form of community building and social interaction for young Let's Play fans. In early 2019, however, YouTube began disabling comments on children's videos uploaded to the platform as part of its response to accusations that it had exposed children to inappropriate adult behavior. Later in 2019, following a ruling by the US Federal Trade Commission that YouTube had violated the Children's Online Privacy Protection Act (COPPA), the platform made additional significant changes to children's content. In January 2020, almost all comments on children's videos on YouTube were disabled, making the kind of analysis conducted for this project increasingly difficult.

Most previous work on the YouTube comments function has understandably focused on how comments become a site for online "hating" and abuse (Lange 2014). I instead focus on ways that comments were used to develop community and support peer pedagogies. Commenting on a Let's Play video allows an audience member to directly address the video with praise or criticism or to make suggestions about the production of future videos. Comments are frequently directed toward the Let's

Player with personal observations, expressions of loyalty, and positive affirmations. Other comments are meant for the broader community or are intended as personal exchanges between community members, although it is impossible for commenters to keep conversations private. Fans frequently respond to each other's posts in agreement or disagreement and with expressions of support. Occasionally the Let's Player responds to fans in the comments, either directly to a fan or to the whole community. Commenting also involves fans in specific community practices. For instance, a degree of status may be earned by being among the first commenters on a new video—fans will respond to a new posting by commenting "first," "second," "third," and so on. Each commenting community develops its own loose rules and practices, and one of the objectives of my research was to identify attributes of the specific commenting communities that develop for Stampy, Stacy, and Karina.

My analysis of the YouTube comments had four steps. First, I scraped comments from a select number of videos using an online tool, the YouTube Comment Scraper (http://ytcomments.klostermann.ca), which allowed me to download all the comments attached to a single video as a spreadsheet file. Next, I read all the comments, which typically included two to three thousand entries, some of them just a few words in length and some of them two to three sentences. Through this process, I noted emerging themes and broke these down into categories such as "praises the Let's Player," "refers to themselves," and "offers advice." Third, I generated a list of key terms emerging from my read-through, related to the relationship being developed between the Let's Player and fans. Finally, I conducted searches of the comments using the key terms to see how often particular themes emerged in the data and to identify typical examples of comments. Chapter 7 in particular reports on the outcomes of this process to provide depth of analysis about commenting practices among Stacy's viewers.

In addition to comment analysis, I considered how fans interact with Let's Players through forms of online content creation or via fan practices. Like other celebrities, popular Let's Players attract support from fans who participate in their world by producing stories, images, and videos to extend and supplement the celebrity's original content to bring the storyworld "alive" for themselves (Jenkins 2013). Fan-produced content enables fans to identify themselves with a particular celebrity, allows them to gain status with the fan community, and provides pleasure as it extends the storyworld created by the celebrity. It may also allow fans to critically engage with the celebrity's content (Jenkins 2013). A fundamental aspect of fandom is that it provides the opportunity to accumulate knowledge about the celebrity and their creations and to display knowledge through the production of cultural artifacts (Fiske 1992). I searched for references to each Let's Player on popular fan sites including the fan fiction site Wattpad, the online art gallery DeviantArt, the FanPop site, and YouTube channels dedicated to the Let's Players. My goal was to gain insights into the appeal of each Let's Player and to understand the kinds of knowledge about the players that fan communities valued. Through this process, I aimed to better understand how each Let's Player aimed to produce an authentic self for his or her audience and how fans took up this image and brought it to life through their own creative activities.

Let's Play Knowledge, Classification, and Framing

One of this book's key aims is to identify what is considered to be worthwhile or valued Minecraft knowledge and practice and to consider this against the backdrop of the "official" culture of schooling. In Bernstein's (2000) terms, Minecraft knowledge and practice are not particularly valuable in formal education contexts unless the game is used in ways that become codified and classified through what counts as school knowledge. Within Minecraft player communities and Let's Play communities, gameplay knowledge and skill are highly valued. As I have argued elsewhere (Dezuanni, Beavis, and O'Mara 2015; Dezuanni 2018), Minecraft knowledge among children can be important social currency in school hallways and playgrounds and during playdates with friends. Fiske argued that "fan culture is a form of popular culture that echoes many of the institutions of official culture, although in popular form and under popular control. . . . Fandom offers ways of filling cultural lack and provides the social prestige and self-esteem that go with cultural capital" (Fiske 1992, 33). From this perspective, learning what counts as valuable Minecraft knowledge and practice can be an important investment for Let's Play fans, not just for their own enhancement but so they can become recognizable to others who value the game.

Chapters 6, 7, and 8 identify the kinds of knowledge and practice Let's Players prioritize and value and trace their similarities and differences. My contention is that unless a Let's Player displays expertise in his or her play and narration, that player is highly unlikely to be accepted as authentic by children watching Minecraft Let's Play videos. Viewers expect Let's Players to be exceptional in some way related to how they play the game. Therefore, I seek to understand how each Let's Player may be recognized as being expert at Minecraft play, while acknowledging that play on the platform involves many different practices cutting across Abidin's (2018) qualities of microcelebrity, including everydayness, exclusiveness, exoticism, and exceptionalism. What Let's Players understand about Minecraft, what they can do on the platform, and their use of game-related terminology establish their credibility and their right to be a figurehead for a specific fan community. By outlining the scope and comprehensiveness of each Let's Player's knowledge and practice and what they emphasize as being important in the game, I establish what they classify as important and essential in Minecraft Play.

The classification of Minecraft knowledge as valuable or important to the community relates to how each Let's Player plays the game. As established in chapter 2, the platform appeals to players for different reasons, with some players placing more emphasis on designing and building, while others aim to establish a world with characters and locations. Some purposely fight "mobs" to gain resources, while others like to set themselves challenges by visiting new and dangerous locations to find rare resources. Of course, Let's Players may record videos involving all of these approaches at different times for different purposes.

My analysis also aims to identify hidden rules of gameplay—that is, less obvious practices or tacit knowledge that informs the values and practices of the fan community. For instance, I am interested in practices that promote what James and colleagues (2009) refer to as "good play," or "online conduct that is meaningful and engaging to the participant and is responsible to others in the community and society in which it is carried out" (xiv). This approach is particularly interesting in the context of children's entertainment, which has a long-standing tradition of seeking to regulate children's moral and ethical practice. Buckingham (2002) argues that children's television plays an important regulatory and ideological role not just in terms of valued knowledge and experience, but in terms of children's socialization into dominant social norms prescribed by adults. He states that children's media often become sites of negotiation over the boundary between childhood and adulthood. From this perspective, Minecraft Let's

Plays may become the site of negotiation about desirable forms of play, at least as far as adults are concerned.

Let's Players bring themselves into being in ways that are intelligible to their community, and within the family-friendly videos discussed in this book, this is generally framed through the development of a casual, playful, and fun persona. Furthermore, Stacy, Stampy, and Karina would be considered by most adults to be safe bets for their children's entertainment, uncontroversial in terms of their content and values. And as each of these Let's Players sets out to entertain children, they are unlikely to seek controversy. In an interview in the *Guardian*, Stampy argues:

> I make sure that in every situation I'm acting in a way that I would hope other people would act. If I get really angry about something, I'm not going to tweet about it and if I play a mini-game and end up losing, I'm going to say congratulations and be gracious about it. People think if you don't swear in videos you're child-friendly, but there's a lot more to it than that. (Dredge 2016c)

While the Let's Players discussed in this book are not considered to be controversial, several high-profile YouTubers have attracted condemnation for their public commentary. YouTube's most successful Let's Player, PewDiePie (103 million subscribers, 24.5 billion views), was widely criticized in 2017 for anti-Semitic behavior. While many PewDiePie fans defended his humor, his actions were clearly not acceptable within the context of broader community standards. He subsequently lost a lucrative contract, worth several million dollars, with Disney.

There is a precarious relationship between Let's Players—the ideas and attitudes they share with fans and the implications for peer pedagogies. My approach to this has not entailed a close reading of the language used in the videos, and I have not completed a critical discourse analysis. Rather, I have been attuned to instances of framing that are particularly careless or potentially harmful. It is informative to identify the values and norms repeated in Minecraft Let's Play videos framed by particular social and cultural logics. Of course, video games have long been assumed to be heteronormatively masculine. Minecraft Let's Plays seemingly expand the notion of the gamer, and the microindustry discussed in this book includes as many female as male gamers. However, this does not necessarily lead to challenges to existing normative relations. One of the aims of my analysis is to consider the social framing around gender, race, and sexuality that occurs in the videos created by the Let's Players. How Let's Players narrate their videos by deploying particular social and cultural norms is an important consideration of how peer pedagogies promote or vary normativity.

In a more direct sense, how Let's Players frame Minecraft knowledge in more and less formal terms, and how they relate that to knowledge development more generally, is of interest. Some Minecraft Let's Players produce content that verges on being instructional and might more accurately be described as belonging to the how-to genre. Comparing different kinds of Let's Player content aims to show how pedagogical framing relates to Let's Player authenticity and the characteristics of microcelebrity. One of my goals, then, is to establish that Let's Players frame Minecraft knowledge along a continuum of degrees of formality and that videos along this continuum appeal to viewers for different reasons. This is particularly interesting in relation to the more specifically educational content produced by Stacy for her Field Trips videos and Stampy for his Wonder Quest series, both of which are attempts to provide official learning content for children. As Stampy and Stacy have branched out into the production of educational content, each has been challenged to maintain an authentic self as they have become more teacher-like.

6   Stampy's Lovely World

Stampylonghead, otherwise known as Stampy Cat or simply Stampy, is the best known of the three Let's Players discussed in this book and one of the most popular children's Minecraft Let's Players on YouTube. Stampy is the creation of English YouTuber Joseph Garrett, who from 2012 to mid-2017, uploaded at least one twenty- to thirty-minute Minecraft video per day. Stampy is currently ranked the 622nd most subscribed YouTuber, with just over 9.2 million subscribers, and is ranked 181st for number of views, with 7.2 billion views, making him a significant online microcelebrity, particularly among preteens. Although Garrett largely stopped production of his Minecraft Let's Plays in October 2018, his videos continue to be watched over 788,000 times each day, and he continues to attract new subscribers (table 6.1).

Stampy is a significant commercial entity whose merchandise can be found in department stores and online, and this has the potential to make him the least accessible YouTuber discussed in this book. However, his self-presentational practice and mode of address allow him to remain accessible, approachable, and authentic, garnering the deep loyalty of his community of fans. Despite his celebrity status, he remains accessible to fans through his Let's Talk vlog videos, in which he discusses his professional decisions, and through his openness about his relationship with fellow Let's Player Bethany Bates (Sqaishey Quack), who often appears with him in his videos.

This chapter explores the characteristics that make Garrett a consummate entertainer whom children identify with as a peer. Garrett argues that while he did not set out to target children, his videos naturally appeal to them, and he has responded by remaining family friendly. He states that this was an organic process rather than a strategy

Table 6.1
Stampy Analytics, 2020

New Subscribers in Previous Thirty Days	Daily Average New subscribers	Views in the Previous Thirty Days	Daily Average New Views	Total Subscribers to Date	Total Views to Date
10,000	300	23.6 million	789,000	9.2 million	7.2 billion

Source: Social Blade (2020d).

(stampylongnose 2016b). Of the three Let's Players discussed in the book, Garrett places the most emphasis on developing entertaining scenarios within his videos. From the perspective of Abidin's four characteristics of microcelebrity (Abidin 2018), he combines the everydayness of his personality with the exceptionalism of his Minecraft knowledge and skill. While each of his video series is themed or built around a particular location, episodes typically feature a specific task, minigame, or building challenge that he narrates in a highly entertaining way. He is often joined by friends, and together they model good friendship practices as they have fun playing Mincecraft.

The chapter presents an analysis of Let's Play videos and video blog posts that Garrett produced to illustrate how he presents himself and the ways in which his activity may be considered pedagogical. Discussion of fan responses to Stampy provides insight into fans' relationship with him and the ways in which his videos perform a peer-based pedagogical function. The chapter also pays attention to Garrett's foray into specifically educational content, the Wonder Quest web series, as a contrast to his more entertainment-focused videos.

Joseph Garrett, YouTuber

Garrett's rise to YouTube stardom was relatively swift. According to several online sources, he studied video production at a university in England with a desire to become a video games journalist. After graduation, then in his early twenties, he left a bar-tending job in 2012 to produce Minecraft YouTube videos full time, and by late 2014, his Let's Play videos made him one of the top five most viewed YouTubers worldwide, with more than 220 million views per month (Cohen 2014), placing him ahead of celebrities like Justin Bieber, One Direction, and Katy Perry. He received somewhat incredulous media attention in the United Kingdom in 2014 as an example of someone "getting rich" on YouTube: "Forget Justin Bieber, the latest You-Tube star is a university graduate from Portsmouth who plays Minecraft full-time" (Woollaston 2014); and "Stampylongnose is the Pied Piper of YouTube, calling a generation of children to their computers every after-noon while apparently bypassing anyone who has been through adoles-cence . . . potentially making him up to £200,000 per month" (Merz 2014).

Garrett worked long hours for his success: between 2012 and 2018 he uploaded over 3,300 videos and self-reported working eleven hours a day on video production and interacting with fans (Burrell 2015). He produced videos for several series on his channel, including non-Minecraft content. His most popular and longest-running Minecraft series, Lovely World, con-sists of 649 videos. Other popular Minecraft series are the Cave Den series, produced with Sqaishey Quack (105 videos, August 2015–October 2016); Ocean Den, also produced with Sqaishey (80 videos, November 2016–May 2018); The Stampy Flat Challenge (20 videos, April–September 2016); and Stampy's Funland (35 videos, February–October 2018). In addition to Mine-craft Let's Plays, he has produced videos for a range of other games, includ-ing Stardew Valley (ConcernedApe 2016), The Legend of Zelda: Breath of the Wild (Nintendo EPD 2017), Pokémon Moon (Game Freak 2016), and Terraria (Re-Logic 2011).

Despite his YouTube success, Garrett has avoided calling himself a "You-Tuber," and in interviews he often says that he considers himself to be a video producer first and a games expert second. He seems to want to avoid the stereotype of the YouTuber celebrity whose success is built on self-disclosure and gimmickry. In an interview with the *Guardian* he says,

> My personal life I keep very secret. For lots of YouTubers, part of their appeal is that they are so real: they share literally everything. I could never do that and would never want to do that. I still consider myself a video producer at heart, not necessarily a YouTube personality. (Dredge 2015)

He uses his "Let's Talk" videos, featured on the separate Stampylongnose channel, to share his perspectives on a range of topics and issues related to the production of YouTube videos. For instance, in "Let's Talk—Questions and Answers—Episode 4" (stampylongnose 2018a), he says he chooses to avoid the tactics used by YouTubers to build a subscriber base. He discussed this topic in more detail in his video "Let's Talk—Is My Channel Dying" (stampylongnose 2017a), in which he addresses the issue of receiving fewer views than he did at the height of his popularity:

> I feel like I have a good understanding of what I could do to get more views. Like the games I would have to play, the style of video, the pace of the videos would probably need to be stepped up. And then my title and thumbnail game would need to be completely overhauled and, you know, I'd have to join the "YouTube game" as I call it. You know, whatever you want to call it. Clickbaiting, or just, promotion, or . . . I'm just not interested in doing that. (stampylongnose 2017a)

Garrett's Let's Talk videos reveal the depth of his knowledge of games culture and the gaming world. For instance, in "Let's Talk Question and Answer Episode 4" (stampylongnose 2018a), he canvasses a range of games topics and issues as he answers fans' questions. He shares his views on several different games, including Overwatch and Fortnight, and why he prefers Minecraft over Roblox and Pokémon Go. His commentary about these games comes across as being well informed. His identity as a games player and expert is reinforced in the video "Let's Talk—How Minecraft Is Changing" (stampylongnose 2018b), where he provides a comprehensive explanation of the different versions of Minecraft available for different devices and how Microsoft's decisions about these versions will affect players. In a later video (stampylongnose 2018c), he explains his disappointment about Microsoft's decision to reduce its support for the version of the game on which he created Lovely World. Garrett's willingness to criticize Microsoft is significant, particularly because Microsoft's approach was a contributing factor in his ultimate decision to cease Minecraft video production.

Garret's video producer identity is on show in a video from July 2013, where he gives a behind-the-scenes tour of his gaming and video production setup (MagicAnimalClub 2013). The video has over 9.0 million views and provides an overview of "how I record, in case any of you wanted to record like me." The video is a particularly interesting for the mundane nature of Garrett's bedroom recording "studio," which is located in an everyday setting that no doubt resembles many of his viewers' bedrooms or living rooms. He shows a standard television, with an Xbox and PlayStation attached, and a laptop computer for editing video and uploading to YouTube. Just a couple of semiprofessional items of equipment capture gameplay and voice recordings. Through the window in the background, viewers see what appears to be an everyday suburban setting. The mundane nature of the video is also reinforced by its amateurish style; it was shot by a friend and looks very much like a home video recording, complete with poor-quality lighting and sound.

During the tour of his facilities, Garrett's knowledge of video production becomes apparent when he starts to discuss sound recording using a high-end microphone and his editing process and software. He also brings out a high-end video camera to share with the audience:

> It's nongaming, but I might show you. Hidden away in my cupboard up here, I do have a video camera as well. A lot of people don't know that I actually do real filming as well, like freelance stuff, and I got a Panasonic 101 which is my main camera, but I'm not going to become too nerdy and talk about all of its features and stuff, but expect more live action stuff coming soon. (MagicAnimal-Club 2013)

This focus on "nerdy" ideas and live-action production is significant because it reinforces Garrett's professional media producer identity, in contrast with his YouTuber identity. This theme is repeated through his subsequent more "professional" projects like Wonder Quest, discussed below. Garrett's balancing of his professional identity as a media producer and children's YouTube entertainer is a delicate one that does not always pay off, as the discussion of Wonder Quest will show. He often seems least authentic when he branches into the production of content that is less well aligned to his fun Stampy persona.

Stampy's celebrity status and his bankability are reflected in a range of commercial and industry pursuits, some of them gimmicky despite Garrett's desire to be taken seriously. For instance, in September 2018, Stampy Cat was acknowledged by Guinness World Records for recording the "fastest time to make and display 10 cakes in Minecraft" (PC Edition). The record is published in the *Guinness World Records: Gamer's Edition* (Guinness World Records, 2017). The story was featured in the publicity for the gamer's edition of the book, in recognition of Garrett's popularity and clearly as an endorsement. In the same month, a search for "Stampy" on Amazon.com listed dozens of products, including The Pyjama Factory Stampy Cat Long Nose Animal Costume; the book *99 Kids Jokes—Stampy Edition* (Lester 2014); Stampy T-shirts; *Stampy Cat Maths: Problems for Elementary School* (Gameplay Publishing 2017); a Stampy Cat edible icing image for a one-quarter-sheet cake; *Diary of a Wimpy Stampy Cat: Airplane Adventures*

(Harrison 2015); and several "away from keyboard" novels featuring Stampy (Mosley 2015a, 2015b, 2015c). It is unclear how much of this merchandise is officially licensed, providing income for Garrett. However, his *Stampy's Lovely Book* received significant publicity prior to its release and was one of the most popular children's books of 2016, selling almost 120,000 print copies (Kantor 2017). In addition, his *Stick It with Stampy! Sticker Book by Stampy* (Garrett 2017) had shipped 200,000 copies as of January 2017 (Publisher's Weekly 2017). Both books have presumably sold significantly more copies since; *Stampy's Lovely Book* is still available in stores and online.

Throughout 2014 and 2015, Garrett appeared in mainstream media including *Good Morning Britain*, where he was interviewed alongside collaborator David Spencer (iBallisticSquid 4.2 million subscribers), an interview that has over 1 million views on YouTube (YouTube, 2014). The BBC's CBBC children's channel visited Stampy at his home asking viewers, "If you haven't heard of Stampy, where have you been?" (CBBC 2014). The BBC also interviewed him in March 2014 alongside a BBC games developer, describing him as a "Minecraft entrepreneur" (Precey, 2014). An indication of Stampy's appeal in 2015 was that at the end the year, Garrett appeared live at the Royal Society of Edinburgh Christmas Lecture in front of 2,000 screaming fans in Dundee, Scotland, the largest audience for the lecture in its 230-year history and featuring its youngest presenter (Royal Society Edinburgh 2015).

Stampy's Voice, Mode of Address, and Stylistic Features

To provide some insight into why children find Stampy so entertaining, I discuss episode 348 of "Stampy's Lovely World," *Minecraft Xbox—Big Barn*, published on October 21, 2015 (860,340 views), as a typical example of a building episode from the series (stampylonghead 2015). The twenty-minute episode begins with Stampy's trademark introduction, "Hellloooo, this is Stampy, and welcome to a Minecraft Let's Play video. And another video inside of Stampy's Lovely World." The video begins in Stampy's Minecraft home, and as he completes the introduction, he moves outside to his deck area, where we see a view of his Lovely World from his point of view. He then goes back inside as he explains what he is going to be doing in the episode, and he introduces the audience to his episode helper, Choo

Choo, a recurring character in the series. Stampy's voice is very upbeat and animated as he introduces his friend, and as Choo Choo makes a grand entrance, Stampy makes a joke about how easily Choo Choo has entered the room. This is humorous because Choo Choo's avatar "skin" features an unusually tall head, which makes it difficult for him to get through doorways. Stampy says in a mocking but friendly tone, "You've really started to master doorways, I'm very proud of you, Choo Choo."

Next, Stampy completes his regular episode rituals. He eats some cake for breakfast, says hello to his dog Barnaby and then heads over to the Love Garden. On the way, he runs into Veeva Dash, another regular series character. Stampy seems surprised to see her, saying he didn't know she would be joining him, but he is happy to see her. He arrives at the Love Garden, which is in a large open space, covered with Minecraft "signs" featuring the names of all the people he has previously added to the garden. Selected fans are added to the garden as a reward for sending Stampy artworks and stories about themselves. When he arrives, he says he is adding Paul because Paul made a blanket with the Stampy design on it. A picture-in-picture image appears on the screen featuring Paul and the large blanket. Stampy says, "It is absolutely huge, and it took him over two months to make, and I think it looks so amazing. I wanted to say, thank you so much for making it and for sending me the picture, and welcome to my Love Garden." Stampy then goes to a new location and chooses his dog, Benton, to accompany him for the episode.

With his regular episode tasks completed, Stampy walks to the town area of his Lovely World, and along the way, he explains that the plan for the episode is that he and his helpers are going to build a pharmacy, but he explains that it is spelled "farmacy": "Pharmacy is spelled with a 'ph' . . . I am going to be building a pharmacy spelled with an 'f,' an f-a-r-m acy." He asks the audience if they get the pun. He explains it will be a pharmacy where you can get medicine, but themed around a farm and will built as a big barn. He notes that the traditional color for a barn is red, and he starts to build as he notes that the barn is going to be twelve blocks wide and seventeen blocks deep. The barn, he says, will not be very big, but it will have a very sloped roof and two levels—the first level where the medicine will be, along with a few animals (he laughs at this and repeats the farmacy pun), and upstairs where the medicine will be produced. As he is building, he asks Veeva Dash and Choo Choo to start building as well; he provides them with instructions on what to do. He explains that the building will have a stone brick ceiling.

After a period of building with continuous commentary, Stampy stands back from the build to see if it is designed correctly and realizes he needs to make an adjustment because the building is not symmetrical. He goes to his crafting table and creates stone brick stairs to use for the barn's roof, explaining the process as he goes. He continues on, explaining each step in the building process, experimenting a little too. He regularly goes back to the front of the barn to see how the build is looking and expresses excitement when he is pleased with his progress. About two-thirds of the way through the build, he notes that whenever he builds, he likes to complete the outside first so that he has a nice blank canvas to work with during the next episode. He also says that he is looking forward to working on the floor of the barn, because there is an open space underneath it, and that means he and the others can have a game of "spontaneous spleef" (a Minecraft minigame in which players destroy blocks underneath other players to try to make them fall down). As he finishes the outside of the barn, he says he is amazed at how much they have been able to complete together, helping each other out. He and Choo Choo move to the front of the barn and briefly admire its design and what they have achieved together. Finally, the three companions play a round of spleef inside the barn as they dig up the ground. He outlines some rules for the game, stating that the last person standing will be the winner, and he blocks up the entrance to the barn so no one can avoid being dug out by leaving the barn. Stampy wins the round. The three then create the barn floor, with Stampy explaining the pattern they are creating on the floor with wood. As he completes the floor, he begins to explain what will be inside the barn. When they are finished Stampy suggests they give each other a pat on the back for their good work. He ends the episode by thanking his helpers and explains that they will finish the build in the next episode. He briefly moves into third-person perspective and looks directly at the audience and says, "Byyyeeee . . . ," his standard way for ending an episode.

From the moment a Stampy Let's Play video begins with his tagline, "Hello and welcome to a Minecraft Let's Play Video," to the end of each episode, he speaks in a highly recognizable tone, interspersed with chuckles and laughter. He often uses intonation to make his voice sound exciting and engaged, and he quickens the pace of his commentary at key moments to heighten the excitement. Garrett describes the Stampy character as "a bigger, brighter, better version" of himself (Burrell 2015). Stampy seems to have a passion for Minccraft. He never seems to get bored with it or has difficulty deciding what to do in the game. He is always positive and fun loving. Newman (2016, 286) suggests "Stampy's pixelated appearance in Minecraft is unambiguously an avatar representing a living, breathing human player," achieving what Newman suggests is the "performance of intimacy and connection with the audience."

Of the three Let's Players discussed in this book, Garrett is the most conventional entertainer, and this is reflected in the planning that goes into each episode. The ritual he performs at the start of each episode provides some predictability for the audience, but also the surprise of revealing the latest fan to be added to the Love Garden, a highly sought prize for fans. Garrett has made it clear that there is a strategy and planning behind each episode (Fun Kids 2015), and this is also clear in the "Big Barn" episode, which fits into the flow of a series of episodes, featuring a loose ongoing storyline complete with recurring characters. An internal episode and series logic enables Garrett to build on a successful formula that he has developed over time. It is clear that Garrett carefully planned the "Big Barn" episode and had likely practiced building the barn at least once prior to the episode, even though he experimented with some aspects of the build and made some mistakes while recording. It also seems clear that he timed the episode carefully so that there would be time to include the game of spleef, which added some excitement to the end of the build that might otherwise have ended less climatically. It is also appropriate because although this was a building episode, some of Stampy's most popular episodes are based entirely around the characters playing minigames.

An appealing aspect of Stampy's Lovely World for children is that it is bright and colorful. From the opening images of "Big Barn," it is noticeable that Stampy has built many of the structures in the world using wool, the Minecraft material that allows a player the most control over color, because it can be dyed with colors obtained from a variety of sources in the game. Minecraft building materials such as wood and stone are muted colors and cannot be changed, so it is difficult to introduce bright colors into the world without using wool. Stampy's abundant use of bright colors is a deliberate design choice to create a world that is cartoon-like and reflects his upbeat, energetic personality. The big barn is bright red, and surrounding it are several other brightly colored buildings; the roadways surrounding the buildings are often patterned, and other structures are typically designed with highly contrasting colors. The overall effect is a world that resembles a kind of fun fair, which is appropriate because dispersed throughout the world are various minigames and fair-like attractions.

The "Big Barn" episode is also a good example of how Stampy's mode of address recognizes the agency and legitimacy of his young fans as Minecraft players. He avoids talking down to them and pitches his commentary in a manner that is appropriate for the age group. His language is not overly technical but not childlike either. He tends to provide simple, clear instructions, and he demonstrates his building process as he goes along in the following way:

> With barns, they are not normally completely filled in. They normally have a little opening in the very middle, which is used, I think, to lift things up into the barn. So I'm going to open that up here, and there's also going to be an opening into the top level. So, if I just break away about four blocks here like this, this can be where the little opening on the front is [demonstrates]. And I'm actually going to use some white wool around the outside like this [demonstrates] because this is just a kind of another traditional color for barns in real life. . . . Actually, I think I have done it a little bit too high. (stampylonghead 2015, 9:48–10:31)

As the final part of the excerpt indicates, he is not afraid to show that he sometimes gets things wrong and uses his mistakes to illustrate that adjustments are often necessary and that persistence pays off. Exceptionalism is combined with everydayness in his building process (Abidin 2018). His approach is exceptional because he is able to quickly and efficiently create a new building that resembles an actual structure. From a child's perspective, he is well informed about the design of barns, and he is able to lead the creation of the build almost trouble free. The effort Garrett puts into researching, designing, and practicing the build is obscured by the ease with which he completes the build during the recording. At the same time, his building process is "everyday" because it is not overly technical or out of reach for viewers who might want to go off and try to build a version of the barn themselves. His designs are not overly complex, and he does not use materials that are too difficult for regular players to obtain.

The "Big Barn" episode also provides a good example of how Stampy models friendship and forms of cooperation and collaboration in Minecraft. Although this episode features nontalking friends, he makes it clear that Choo Choo and Veeva Dash are essential to the building process. Presumably the characters are nontalking to enable Stampy to record the episode in a predictable way. There Is also a sense in which Stampy's nontalking friends represent Stampy's fans, many of whom request in the comments stream to be allowed into Stampy's world. In other episodes and other series, Stampy's videos include characters whose commentary is recorded, such as iBallisticSquid and Squaishey, both Let's Players with a proven ability to entertain fans. Although the "Big Barn" episode friends are nontalking, they are essential to the episode, not just in terms of completing the build but as part of the entertainment and of Stampy's message of friendship and cooperation. His friendly and humorous introduction of Choo Choo at the start of the episode adds warmth and a welcoming atmosphere to the video, as does his greeting of the unexpected Veeva Dash. The game of spleef with the friends adds fun and excitement to the episode and models a way for friends to play together. More than this, though, his explicit commentary around the need for cooperation in the game and his message that more can be achieved by working together provides pedagogic framing for a version of positive play.

Stampy's Authenticity

To understand how Stampy may be considered a peer to his fans, it is necessary to understand how he remains authentic against the backdrop of his significant success as an online celebrity. Drawing on Marwick (2013), I argue that Stampy's authenticity is established through his insistence on producing entertaining videos to a high standard; the exceptionalism of his Minecraft knowledge and play; and his willingness to display aspects of his hidden inner life with his viewers, despite his claim that he aims to remain a private person. He creates safe and fun spaces for children's entertainment and is honest about the decisions he makes affecting his viewers. Through these practices, Stampy/Garrett comes across as an everyday person who is down to earth, genuine, accessible, and talented.

A significant degree of Stampy's authenticity is created through his well-established Minecraft expertise and his games knowledge in general. It is clear from his play and commentary that his design and building skills are highly advanced. While he plays Minecraft in a recognizable way, he generates unique and original approaches to play that continually challenge his audience to consider the limits of their own Minecraft play. He shows what is possible with Minecraft, using his knowledge and skill to develop entertaining and informative scenarios. This is important within a sandbox platform like Minecraft, which is open and generally nondirective. As Garrett suggested in a BBC interview "I come up with stories within the game, I give people lots of ideas for things that they can play with their friends and I just talk about the things the children are interested in" (BBC 2014). As I noted in chapter 5, children do not necessarily know how to have fun in Minecraft or how to navigate some of the game's more complex features. As an open sandbox game, one of the challenges of the game for children is knowing what to do with their creative freedom, especially if they are playing on their own.

In addition to his status as an expert Minecraft player, Stampy's authenticity is related to his everydayness. A good example is the consistency Garrett displays as he moves from the production of his Let's Play videos to disclosing aspects of his personal life. This includes the development of his romantic relationship with fellow YouTuber Bethany Bates (Sqaishey Quack). As Garrett slowly revealed his relationship with Bates during 2015, he shared a greater level of intimacy about himself than he previously had. An indication of fans' interest in the couple's relationship is the presence of numerous stories on the fan fiction site Wattpad about the two. Stories written by fans include "Stampy and Squaishey," thirteen parts (3,200 reads); "Stampy and Sqaishey Love Story," fifty-four parts (87,000 reads); and "Adopted by Stampy and Sqaishey," twenty parts (4,000 reads). Stampy and Sqaishey have also recorded numerous videos together, particularly for the Cave Den and Ocean Den series that feature their ongoing conversations revealing insights into their relationship, at least in terms of how they play together in Minecraft.

At various stages of his YouTube career, Garrett has uploaded vlog posts that provide his audience with insights into his life. These vlogs are produced with low production values and resemble home movies that provide a sense of intimacy and closeness that more highly crafted videos do not. They resemble the kinds of videos a family member or close friend might share. A good example is a 2015 vlog produced to share the experience of attending the 2015 London Minecraft convention, "MineCon 2015—Day 1 vlog" (MagicAnimalClub 2015; 2.9 million views). The video starts with Stampy/Garrett and his friends sitting in a living room, and he directly addresses the audience in selfie style, sharing the news that he and his friends are about to go to MineCon. This is a significant moment, because MineCon was a highly popular convention for Minecraft fans, and in 2015, it was held in London, a relatively short drive from Stampy's home. In addition, Stampy explains that it is his first MineCon and that he is appearing onstage at the event.

While explaining the trip to MineCon, Garrett shares some new Stampy merchandise that has arrived at his home. He does this in a casual manner, in the way that he might share the merchandise with a friend who has dropped in for a visit; he does not plug the merchandise in an overt manner, and his promotional technique does not come across as being cynical or crassly commercial. As he speaks about the merchandise, Bates casually leans on his shoulder, and he and his friends talk over each other with friendly banter about the merchandise. Fans are ostensibly invited into an intimate moment within the friendship group. The video then cuts to the MineCon venue, where Garrett talks directly to camera as an "everyday person" about what it is like to be at MineCon, albeit one who will be onstage. There is an exclusivity about this because he is walking around the venue before it opens to the public, and he talks about having a special panelist pass. As he records, he is also followed by some YouTubers who are taking footage of him. Nonetheless, Stampy's manner is casual and relaxed, and fans are positioned as being part of his inner circle. Toward the end of the video, Garrett stands on the steps outside the venue and shares a painting of himself and Bates that a fan and her dad sent to him, which, he says, "will be put up above the mantelpiece and admired very much." This personal thank you to the fan comes across as being sincere and heartfelt. It is also an acknowledgment of his relationship with Bates (early in their relationship) and a shared intimate moment with her and with his fans.

Vlogging also allows Garrett to speak directly to his audience about why he makes videos, how he attracts subscribers, and why he makes specific decisions about his channel. In a video from May 2017, "Let's Talk—The Future of My Channel" (stampylongnose 2017b), he explains that he is changing his approach to making videos: he will no longer upload a Minecraft video each day. He explains that he wants to reduce the number of videos he makes so he can focus on the quality of the videos and reduce the amount of stress associated with making multiple deadlines:

The big thing is this Friday will be the first day in a very long time where I won't be uploading a Minecraft video. So for probably about four and a half years . . . I've uploaded a Minecraft video every single day and I'm ending that streak and in a way I'm kind of a little bit sad about it. But also, I'm kind of looking forward to it because I know once I've kind of ended that streak and I've had the first day where I don't upload a Minecraft video, then any other days after that, like, I'm not going to be stressed about it.

Throughout most of the video, Garrett talks about his work processes and how less focus on Minecraft will allow him to pursue his other video production passions. Toward the end of the video, he also reveals that he has had some negative experiences working with people in the YouTube community and he's looking forward to being in control of his own production processes. He says, "I've been forced to have to kind of, you know, be associated with or, you know, kind of be with just people in the community that . . . it's just not been fun to be with them." This final statement seems to indicate that Garrett has become somewhat disillusioned with the industry and offers a rare insight into the challenge of dealing with success and maintaining a persona as a happy, fun, and "everyday" person. The overwhelming majority of the 2,600 comments under the video show support for Garrett, saying, for instance:

Start the trend #StampyForLife because Stampy has done everything he can to keep his viewers happy—most people are being supportive about what he said in this video—but if some people are mad about it, they only care about the videos and not for Stampy himself! Stampy needs to be appreciated for everything he does and not just for the amazing videos he uploads everyday! Stampy, you are an incredible person, keep being you, and stay Stampy! "Thanks for watching, and I'll see you all later! Byyyyyyyyyyyyyeeeeeeeeeeee!"

It is striking that the response from this fan, and hundreds more like it, are couched in very personal terms that address Stampy as a friend rather than an abstract entertainer or star. The comments largely show care and compassion and grant Stampy permission to slow down. The request to "keep being you, and stay Stampy" seems an exhortation for Stampy to remain fun loving and happy whether he is making videos or not. The fan seems to assume that Stampy's character, presented in his Let's Plays and vlogs, is consistent with his real-world personality, an indication that he has successfully presented himself as a kind of real-world friend as much as a character.

Stampy Fandom

Perhaps the clearest example of both the fandom that surrounds Stampy and Garrett's challenge in meeting his fans' expectations is the Love Garden within his Lovely World. The Love Garden is a series of honor boards, made from Minecraft signs, that record the names of fans Stampy wants to acknowledge. Part of the challenge for Garrett is that only a small number of fans can be highlighted from the vast number who watch his videos, so being named is ultimately a kind of prize. Being added to the Love Garden brings fans directly into Stampy's world, and the acknowledgment provides the chosen fan with a certain status. Fans may be acknowledged for a range of reasons, but mostly for creating a tribute to Stampy, typically in the form of fan art. In episode 354, "Minecraft Xbox—Chicken Trail," he adds a fan for sending him a picture of Stampy and Sqaishey drawn as the *Toy Story* characters Woody and Buzz Lightyear. Episode 319, "Minecraft Xbox—Clock Shop," features a fan who sent him art that she made while in the hospital: a paper plate featuring Stampy and his collaborator Squid. In episode 398, "Minecraft Xbox—Flying Fish," he adds a fan who has sent him a photograph of her snowcat (a snowman that looks like a cat), and in episode 498, "Minecraft Xbox—Sheep Shuttle," he acknowledges a fan who has made a three-dimensional model of Stampy's house. In each case, he shows a photograph of the artwork as an overlay on top of his video and explains why he is adding the fan.

The Love Garden provides Stampy with a way to show his appreciation for fans' commitment to him, but it also allows him to demonstrate kindness and thoughtfulness through whom he chooses to include and what he says about them; it is a way for him to share his values. A key purpose of the Love Garden is that it creates a sense of community among fans. For instance, a search of the comments for the "Big Barn" episode reveals many affirmations for Paul, who was added to the Love Garden for creating a large blanket featuring Stampy. Fans' dedication to the Love Garden became obvious in mid-2017 when it faced a crisis because Stampy's world began to "lag" (process slowly) because the number of signs he had used to make the garden required too much processing power to regenerate each time he entered the space. As a result, he contemplated removing the Love Garden, as he explained in a video, "My Lovely Problem" (stampylonghead 2017). The four-minute video attracted almost a million views and received over 13,000 comments. Many of the comments in support of keeping the garden argued that it was an important part of the world and that Stampy's Lovely World wouldn't be the same without it. Quite a few of the comments were also nostalgic, referencing the amount of time fans had been watching Stampy and that the garden was a record of time passing, as a kind of archive of fandom. For instance, one fan writes:

> Stampy. The love garden is amazing. You spent so long making it and even its extension. It's a piece of history and Stampy fans will turn into haters if this massive piece of history is destroyed. A love book just wouldn't be the same. I have been watching for a very long time now and if the love garden was taken away it would upset me even though it isn't my world.

Ultimately Stampy chose to keep the Love Garden in place, though many fans agreed that alternatives such as a "Love Book" with the names of chosen fans could stand in for the garden. As a physical space in the world with a presence over time, the garden seems to hold meaning for many fans, even if they have never been chosen for inclusion. Defense of the Love Garden is a defense of the fan community. In a broader sense, it is a defense of My Lovely World and the way Stampy has chosen to design his world and bring it to life over several years. For many viewers, the dependability of being able to watch a new Stampy video each day, including honoring a chosen fan each day, seems to have been an important part of the experience. In response to "My Lovely Problem," one fan says:

> You know, I watched Stamps daily for probably 3 years at one point, I'm now about to turn 21 and this is the first vid I've clicked on in years. I just wanna say thanks to you and all your friends for making me laugh daily throughout that time, enjoy childhood while you can kids, these are your best days of your life.

The fan's comment is somewhat evocative of the Peter Pan myth that might apply to Stampy in more general terms—the story of the boy who never grows up. The Stampy character, played by the adult Garrett, is full of fun and happiness in a kind of Neverland. He acts as a captain as he takes his audience on adventures and shows off his many skills and talents. It is productive to think about Stampy's traits, and his appeal to fans as a fun, childlike but loyal hero who shows other children how to have fun. Unlike Peter Pan, though, Garrett recognizes his role as an adult and the responsibility he has toward his child fans. These two roles of childlike hero and adult guide come into tension at certain key points in the pedagogic relationship between Stampy and his viewers.

Stampy's Peer Pedagogies

In Bernstein's terms (1973, 2000), the videos on Lovely World might be considered moderately classified and framed in their presentation of Minecraft knowledge. As seen in the "Big Barn" episode, Stampy demonstrates a way to build that provides a model for designing and building a barn, but he is not insistent that his is the only or even the best way to build. Having said this, by playing in particular ways to provide available designs for his fans, Stampy inevitably classifies some knowledge and skills as being more important than others. This leads to knowledge transfer about better ways to play Minecraft, and Garrett shares Minecraft literacies in the process, including how to build with particular materials, how to use the conventions of particular styles of play, and how to interact with others in the game. Furthermore, Stampy's videos frame Minecraft knowledge in a manner that is open to experimentation and playfulness. Although he provides structure and direction in his videos, he is never so rigid or demanding that only certain kinds of play count as being legitimate. It would be fair to say that Stampy's Let's Play videos leave room for viewers to make their own judgments about what is and is not important.

One area where Garrett is more didactic in his approach to gaming is through his Let's Talk videos and his desire to teach children about some of the negative aspects of online culture. For instance, in "Let's Talk—Questions and Answers—Episode 4" (54,000 views) (stampylongnose 2018a), Garrett introduces an element of critical thinking about games, gaming culture, and Internet culture in his answers to fans. He discusses his views on people who have started to "hate on Minecraft" (unfairly criticize it), and he talks about how he hopes his videos make a positive difference in the world, saying that it is possible to change the world with art and culture. He specifically says it is important to be a positive influence on the Internet to counter widespread negativity. In his video "Let's Talk—Hate Comments" (stampylongnose 2016a), he addresses trolling directed toward him and others and aims to establish some guidelines for acceptable online behavior:

> The "troll" has become part of YouTube culture, you know. I think troll has just become another name for bully. Like, a troll seems like more of a jolly thing— look at me I'm just trolling, don't take it personally, I'm just joking, I'm just trolling. But if you're trolling and acting mean, it's no different to being a bully. It's

just another name for it. . . . If you're directly attacking other people, then that's where the line is drawn. It's no longer ok. (stampylongnose 2016a)

This normative approach to advice about online behavior leaves little room for interpretation or negotiation and is more didactic in its delivery, both because Garrett is speaking directly to the camera but also because his passion for the topic is obvious and he seeks to establish a position for children to follow. Although his Let's Talk videos are watched by far fewer viewers than his Let's Play videos, they nonetheless help to establish Garrett's social position and become an avenue for him to share his opinions and views in ways that are less available to him in his Let's Play videos. Despite their serious content, they come across as a consistent and authentic extension of Stampy/Garrett, who is sharing his expertise, knowledge, and experience with his fans in an accessible way.

An example of where Garrett has been less successful in maintaining authenticity as he balances his persona as the fun Peter Pan figure with his role as a responsible adult was his involvement in the production of the Wonder Quest series. Garrett's motivation for Wonder Quest was his sense of responsibility as a role model:

> It's something I'm always actively thinking about when I'm making videos. It was the motivation behind Wonder Quest: I realised I had this audience of children, so let's do something good with that. That even goes beyond the videos to real life and what I'm tweeting about on social media. I've become this Stampy character, which is still the real me, but it's almost like the perfect version of me, or the cartoon version. I make sure that in every situation I'm acting in a way that I would hope other people would act. (Dredge 2016c)

However, the much more schoolish approach to knowledge sharing in the Wonder Quest series was not overly successful. By 2015, Stampy's success as a Minecraft Let's Player was well established, and he was widely recognized as the most successful Minecraft Let's Player for children, with over 2 million subscribers. In early 2015, he began a collaboration with Maker Studios, a successful YouTube multichannel network (subsequently purchased by Disney in late 2015), to make videos for an educational YouTube channel. Speaking about the launch of Wonder Quest at industry event MIPTV, Garrett suggested children would learn from the channel because of Stampy's popularity: "If you take their engagement and put it into a more productive space like education or the arts, they're going to be involved in that, they're going to be engaged" (Wonder Quest 2015). The series was promoted as a "learning adventure" or "edutainment" series (Dredge 2015) and described as follows:

> An all new Minecraft adventure taking place in the land of Wonderberg. In episode One, Stampy is summoned to save the day and stop the evil wizard, Heinous. Stampy teams up with the good wizard Keen to find all the missing wonderments and restore wondering to the town. Can Stampy and Keen stop Heinous and his two evil henchmen, Flunky and Lackey? Or will Wonderberg lose its wondering forever? Find out on this season on "Wonder Quest"! (Wonder Quest 2015)

Wonder Quest was made up of three separate elements across two seasons. The main series consisted of twelve scripted and high-production-value episodes made within Minecraft with a focus on a particular educational concept or topic. This series was supplemented by an accompanying I Wonder cartoon series made using traditional drawn animation, which explored each educational concept in more depth. Third, a series of Side Quest Let's Play videos were produced and hosted on Garrett's main channel and made as typical Let's Play videos. Wonder Quest also featured a number of other YouTubers, including iBallisticSquid (4.2 million subscribers), ShayCarl of the Shaytards (4.9 million subscribers), EventubeHD (6.5 million subscribers), and AmyLee33 (1 million subscribers). YouTube acquired the rights to Wonder Quest in part as content for its YouTube Kids App, launched in 2015 (Dredge 2015), making Stampy an important cornerstone product to ensure YouTube Kids' success.

The series was initially successful, presumably due to Stampy's popularity, with the first video attracting over 7 million views. However, views of the videos quickly dwindled, and only twenty-four episodes were made. Several videos in the second season attracted under 1 million views each, and to date, the Wonder Quest channel has attracted just over half a million subscribers (compared to Stampy's main channel with 9.2 million subscribers). One explanation for the series' relative lack of success was that it was much less spontaneous than Stampy's usual videos. As Garrett stated, "It's different to my normal videos just playing and talking about Minecraft. It's a completely scripted show, and the production values are much higher: there's an original score and lots of sound effects and overlays" (Dredge 2015).

The Wonder Quest videos were an experiment in applying Let's Play content to a new genre, funded and produced industrially, but the resulting stylized nature of the videos moved away from the spontaneous nature of genuine Let's Plays. Content was highly classified in the videos to align to more school-like knowledge. Garrett suggested, "I might be estimating the size of trees or learning about the water cycle. There's always something Stampy needs to learn in order to get past the challenge" (Dredge 2015). Episode 10 of series 1, for example, features Stampy learning about bridge supports to build a suspension bridge, and he explicitly learns about engineering from his companion, Wizard Keen, who says, "It's an important part of engineering, Stampy, designing, building and then testing. And when it doesn't work, you redesign and you try again." The episode shows the disaster that might occur if the bridge is not well built. The problem with this from a Minecraft perspective is that Minecraft bridges do not follow the usual laws of physics, and Stampy has previously built hundreds of Minecraft bridges without worrying about specific design rules. The worthwhile lesson therefore becomes somewhat meaningless for most regular Minecraft players who recognize the in-world inauthenticity of the scenario.

Garrett's lack of experience as an educator and his misunderstanding of Minecraft's educational affordances was revealed in interviews he conducted about Wonder Quest (Dredge 2016b). He argued that viewers would respond to it primarily as entertainment rather than education, and he stated that he aimed to speak to his audience as a friend in the Wonder Quest videos, without recognizing how this might compromise the authenticity of his Stampy persona as understood in the context of Lovely World. Finally, he assumed that Minecraft's popularity and its ability to attract children's attention would transfer to their willingness to engage with educational content outside school. He argued, "When people think of games, it's something you play from beginning to end with one story. Minecraft is more a plaything like plasticine or Lego. There's so much depth to it and what you can do within it" (Dredge 2016c). However, Garrett did not recognize the limitations of applying relatively didactic processes on a platform designed for experimentation and play. Of course, Wonder Quest did attract a reasonably healthy audience (although it was smaller than for his usual Let's Play videos), and children dedicated to learning school-like knowledge would no doubt learn from the videos. However, the videos fell into a trap identified by the well-documented history of the difficulties of introducing digital games into education (Ito 2009). In producing the Wonder Quest series, Stampy made the mistake of treating his fans as students rather than peers. Let's Plays are not typically created to teach someone something, even if children learn a lot from them.

7   Animal Rescue with StacyPlays

StacyPlays is the YouTube channel of American microcelebrity Stacy Hinojosa, who is in her mid-thirties. The channel differs from the others discussed in this book because its main series, Dogcraft, builds an ongoing coherent narrative about animal rescue and Hinojosa's own experiences of animal companionship. This storytelling focus culminated with the publication of two New York Times best-selling novels: *Wild Rescuers—Guardians of the Taiga* (StacyPlays 2018) and *Wild Rescuers: Escape to the Mesa* (StacyPlays 2019). The StacyPlays channel creates a strong sense of community among young viewers who identify with Hinojosa's love of animals and her openness about her three dogs, Page, Molly, and Polly, and her cat, Milquetoast, all of which feature on both her Let's Play channel and her vlog series, Stacyvlogs (394,000 subscribers). Her vlogging channel description demonstrates the close parallel between Hinojosa's life and her Minecraft Let's Plays, stating, "Join me and my dogs and cat on our adventures in the mountains of northern Utah! I also play a lot of Minecraft on my gaming channel, StacyPlays" (stacyplays 2018a). Many StacyPlays videos involve rescuing dogs and creating dog-themed builds. The channel is described as "family friendly" and aims to "avoid the use of offensive language, gun violence or adult themes." This chapter argues that Hinojosa comes across to children as a fun, cool adult who shares their passion for pets and Minecraft. As a consequence, many of Hinojosa's activities provide designs for young Minecraft players in terms of ideas for building and for ways of becoming in Minecraft and in the world, with a particular focus on kindness toward animals.

Animal companions are a familiar trope in children's entertainment, providing what Melson (2009, 44) calls "Love on Four Legs." In the case of

StacyPlays, Hinojosa's focus on her dogs and cat enable her to create a high level of intimacy. She frequently shares stories about her pets' adventures, challenges, illnesses, injuries, and fun, particularly on Stacyvlogs. Hinojosa regularly posts to her vlog channel, often with her pets also on camera or nearby. She frequently talks about the importance of rescuing animals from shelters and emphasizes that her cat, Milquetoast, is a rescue cat. Animals become a key point of emotional and informational involvement for children as they interact with Hinojosa's content, establishing a robust network of fan participation. Papacharissi (2018, 1) writes, "Balance between sentiment and information sharing renders networks, and the relationships that sustain them, lively, but also lovable." Hinojosa's world building within Minecraft creates opportunities for viewers to emotionally invest in StacyPlays' animal characters. Her first novel extends the idea of a deep connection between humans and animals, as it is about "a girl raised by a pack of wolves and her quest to protect their shared forest home" (StacyPlays 2018). The peer pedagogies that Hinojosa invites are therefore focused not just on Minecraft play but also on the social, emotional, and ethical practices of interacting with animals.

Stacy Hinojosa, Minecraft Let's Player

According to her LinkedIn profile, Stacy Hinojosa came to Minecraft Let's Play production via her work in marketing for AOL, Alloy Digital, and Teen.com (2019). She graduated from college with a journalism degree in 2005 and describes herself on LinkedIn as a "digital media executive in Los Angeles with ten years of experience conceiving and directing editorial and video content for the 12–35 demographic." For Alloy Digital, her work is described in the following professional terms:

> Managed all aspects of the Teen.com brand, website and YouTube channel including editorial and video direction, branded content, social media strategies and advertising campaigns. Created large network of publicists, TV and film executives and YouTube creators to collaborate and create over 400 original videos for YouTube.

She shifted into the production of her own Minecraft videos while producing content for Joey Graceffa, a YouTube microcelebrity with a large subscriber base (9.3 million subscribers as of April 2019). The StacyPlays channel was created in March 2013 as a means for Hinojosa to communicate

Table 7.1

StacyPlays Analytics, 2020

Subscribers Previous Thirty Days	Daily Average New Subscribers	Views in the Previous Thirty Days	Daily Average New Views	Total Subcribers to Date	Total Views to Date
10,000	330	6.8 million	220,000	2.00 million	813 million

Source: Social Blade (2020f).

with Graceffa's fans, and Hinojosa often refers to Graceffa as her best friend, reflecting a common tactic in which YouTubers support each other to build a subscriber base. While there is no reason to doubt the sincerity of the friendship between the two YouTubers, it also seems likely that Hinojosa's skills as a marketing professional enabled her to leverage Graceffa's popularity to build her own subscriber base.

In the YouTube context, the StacyPlays channel is a moderate success, with a Socialblade ranking of B, and placed 6,777th overall for subscriptions (that is, there are 6,776 YouTubers with more subscribers). Socialblade places the channel in 21,133rd place for overall current success, using its ranking system to account for current views and "other factors" (Social Blade 2020f). Given Hinojosa's YouTube ranking, it might seem surprising that she has such a strong presence in children's culture. Despite her moderate YouTube success, however, she is a successful children's social media entertainer. She was contracted alongside other children's Minecraft social media entertainers to perform in episode 6 of the Minecraft Storymode game adaptation, produced by Telltale Games; other celebrities included Stampy (9.2 million subscribers), LDShadowlady (4.8 million), DanTDM (22.4 million), and Captainsparklez (10.7 million). She also featured in an episode of Stampy's Wonder Quest series (see chapter 6). Hinojosa sells merchandise on her own website (shopstacyplays.com), including cat- and dog-themed backpacks, pins, fidget spinners, mugs, lanyards, lunchboxes, pencil cases, and posters. Some of these are available on Amazon.com, along with her books, and other retailers such as Walmart carry her books.

Hinojosa has featured on panels at major industry and fan conventions, including VidCon (2016), PAX South (2017), and MineCon (2016). These events provide her with opportunities to present herself as both a professional content producer and as being accessible to her fans. She has vlogged about several of the events, posting the videos to her Stacyvlogs channel, providing behind-the-scenes insights into what it is like to be a YouTuber at a convention. Her 2016 MineCon (stacyplays 2016b) appearance is captured in vlog footage of her in the lead-up to her appearance, meeting fans, checking out the stage setup, meeting with other family-friendly Minecraft YouTubers such as Sqaishey Quack (966,000 subscribers), and her fans' reactions as she takes to the stage. The video provides insight into how Hinojosa balances celebrity with authentic self-representation at both the event itself and for her online fans viewing the video. It is mostly presented in vlog style as a selfie shot as she walks around the venue, giving the impression that viewers experience MineCon as Hinojosa experiences it. The footage is rough and seems only lightly edited to capture highlights. It is home video footage of the type many people capture when visiting a new place. There is no way to know if the shots were prepared in advance—it is more than likely she walked through the venue prior to recording—but the video comes across as being spontaneous. Her interactions with fans are generous, and at one point after recording herself meeting a young fan, she says she is going to turn off the video so she can "hang out" for a while. The video also provides a model for how to be a YouTuber. She asks the MineCon audience of mostly young children how many of them have their own YouTube channels, and there is an enthusiastic yes from many in the audience.

StacyPlays, Minecraft Celebrity, and Authenticity

Hinojosa's attendance at live events like MineCon provides an opportunity for her to reduce social distance between herself and her fans. Even if a fan is not fortunate enough to be one of the relatively few to attend a video convention in person, they can watch Hinojosa's "home video" of the experience. Just as Garrett's Let's Talk videos provide Stampy fans an opportunity to feel intimately connected to him, Hinojosa's vlogging allows her to connect to fans in a direct, intimate, and honest way on a regular basis, reflecting several of Marwick's (2013) characteristics of microcelebrity authenticity.

Hinojosa also displays particular kinds of Minecraft expertise, although in a different way from Garrett. A narrative running throughout her early videos is that she is an "accidental" YouTuber who doesn't know how to play Minecraft very well. While Garrett seems to have come to Minecraft as an experienced player, Hinojosa is initially a relative novice, and in her early videos, she jokes about how frequently she "dies." In the seven years she has been creating StacyPlays videos, Hinojosa's skills and knowledge obviously improve, providing viewers an opportunity to see her learning how to play Minecraft. How a viewer experiences StacyPlays videos obviously depends on if they watch in sequence as videos are uploaded, or if they come to her archive as a new viewer after several years. Fans are also likely to rewatch videos, viewing her earliest videos simultaneously with her latest ones; indeed, there is no way to know how the videos are watched, short of conducting in-depth audience research. It is unlikely, though, that fans watch only in sequential order and watch the videos only once. The videos therefore represent an archive of Hinojosa's development of Minecraft knowledge over time, where one of the pleasures of viewing may very well include tracing this change.

Vlogging allows Hinojosa to share intimate life moments with fans, particularly related to her pets and her interactions with animals in a broader sense. For instance, her vlog post "Page gets surgery" (stacyvlogs 2017a) focuses on her dog Page being treated for a possible skin cancer. The video includes footage of all aspects of Hinojosa arriving at the vet, shots of the dog undergoing a procedure, Hinojosa nervously waiting while her pet recovers, and footage of postsurgery care, all with commentary that demonstrates her love for her pet. The video has over 3,800 YouTube comments, most of them expressing sympathy for Page and Stacy, with many of the posts recounting viewers' own experiences with vets, including the death of their pets. One commenter says:

> When I saw pages stitches I started to cry get well soon page and Stacy when you started to talk about page was geting surgery i was like **OMG is page going to be ok what happened** love you Stacy and page and all of the dogs and cats <3.

Stacy's posts also occasionally reveal intimate events featuring her family members. One post, "My mom has cancer" (stacyvlogs 2017b), discusses the impact of her mother's diagnosis on her own life. Although she avoids becoming emotional on camera, several edits suggest she stops during recording. She shows footage of life inside her family home, including some interaction with her father and some brief shots of her mother in the hospital, without showing her mother's face. The main purpose of the post is to explain why she has not vlogged for several months, with a brief written explanation under the video: "Hope this explains what's been on my mind the last several months. I'm so happy she is doing so well after her surgery. Thanks for all the support." The disclosure of these deeply personal moments invites Hinojosa's fans into her life in an intimate way that seems to be a genuine request for support. Of the more than 5,000 comments on the video, most express sympathy and care, with many recounting examples of family members who have also had a cancer diagnosis. Many fan comments receive replies from other fans, also expressing understanding and sympathy. The comments overwhelmingly give Hinojosa permission to take time off from making videos to spend time with her mother.

Hinojosa's broader online presence builds a picture of a friendly person who maintains her humility, even while interacting with other microcelebrities. For instance, an online search for information about StacyPlays brings up an entry on the Famous People website. Under the heading "What makes Stacy Hinojosa so special" the entry states:

> Stacy is this chubby, bubbly girl who fulfils every criteria of your best friend. She is someone with whom you can share a laugh and would not hesitate to spill your guts to. She is extremely talented and funny. Her friend, Joe Graceffa, seems to have a riot while he games with Stacy. She is very-very respectful of her adoring fans and loves the attention that they shower on her. (Famous People 2018)

The language of the entry suggests it has been written by a fan, and the emphasis placed on friendship reinforces the sense that a significant part of Hinojosa's appeal is that despite her microcelebrity, she remains accessible and likable.

StacyPlays's "Potato Flakes"

Throughout this book, I have argued that peer pedagogies are networked and multifarious and center on a shared passion or interest. Let's Players are the center of fan-based networks and leaders within their communities, but they are also participants within the community. Hinojosa actively cultivates her fan network across several platforms, including Twitter (740,000 followers), Facebook (31,000 followers), and Instagram (410,000 followers). She calls her fans "Potato Flakes," after her love of a type of milk containing potato flakes (StacyPlays Wiki 2019). Her fans appreciate how accessible Hinojosa is to them as an active member of the community. An example of her openness is a tweet from June 2018 in which she invites people visiting

Disneyland that day to keep an eye out for her: "Not going to Disneyland tomorrow because of my book signing in LA . . . but I'll be there tonight so say hello if you see me." Several fans respond with disappointment that they have just missed her, and some ask if she can go on a different day because that's when they will be there.

The sense of accessibility Hinojosa has developed is also actively cultivated in her videos. In many episodes of the Dogcraft series, she breeds a Dalmatian puppy and names it after one of her fans, with the ultimate goal of having 101 Dalmatians. She rewards fans for a range of things, including responding to her tweets in interesting ways or sharing stories of their love for animals. She also begins many episodes in her "arf gallery," where she shares art sent in by her fans, many of them images of her or images representing events from previous episodes. Throughout her videos, Hinojosa continually addresses her audience and actively encourages them to make comments. She creates opportunities for commenting by asking questions, encourages feedback, and rewards her fans for participating. In episode 20, Hinojosa names a Dalmatian after a fan because that person commented, "Curse you Stacy do you know how many times I've been forced to rescue a dog because of your videos? My house is filled with dogs." This is presumably in response to Hinojosa's catchphrase at the end of every episode: "Page and Molly love you. Go rescue a dog." Later in the episode, she highlights a fan who has named his pig "Page." She returns the favor by naming a pig in Dogcraft after the fan and shows his photograph during the episode to thank him.

Potato Flakes develop StacyPlays content on other platforms as well. For instance, a search for StacyPlays on the user-generated fiction platform Wattpad produces over 10,000 stories written by fans. A significant number of these are within the Wattpad "adopted by" subgenre, in which fans write stories about being orphaned and adopted by a celebrity. Wattpad is described as a social storytelling platform (Wattpad 2019). Established in 2006, its founders claim it had over 70 million active users as of 2019, with over 400 million story uploads (Wattpad 2019). Bold (2018) describes Wattpad as

> a network of user generated content, which has also been described as the YouTube for stories (without the videos). Wattpad is an experimental platform for aspiring and experienced authors allowing them to publish their work, get feedback, and connect with other writers and readers. For readers, it is a platform—available

on laptops, computers, mobile phones and tablets—with a diverse array, across a range of genres (mainstream and niche), of content available for free. (19–20)

"Adopted-by" stories on Wattpad entail the main character of the story becoming orphaned and subsequently adopted by a celebrity. In a typical "adopted by" fantasy, a child or teen living in a stereotypically horrible orphanage is rescued by a celebrity who is either visiting for the purpose of adopting or for some other reason, when they fall in love with a child. After adoption, the child/teen goes home to live with the celebrity. There is a dearth of scholarship about adopted-by fan fiction. However, Novy (2004, 2) argues that mainstream literature about adoption "is a way of thinking about the family, exploring what a family is, that is at the same time a way of thinking about the self, exploring distance from family."

"Adopted . . . By Stacyplays?!" by young writer RubRubaaduubdub (2020) (1,700 reads) is a typical example of an adopted-by fantasy. The story provides particular insights into the importance of StacyPlays to her fans, at least in the fictional world of the story. Interestingly, the story is told through the first-person point of view of each of the two main children and Stacy in turn, so we read what the author imagines Stacy's perspective would be. When the two main characters, best friends Robin and Ember, meet Stacy, who has come to the orphanage specifically to adopt a child, they tell her they are her biggest fans and are the only ones at the orphanage who know about her videos. Upon hearing this, Stacy decides to adopt them both. On the first night after the girls arrive at Stacy's home, Ember has a dream in which she is a baby who is abandoned by her parents because they chose adoption over abortion. She says "These can't be my parents! I start to sob. THESE STUPID UNLOVING MONSTERS." The story then switches to Stacy's point of view:

> I walk over to her and crouch down to her level. "What's wrong sweety?" I ask calmly. "I—I my . . . par-parents!" She sobs. I pick her up cradle her in my arms running my hands through her hair. "It's alright sweety. Your with me now." I say trying to soothe her. I continue to say soft calming words.

As the story unfolds, the girls and Stacy have to deal with the challenges and routines of family life, including Ember's misbehavior at school, but these challenges are resolved without the girls being returned to the orphanage, which is their biggest fear. Stacy is a supportive and loving mom, and we read from her point of view that she cannot imagine what life would be like if she had not adopted the girls: "I smiled to myself and thought the awful thought of *what if I didn't choose to adopt them?* I smacked myself in the head and asked myself, 'How dare you ever think that, *ever?*'"

The fantasy outlined in the story may be read as a performative repetition of the norms of parental care and children's desire to be unconditionally cared for, loved, and accepted. Being adopted by someone famous adds a level of intrigue, but this does not override the desire to have a close and loving relationship. The story raises many questions about the social and psychological implications of children's perspectives on parenthood, love, and responsibility. For the purpose of this chapter, though, I want to emphasize how fan fiction reveals particular insights into the world of fandom that is otherwise difficult to access. In the case of "Adopted by StacyPlays" stories, it provides insights into the kind of relationship fans imagine they might have with Stacy. Writing about the "hurt-comfort" fan fiction genre, Jenkins (2013) argues that fans write stories in which characters undergo physical and emotional pain, providing an opportunity for the characters to experience emotions and connections to other characters that would otherwise go unfelt. He argues that the emotions evoked by these stories may be fraternal, maternal, or romantic, "depending on the fan's interpretation of the series; what matters is that affect gains overt expression within scenarios of growing intimacy and trust between the two protagonists" (174). While Jenkins is writing about fan fiction about television series, primarily about adult male protagonists, his point about fans' exploration of intimate connection and trust rings true for how adopted-by stories aim to express emotions about Let's Players.

Stacy's Voice and Mode of Address

Watching a StacyPlays video is akin to watching over someone's shoulder who is playing Minecraft in a relatively unremarkable way. The Dogcraft series videos are not as preproduced as Stampy's Lovely World videos. While Hinojosa has a directed approach and undertakes planned activities, her style is relatively casual. However, the series has two points of difference that make it unique among Minecraft Let's Play videos for children. First, Hinojosa produces her videos in the "Copious Dogs" modified version of Minecraft that includes a wider range of dogs than is available in standard Minecraft (Snubmansters 2015). Copious Dogs was produced by two independent modders, Zone and "WolfpupKG," and was first released in 2013. The modification allows Stacy to interact with dogs in ways not possible in Minecraft's standard version; for example, she can play fetch with the dogs using a special "throw bone" (episode 20). She also uses the "Shaders" texture pack (https://shadersmod.net/) that looks stylistically different from standard Minecraft. These attributes make the style of play reproduced in the videos attractive and somewhat exotic because it differs from the version children typically play themselves.

Despite the constructedness of Hinojosa's world, it is not overly structured. She plays to have fun and entertain her viewers, but her play is relatively casual. While she builds up the world over time, her structures are not particularly impressive. She does not present herself as a Minecraft expert, and her play reflects this. She builds by trial and error, working things out as she goes along, and her commentary is not so much instructive as it is explanatory. It is typically about gameplay and Hinojosa's interactions with her dogs. This contrasts with other Let's Players such as Grian (2019), who place much more emphasis on the technical aspects of building. Of Abidin's (2018) four overlapping features of celebrity, outlined in chapter 3, Hinojosa most clearly reflects everydayness in terms of her casual style of play and exoticism with respect to the modified Minecraft version she plays.

It is notable that Hinojosa persists when she has a challenge, and she makes this transparent for her young viewers. For instance, in episode 20 (stacyplays 2014), she builds a "mob grinder" so she can more easily collect string by killing trapped spiders. She builds this "off camera," but during the episode, no monsters become trapped, suggesting she has built it incorrectly. She explains that she aimed to teach herself how to build a trap watching others' YouTube clips and that she doesn't know why hers is not working. She invites her viewers to let her know if they know how to build one more successfully. In a later episode, she solves the problem. This contrasts with Let's Players like Stampy and Grian, whose videos tend to be displays of competence and exceptionalism. An aspect of Hinojosa's relatability is that she plays in a familiar and accessible way. She does not undertake large technical builds. Rather, her videos come across as being similar to watching a friend play—albeit a friend with really cool ideas and lots of persistence. She also fights monsters, but not in a particularly organized way. She fights to acquire resources to help develop her world. She is a competent fighter, but her commentary does not focus on fighting techniques or abilities.

Hinojosa's second point of difference is that the Dogcraft series has a specific purpose because it allows her to focus on her passion for saving animals. In episode 1, she tells her audience that Dogcraft allows her to fulfill her fantasy of saving as many stray dogs as possible. She builds a narrative that parallels and complements aspects of her offline world in a manner that builds "worldness" for Hinojosa across the online and offline worlds. As discussed in chapter 2, Klastrup (2009) describes worldness as a blending of in-game play and experiences of the world across other platforms and offline. Hinojosa's Minecraft play and the challenges she faces both in the world and out of it as she produces her series are reminiscent of the trials and tribulations Klastrup faces in her Everquest play. The added layer of video production, including intense commentary about online play and offline life, potentially produce an even richer sense of worldness for Hinojosa than Klastrup detailed. This is relevant because this sense of worldness helps produce authenticity for StacyPlays' fans.

The StacyPlays persona is normatively feminine, caring, and maternal. In this sense, she represents as a cool mom or aunt who plays Minecraft. She is fun but acts responsibly. Her language is casual and peppered with a tempered version of Valleyspeak slang, using phrases such as, "oh my God," "this is amazing," "cool," and "aww," and she often uses uptalk, with a rising inflection at the end of sentences. This includes the occasional use of "girly" phases such as "Isn't that cute?" and "That would be pretty," and she sometimes screams or "squeals" when something scary or fun happens. However, she never swears, and her content is very child-friendly; Stacy is fun, safe, and trusted. Interactions with her Minecraft animals and real-life animal companions are maternalistic and anthropomorphic. Melson (2009, 46) argues that pets enable humans to take part in intimate talk in a manner similar to that of "motherese," the conversational form of speech used toward babies. She suggests "people speak to their pets in a higher-pitched, soft singsong, often ending an utterance with a rising inflection, as if posing a question, and inserting pauses for imaginary replies." Melson introduces the term *petese* to describe how people address their pets, and StacyPlays' videos are replete with petese:

> One of the most important yet unrecognized functions of pets—from dogs to goldfish—for children may be their *thereness*. (This constant availability may be a major reason why many children bestow the honoric "my best friend" on their pets.) Their animate, responsive proximity makes children feel less alone in a way that toys and games, television or video, even interactive media, cannot. Pets, like all living animals, situate a child in a give-and-take universe of fellow beings. (Melson, 2009, 59)

StacyPlays videos bring together a particular group of children's love for gameplay, video consumption, and pets. However, they do more than this because they provide available designs (New London Group, 1996, 74). They suggest how children might play Minecraft in particular ways, but also how to have caring dispositions toward pets and other animals. In this sense, the videos provide pedagogies related to the ethical care of animals. This does not always go well for Stacy, however, as she sometimes misreads her audience's expectations, as I show in the next section.

Stacy's Peer Pedagogies

A close analysis of an episode from Dogcraft provides insight into both Hinojosa's use of stylistic techniques for appealing to her viewers and the connections she develops with them, as illustrated by fan comments on her videos. Episode 89 of Dogcraft, "The Creeper Simulator" (1.1 million views; stacyplays 2015),is a twenty-nine-minute episode that follows on from a previous episode in which Stacy built an obstacle course for her dogs to test them in a light-hearted manner to see which is the best-trained dog. The outcome is lightly comedic, because the dogs' "behavior" is reliant on the game's programming, which causes dogs to respond in slightly unpredictable ways. For instance, they do not always follow their owner in expected ways. At the start of the episode, she goes to the Dalmatian Plantation and names a dog after a fan named Sam who sent a photograph to her of something she has built in Minecraft, replicating one of Stacy's builds, as well as a picture of her pet dog. Hinojosa says of the photographs:

> Today we're adding Sam and that is because Sam sent me a picture of a build that she did that is actually a build I did in my Book Craft series; and she sent me a really nice letter too. It was just a really, really nice letter. She's such a fan of Bookcraft; she doesn't have the book but she's still trying to build the builds. I'm gonna see if I can try to get her the book; she lives in New Zealand and has the most adorable dog named Oliver and it was just really nice getting your letter

Sam. A lot of times I think that it seems like you have to draw me something or do something really artistic in order to get into the Dalmatian Plantation, but the truth is I love getting letters too and so I am happy to name a puppy after Sam.

Following this, Stacy goes to her barn to kill a number of pigs so she can feed her dogs, and she breeds some new pigs, which she explains she will eventually kill for food. She expresses sadness about this but says that it is necessary to feed her dogs. Next, Stacy goes to the "arf gallery" where she shares art from approximately eighteen fans, which has been made in response to Hinojosa's different Minecraft series, including her Xbox series, and Cake Quest with Sqaishey. Following this, she points out "bone mountain" in the distance and mentions a post she has seen from some fans: "There's bone Mountain. I saw a funny comment about someone who is also on the committee that Lizzie is on for dogcraft citizens for the completion of bone mountain. It's gonna happen guys, it's gonna happen soon, I promise, okay?"

The majority of the episode subsequently involves a comical scenario in which Stacy leads her dogs through the obstacle course to determine which is her best "defense dog." This includes a bridge over a lava pit, a "ring of fire," and a "creeper simulator" that is meant to simulate a creeper blast. She takes the dogs through the course in turn and then allocates each of them points based on how well they "performed." All the while, because it is night in the game, the game generates "mobs" such as zombies and creepers, which Stacy has to kill, adding an element of chaos to the scenario. The video recording includes dramatic background music to emphasize the competitive nature of completing the course, which, at least to an adult viewer, comes across as being parodic of serious dog show competitions.

Although there is an overall structure to the video, Hinojosa's commentary is largely spontaneous. There are moments of surprise when she is suddenly attacked by "mobs," including a spider and a baby zombie, and again later when the creeper and zombie attack her and the dogs during the obstacle course. There is an overall objective for the video, which ends up being structured like a Minecraft minigame, similar to those discussed in chapter 6 in relation to Stampy. However, Hinojosa's minigame is less well planned than Stampy's typically are, with greater emphasis on everyday gameplay than on demonstrations of expertise. Stacy's video is fun to watch because of the behavior of the dogs and what Stacy says about them, whereas Stampy's videos are fun because his minigames provide opportunity for genuine competition.

The video has attracted 2,534 comments since it was posted in 2015, with the most recent appearing in 2019. Analysis of the comments indicates they fall into several categories. The majority are comments directed toward Stacy. These include suggestions for improvement, ways Stacy can enhance Dogcraft, or ideas for new builds. In 2015, for instance, one commenter says:

> An idea for the rebuild of the Dalmatian Plantation: Small fenced areas for each of the dogs, with their names on the top. You could turn it into a museum, almost like a hall of fame: fan edition! Pongo and Predita could be the mascots, greeting you when you walk in, and cookies could line the walls! Then you will for sure know that there are exactly 101! Just an idea :)

In numerous comments, fans ask Stacy to be added to the Dalmatian Plantation or for some other form of direct acknowledgment. Some comments ask Stacy to disclose personal information about whether she has or boyfriend or how old she is. Many more comments, however, are expressions of fandom that pay Stacy compliments for being a good YouTuber or complimenting her physical appearance. Typical examples are from CH (in 2017) who says, "Hello stacyplays I love your video I think you are funny, smart, and creative. I love your builds," and NT (2016), who says "I love your videos you're so pretty you're amazing." One fan, LLL (2015), says,

> Hi Stacy my name is faith and I'm eleven your like my favorite YouTuber. I just recently subscribed to your channel and proud to be a potato flake. Dogcraft is my favorite series. I love animals as much as you do I had to stop watching never alone when your fox died. I'm abessed with st. bernards (as you can tell). I also love sled dog saga. I have two schnauzers we adopted there names are Timothy and Tiffany. I will have to send you a picture sometime your awesome love one of your biggest fans faith.

Episode 89, however, generated an unusual number of negative comments for Hinojosa about the way she treats her dogs, with concern about whether they might be hurt and about the fairness of the "contest." A significant number of commenters reacted, suggesting she had favored one dog over another, although different fans felt she was biased in different ways. "JF" says: "YOU ARE SO MEAN TO Basil!, SHE DOES NOT WANT TO JUMP!!!!!!!!!!!!!!, SHE LIKES TO WALK!!!!!!!!! DISLIKE THIS VIDEO!!!!!!!!!!!!!!!!!!!" Another fan, "BRM," says: "That's so unfair Stacy if you give Everest lots of tries you have to do the same with the rest and you didn't tempt them to come. only Everest why do you hate wink and the others." A comment in the same vein from 2016 by QC generates a debate among Stacy's fans, with thirty-four replies either agreeing with QC or passionately defending Hinojosa. It is particularly notable how passionate her fans are about the animal characters she has created. In a sense, fans' willingness to criticize Stacy reinforces that she is part of the community and just as answerable to the community's expectations as anyone else. What is somewhat surprising in the example, though, is the perception that she has betrayed her dogs in the episode. This seems partly to do with the perceived harm Stacy has done to her dogs, not just in terms of being unfair to them in the competition but because they are "physically" harmed by the task and the monster attacks.

Unlike standard Minecraft, the "Copious Dogs" modification represents harm to animals by the amount of blood that appears on them: the more injured the animal, the bloodier they become. By the end of episode 89, Stacy's dogs are very bloodied, causing concern for some fans. RS says "yes you thought it was fun . . . . to see the wolves bloody and hurt . . . . take it down." There is contested pedagogy here in which fans may learn as much from other fans as they do from Stacy about a moral and ethical code for treatment of animals. In addition, fans' reactions to Stacy's treatment of her dogs taps into a more general sense that when Stacy unexpectedly crosses a line in her videos, some fans feel she has broken their trust in her. For instance, in the comments to episode 89, RW says, "Watching the episodes where Stacy kills pigs, I get the same feeling as I got when I saw the videos where Samgladiator and Stamps swear." This fan's reference to a negative feeling prompted by being let down by Let's Players who are typically safe points to the risk for Let's Players of seeming to be fake or untrustworthy.

However, for every negative comment that appears on the video, several others indicate that most fans are willing to forgive Stacy for what they see as small error. For instance, as a general comment of support on the video, in 2015, AY writes:

> Stacy, you are the most amazing and inspiring person. in some of your recent videos you have been getting hate from viewers, and you have replied to them explaining "this and that," and why your video maybe lacks something, which shows that you really care and love to make your videos. i love when you do vlogs

because i always love seeing you <3. your youtube channel is well organized and (my favorite part) appropriate. your 400k subscriber video was so cool! and i know that you will be uploading a 500k sub video in no time! i have become a better person because of you. you have come so far since i have started watching your channel, and your videos are amazing, don't let those haters hate }:(you are better than they will ever be <3 <3 <3 :)

Many of the comments on episode 89 are self-focused, with fans discussing their own pets or themselves. Mostly they share the names of their pets and talk about pets in general, but in quite a few comments, fans discuss pets' becoming ill or dying. In 2015, GC says,

Hey stacy i just wanted to say how much i love you and your videos. Thank you for helping me through some hard times like my dog Tiny dying while I was on vacation last year during the summer. I can't thank you enough! Tell Paige and Molly me and my dogs, Chubby the bear and Mr. Cookei, say hi

A small number of self-focused comments also disclose or claim personal illness, including some in which children reveal they have a cancer diagnosis. Many more self-focused comments, however, are from fans who claim a name, saying they are also called Stacy, share the name of the animals in the episode, or share the name of the fan who has been added to the Dalmatian Plantation.

Fans also seek connection with other fans through the comments stream. Some comments, for instance, seek a response from other fans who are viewing the video in a similar temporal moment. For instance, AC received twenty-three responses to her question, "Who's in the 2016 squad?" Some comments seek technical advice from Stacy or the community. Quite a few comments ask other fans or Stacy herself how she has produced her video using modifications of the original Minecraft platform. A small number ask about becoming a YouTuber or about Stacy's recording setup. Sprinkled throughout are comments that might be described as random troublemaking or purposely mischievous or hateful comments.

The comments might be considered performative (Butler 1990), because they bring fans into being as they seek affirmation and acknowledgment through expressions of connection to Stacy and other fans. The comments also police acceptable behavior within the community, constituting forms of normative practice that encourage particular kinds of behavior and that allow StacyPlays fans to be recognizable to each other—and for Hinojosa to remain recognizable to her community. Trust and declarations of love are often central to acts within processes of relationship building among Hinojosa's fans, with Stacy being positioned more like a family member or a friend than a celebrity or entertainer. In this sense, Hinojosa's authenticity is based on the personal connections she invites, in which she is positioned as someone who can be trusted, particularly as an animal lover, pet carer, and friend. The "Creeper Simulator" episode tests the bounds of acceptable normative practice within the community and her fans' trust in her, because she inadvertently threatens the image she has developed for herself, inviting significant criticism. While this criticism acts as a reminder to Hinojosa about the need to retain authenticity, it also potentially restricts her ability to be creative or innovative. This applies to her production of videos that are more directly didactic, as outlined in the next section.

StacyPlays, the Teacher

While Hinojosa does not set out to be explicitly pedagogic in her Dogcraft videos, she nonetheless produces learning opportunities for her young fans. As discussed in chapter 6 with regard to Stampy, her Let's Play videos are pedagogic because they provide a model for how to play Minecraft in a particular way. Stacy's approach differs from Stampy's because it is less focused on straightforward entertainment in the form of building, adventures, or minigames, although her approach includes elements of these. Her Dogcraft series creates a narrative over time, allowing her fans to get to know her animals as characters with their own attributes and story arcs, which explains why some viewers seem to be fans of particular dogs as much as they are Stacy fans. This is at least partly due to Hinojosa's abilities as a storyteller, as exemplified in the expansion of the Dogcraft world into the "Wild Rescuers" novels.

Hinojosa takes a much more didactic approach to storytelling in her Bookcraft series, which consists of sixty-nine videos created between 2014 and 2015 (and reprised in 2019). In the series, she chooses favorite books from her childhood and creates items from the books in Minecraft. She tells her audience which books she is going to focus on in advance so her viewers can read the books before watching the episodes, although she says she is not "assigning homework." The first book she "builds" is *The Twenty-One Balloons* by William Pène du Bois. The series is more didactic than her general Let's Play videos in that as she plays, she recounts the book's plot and explains what she likes about it. In each episode, she has a "word of the day," which she adds to a "book" within the game, and she provides a definition for the word. In episode 12, the word is *genuflect*, and Stacy explains how the word is relevant to the adoration given to the main character of *The Twenty-One Balloons*, Professor Sherman, as he parades through the streets of San Francisco. As the series goes on, Stacy and other Let's Players build a range of structures from several books, including *Charlotte's Web* by E. B, White, *Hatchet* by Gary Paulsen, *The Hundred and One Dalmatians* by Dodie Smith, *Misty of Chincoteague* by Marguerite Henry, *Island of the Blue Dolphins* by Scott O'Dell, and *A Christmas Carol* by Charles Dickens. Along the way, she and her helpers explain the significance of the builds, and Stacy reads excerpts from the books. Eventually a community that acts as a book club formed around the videos. Participants can post photographs of themselves on Twitter as they read the books, and Stacy shares the images in the Bookcraft videos. The pedagogical classification in the series is quite strong, given that Hinojosa chooses literature that she feels will be appropriate for her viewers. The pedagogical framing is also relatively strong, although there is a lot of playfulness in the way she presents the stories. The atmosphere created is more akin to a moderately serious book club than a classroom where children will be assessed on their understanding of the books.

Hinojosa also takes a somewhat didactic approach in the production of her Minecraft Field Trips series (three videos in 2017), which blend professionally recorded footage of Stacy "in real life" visiting locations in Minnesota that resemble Minecraft's Taiga biome, with footage recorded within Minecraft. Hinojosa explains the inspirations for elements within Minecraft, including natural resources of the forest biome (episode 1, "Minecraft IRL—The Mega Taiga," 577,000 views), wolf pack behavior (episode 2, "Meeting Wolves," 501,000 views), and historic mining practices (episode 3, "Riding in a Minecart," 519,000 views). The trailer for the series states: "Who wants to go on a field trip with me? We're going to the Mega Taiga this weekend on a 3-day virtual field trip to learn more about the natural elements that exist within Minecraft" (stacyplays 2017a).

The production style of the three videos draws on educational video conventions in several ways. They include a distinctive "Minecraft Fieldtrips with Stacyplays" badge that separates the videos from her regular Let's Play content. Hinojosa talks directly to the camera as a voice of authority, and she interviews a number of experts about the topics she is addressing. Informational sequences are accompanied by graphical overlays, called "field trip facts," that summarize what she is saying. For instance, in episode 1, an overlay includes the fact that "beavers can chew through a 6-inch tree in just 15 minutes. One beaver can chew down hundreds of trees in a year." Minecraft footage in the videos is used for illustrative purposes, to connect the game back to the field trips. The videos are didactic because they directly aim to teach fans about the real world and to explain the similarities and differences between Minecraft as a game and its real-world inspiration. There are connections to Hinojosa's novel *Wild Rescuers—Guardians of the Taiga* in that she includes pages at the end of the novel with a link back to the Field Trips videos, and further information about wolf research (StacyPlays 2018, 193–201).

The response to Field Trips videos is highly positive. For instance, the first episode received 19,000 "thumbs up" and just 196 "thumbs down," and the vast majority of the comments are very positive, with many describing Stacy as a great teacher. In 2017, HM says: "This reminds me when we had to study biomes in science class in high school (which I hated). Only now, Stacy made this really interesting. I love it"; and CC says: "Stacy, I love you so much! I am in fifth grade, and you talk about so much stuff that I am currently learning in school! You are like a 2nd teacher! Also, I adored the field trip facts. U rock Stacy!!" The majority of comments exuberantly praise the videos. The following comments all come from 2017, just after the video's release: "OMG I LOVE THIS SERIES ALREADY!" (HM); "the tiaga is so beautiful!!!!!!" (DP); "I love how much you love the nature and learning" (GH); and "I've NEVER been more exited for a stacyplays series!" (JA).

In a sense, the content of the videos is highly classified, and the relational style, while relaxed, is more tightly framed than the content in Hinojosa's Let's Play videos. The point of the videos is to provide children with an accurate account of the Taiga biome. Hinojosa sets out to use Minecraft as an opportunity to introduce children to accepted knowledge, much as a classroom teacher does. As a "field trip," though, the framing of information is casual in comparison to how it might be provided in a textbook, a classroom setting, or a directly informational video. In this way, Hinojosa is able to take her fans on an exploration rather than into a classroom setting, and this allows her to show herself learning alongside her fans. Much of the information she acquires while conducting interviews for the videos seems to be new to her. This places her in a more peer-like position than she might otherwise be in, allowing her to remain authentic and relational. These videos contrast in an interesting way with the approach Garrett takes in his Stampy's Wonder Quest videos, where Stampy is presented as an authority, somewhat disrupting his authenticity as a peer.

GamerGirl, who also goes by KarinaOMG, is the Let's Play channel of twelve-year-old Canadian-born YouTuber Karina Kurzawa, who is not only the youngest Let's Player considered in this study but also the most diverse social media entertainer. In addition to her successful GamerGirl Let's Play channel (3.9 million subscribers), she shares a highly successful YouTube channel with her younger brother, Ronald (SIS vs BRO, 12 million subscribers), and a fashion and lifestyle vlogging channel, Karina Kurzawa (1 million subscribers). The siblings have a dedicated app on the Google Play store that aggregates their videos and offers challenges and games. In addition, Karina has 451,000 followers on Instagram, where she shares lifestyle and fashion images of herself. Karina began uploading videos to YouTube when she was nine years old on the channel FUNwithKARINA. In the eighteen months from October 2017 to January 2020, the GamerGirl channel increased its subscriber base from 800,000 to 3.9 million and views from 244 million to 1.49 billion, vastly outpacing growth on Stampy and Stacy's channels. While Stacy Hinojosa's daily average views in January 2020 was about 220,000, Kurzawa's was approximately 1.5 million.

KarinaOMG mostly produces Let's Play videos for Minecraft (464 videos), Roblox (804 videos), and The Sims 4 (112 videos). She began, but did not persist with, making Fortnite videos with her younger brother (20 videos). Her more than 1,300 gaming videos are typically between fifteen and thirty minutes in duration, and she uploads between three and six of these each week, in addition to weekly Sis vs Bro and occasional Karina Kurzawa videos, making for a very hectic production schedule.

This chapter focuses on KarinaOMG as the Minecraft Let's Player closest in age to most of her subscribers and consequently the most obvious peer

Table 8.1
GamerGirl Analytics, 2020

Subscribers Previous Thirty Days	Daily Average New Subscribers	Views in the Previous Thirty Days	Daily Average New Views	Total Subscribers to Date	Total Views to Date
70,000	2,300	47 million	1.5 million	3.9 million	1.5 billion

Source: Social Blade (2020c)

of the three Let's Players discussed in the book. It also focuses on Karina as a social media entertainer and argues that it is impossible to separate her Let's Play productions from her cross-platform activity because her fans are highly likely to interact with her across several platforms. Despite Karina's rapid success, she seems to have remained reasonably grounded, although several of her "SIS vs BRO" videos with Ronald focus on the spoils of their success. These videos attract as much negative commentary as positive. For instance, a walk-through vlog of their family's palatial new home in Spain, "Spain HOUSE TOUR!!!!!" (13.9 million views; SIS vs BRO 2017b), received a significant number of critical comments and negative response videos from other YouTubers. This creates a challenge for Karina's authenticity as "the kid next door," although her mode of address remains recognizable, particularly in her Let's Play videos. A significant part of Karina's appeal as a Let's Player is that she is friendly and fun and her commentary is competent. Her authenticity is built on a pedagogic process that is loosely classified and framed in that she tends to choose easily replicable building projects, which she describes in a casual way that encourages experimentation. More than this, her mode of address is very much an illustration of everyday Minecraft play, and the focus is on her performative practice as a YouTuber rather than on Minecraft itself.

KarinaOMG, YouTuber and Social Media Influencer

KarinaOMG's YouTube activity occurs within the context of her family's successful social media entertainment business, which they have built in just three years, with the majority of their sustained activity beginning in 2016. The Kurzawa family, originating from Ontario in Canada and now based in Spain, has created its business using digital labor on YouTube by

Table 8.2

The Kurzawa Family YouTube Business

Karina	Ronald	Karina and Ronald	Freddy (Father)	Total Family Subscribers and Views
Gamer Girl: 3.9 million subscribers 1.4 billion views Karina Kurzawa: 1 million subscribers 41 million views	RonaldOMG: 2.9 million subscribers 1.1 billion views	Sis vs Bro: 12 million subscribers 5 billion views	Freddy Goes Boom: 1.1 million subscribers 274 million views	Approximately 20.9 million subscribers 7.81 billion views

Source: Social Blade (2020c, 2020g, 2020h, 2020i, 2020j)

monetizing channel subscriptions and through paid sponsorships. As You-Tube's "basic currency" (Postigo 2016, 344), subscriptions are rewarded with advertising revenue via Google's AdSense system, and family-friendly content, which is also often ad-friendly content according to Google/YouTube's filtering system, can be particularly lucrative (Cunningham and Craig 2019, 68). Posting videos featuring family friendly content to YouTube has been financially rewarding for a significant number of families (Luscombe 2017). In addition to Karina and Ronald's separate gaming channels, their father has a channel, "Freddy Goes Boom," where he posts Fortnite and Roblox videos (1.1 million subscribers). In total, the Kurzawa family has five channels with a combined subscriber base of approximately 20.9 million and a view count of approximately 7.81 billion. If the family's subscriptions were combined as a single channel, they would notionally be ranked the 126th most subscribed channel on YouTube (as of January 2020).

This subscription base likely places the family among the more successful earners on YouTube, producing millions of dollars in income every year. Video production is evidently more than a hobby or after-school job for Karina. Her videos are mostly well produced, suggesting she is not responsible for producing them on her own. The family seems to work as a team, with her mother often recording the videos and her father editing and postproducing them. Combined with her work across other social media platforms, KarinaOMG appears to spend several hours each day creating social media content and interacting with fans. Table 8.3 provides an

Table 8.3
KarinaOMG Social Media across Channels, July 2018 and March–April 2019

	Gamer Girl	Karina Kurzawa	Sis vs Bro	Instagram
2018				
July 1	"Finding ICE TREASURES!" (Roblox), 71,400[a]/494[b]			
July 2	"Becoming INVISIBLE" (Roblox), 72,400/566			
July 3	"DYING AT 3AM!!!" (Roblox), 112,000/846			
July 4	"Stuck in Crazy Hotel and ESCAPING IT!" (Roblox), 5.1 million/3,400	"My Makeup Collection": 815,000/ 5,600	"Tie Dye Backpack Challenge!" 9.4 million/ 132,000	"Summer!!!" (profile image): 11,700[c] "Which one is your fav?? (swimming) 13,800
July 5	"Creating MY SPIDER ARMY!" (Roblox), 611,000/ comments disabled	"I Quit My Summer Camp!" 1.2 million/ 4,900		"New Phone Case!!!!" (selfie): 13,600
July 6	"New Vampire Added to the Family!" (Sims 4), 400,000/ comments disabled	"My fake account on Instagram! 552,000/ 3,500		
July 7	"The Ultimate Hide a Seek UNDERWATER with Ronald" (Roblox), 480,000/ comments disabled	Summer Haul!!!" 337,000/ 5,200	"GOING ON SUMMER VACATION!!!" 6.6 million/9,400 Explicitly sponsored	"Summer Smoothie" (selfie): 13,000

Table 8.3 (continued)

	Gamer Girl	Karina Kurzawa	Sis vs Bro	Instagram
2019				
March 23			"REACTING TO OUR OLD VIDEOS!!!" 2.6 million/ comments disabled	
March 24	"MAKING GIANT DONUTS!" (Roblox), 364,000/1,045			
March 25				
March 26	"I WILL DO ANYTHING FOR PIZZA!" (Roblox), 189,000/710			
March 27				"Fav Smoothy?" Mine Is Berry": 29,000
March 28	"Working Out Until My Arm Fell Off!" (Roblox) 75,000/343			
March 29				"At the top of London Eye!" 28,000
March 30	STANDING ON A VOLCANO! (Roblox) 251,000/945		"PAUSE SLIME CHALLENGE!!!" 6.9 million/ comments disabled	
March 31		"Going Treetop Trekking :)" 119,000/ comments disabled		

Table 8.3 (continued)

	Gamer Girl	Karina Kurzawa	Sis vs Bro	Instagram
April 1	"PEOPLE DYING FROM MY COOKING!" (The Sims 4), 104,000/559			
April 2				
April 3	"I'M A BIG BABY!" (Roblox) 410,000/784			
April 4	"			
April 5	"THIS GIRL STOLE MY MEDAL!" (Roblox) 384,000/938			
April 6			"Making Slime in Alphabetical Order!!!" 7.9 million/ comments disabled	
April 7	"BUILDING MY OWN WALMART STORE!" (Roblox) 353,000/1,038			
April 8				OMG My First Time Paragliding! It Was So Much Fun" (video footage from action camera) 24,000
April 9	"JOINING THE ARMY OBBY!" (Roblox) 239,000/635			"At the Top of Table Mountain!" 30,000

a YouTube views

b YouTube comments (comments on Karina's videos were disabled in early 2019)

c Instagram likes

Sources: GamerGirl (2020), Karina Kurzawa (2020a, 2020b), SIS vs BRO (2020),

overview of Karina's social media activity during two time periods, first in July and August 2018 (summer vacation break) and again in March and April 2019.

This overview of Karina's creative activity provides interesting insights into her practice as a social media entertainer. The breakdown indicates a strategy behind her production process as videos for her two main YouTube channels are released according to a predictable schedule. Furthermore, the schedule changes at different times of the year, perhaps reflecting the time the audience has to watch the videos—for instance, more often during summer vacation. She is also more likely to have time to produce videos during summer break than during the school year. The breakdown also shows the inconsistency of her vlog production for the Karina Kurzawa channel, with a significant break of almost four months between video uploads in early December 2018 and April 2019. Despite this inconsistency, these videos still attract regular attention from fans, with over 650 new subscribers per day and over 54,000 viewers per day. The channel presumably benefits from the popularity of her other channels and her regular Instagram activity, suggesting that success on one platform promotes success on associated platforms. It is also interesting that Karina makes a greater number of gaming videos than videos for the SIS vs BRO channel, even though the latter is much more popular.

Table 8.3 reveals that an occasional source of income for Karina and her family is direct sponsorships and product placement on the SIS vs BRO channel. The "GOING ON SUMMER VACATION!!!" SIS vs BRO episode from July 7, 2018 (12 million views), begins with Karina stating, "This video is sponsored by *Hotel Transylvania 3: Summer Vacation*." Karina and Ronald watch the film trailer at the start of their video (the audience watches with them, over their shoulder). The two say how much they have loved the previous Hotel Transylvania movies and that they can't wait to see the new one. The two then receive a mystery suitcase containing Hotel Transylvania 3 merchandise, and they spend the middle part of the episode unboxing the items in the suitcase. They receive an invitation to an advance screening of the movie, and they pack for their "vacation." The video then cuts to the two at the Sony Studio lot where they watch the movie and meet other kids. They end by directly plugging the film and thank the movie for sponsoring them. Two other videos from the July and August period are also direct sponsorships: one for a game from Mattel called "flushing frenzy," in which players have to catch poop (6.6 million views), and another is sponsored by *Hotel Transylvania 3: Summer Vacation*, which involves Karina and Ronald using Squishy markers (9.5 million views).

Table 8.3 also shows that a substantial amount of Karina's content, particularly on her Instagram account and vlog channel, consists of travel images and video, with the family taking trips to Poland, London, and South African in the time frames represented by the table. Karina is shown undertaking a range of activities including ziplining, kayaking, cave exploring, treetop trekking, and paragliding. Across the whole corpus of her videos and photographs, Karina is shown enjoying many other international trips and fun activities and in their video "25 Things You Didn't Know About SIS vs BRO!!!" (SIS vs BRO 2018g), Karina claims to have visited thirty countries. Taken as a whole, Karina's social media presence represents a mix of her "everydayness" and "exclusiveness" (Abidin 2018). She has an everyday presence in her videos as a kid who enjoys video gameplay, going to the movies, shopping, hanging out with her brother, and having fun. This is complemented by her presence as the kid who has everything: a successful social media career, a large home, popularity, and regular travel to exotic places.

KarinaOMG Celebrity

The production of KarinaOMG as a "girl next door" who is living the high life relies on her providing almost daily posts, allowing fans to consume her content on a regular basis. Unlike other social media entertainers, however, her activity is relatively restricted and localized. Although she is a successful YouTuber and meets Abidin's (2018) definition of microcelebrity, she has a relatively low profile, particularly in mainstream media. Extensive online searches show that in contrast to Stampy, she has not been featured in news reports or interviewed for mainstream media stories, and she does not feature in industry review stories. Unlike Stacy, she has not appeared onstage at conventions, and she does not collaborate with YouTubers outside her family. The only evidence of attendance at a convention was for VidCon 2018, which shows Karina and Ronald attending the convention for the first time. They attend as fans making a vlog about other YouTube celebrities (SIS vs BRO 2018e). As successful YouTubers, they have "creator" passes to attend the event, and they record footage of themselves interacting with some of their fans—for instance, posing for selfies with other children. On the whole, however, their presence at the event seems to have been low key. There is little evidence that KarinaOMG seeks to create celebrity outside the online environment, such as with public appearances. Karina and the other members of the Kurzawa family do not seem to actively pursue relationships with other members of the Minecraft family-friendly Let's Play microindustry or any other community of YouTubers. Karina's celebrity is produced entirely online as part of her family's activities and there is almost no evidence that she has visibility beyond the online environment.

The Kurzawa's approach contrasts significantly with the approach of other high-profile YouTuber families, such as the Butlers from Idaho, whose Shaytards channel (Shaytards 2019) helped to establish the family YouTuber genre (4.9 million subscribers, 2.8 billion views), and the Burgos family from Ontario, Canada, who run the Eh Bee Family channel (8.8 million subscribers, 2.3 billion views). The Shaytards, run by father Shay Butler (ShayCarl) and mother Colette Butler (Katilette), featured daily vlogs of everyday family life from 2012 to 2017 involving their four children. The family has been the subject of extensive online publicity and coverage on mainstream media, has made numerous public appearances, and has collaborated with a host of other YouTuber creators. Shay Butler and colleagues founded the highly successful Maker Studios, a multichannel network (MCN) that aggregated other YouTuber channels and was eventually bought by Disney.

The Burgos family also has a significant social media entertainment presence in addition to their Eh Bee Family YouTube channel (Eh Bee Family 2019a). This includes the Miss Bee YouTube channel featuring twelve-year-old Gabriela (1.2 million subscribers, 81 million views), the Mr. Bee channel featuring their thirteen-year-old son (471,000 subscribers, 51 million views), and the Mama Bee channel, featuring their mother (93,000 subscribers, 1 million views). The Eh Bees have been covered extensively in mainstream media, including on *Good Morning America*, the *Today Show*, *Mashable*, and *CBC News* (Eh Bee Family 2019b), and the family has multiple brand partnerships with companies such as McDonald's, Google, Walmart, Nintendo, Disney, and Apple (Eh Bee Family 2019b). The family has 10.9 million followers on Facebook, 1.8 million Instagram followers, and 119,00 Twitter followers. Twelve-year-old Gabriela Bee is also a contrast to Karina, in that she has aggressively pursued opportunities beyond YouTube. She has 571,000 Instagram followers and is engaging in a singing career, which includes posting performance videos. Both the Shaytards and Eh Bee Family are more exposed to a range of traditional media outlets and are more connected to traditional forms of celebrity than the Kurzawa family seems to be.

The benefit of comparing the Kurzawa family's activities to other YouTuber families is that it puts into perspective both the Kurzawa family's significant YouTube success, given their relatively contained social media activity, and the extent to which the family has limited its creative labor and collaborative activities. The family moved from Canada to Spain in 2017, which restricts the extent to which they can pursue mainstream media opportunities. In addition, less revenue seems to come from the sale of branded merchandise than is the case for other YouTubers. Unlike Stampy, for instance, virtually no branded Sis vs Bro or KarinaOMG merchandise is available in department stores. Karina and Ronald sell a small number of branded T-shirts on their own website (https://www.sisvsbro.com/), but this does not appear to be a key source of income. The main creative labor that Karina undertakes, then, is digital. It involves video production, appearing in Instagram photographs or taking selfies, writing social media posts, and responding to fans on Instagram. Given the scale of Karina's YouTube presence, it is surprising that so little visible online fan activity is dedicated to her. Apart from comments attached to videos on Karina's GamerGirl channel and her Instagram account (YouTube disabled comments for the SIS vs BRO channel and Karina Kurzawa channel in early 2019), there is limited evidence of online fan activity for either the GamerGirl channel or for SIS vs BRO. For instance, only a handful of Wattpad stories are dedicated to KarinaOMG, and few traces of other forms of creative fan activity on fan art sites, a significant contrast with the creative activities of fans dedicated to Stampy and Stacy.

The main online fan presence for Karina is the KarinaOMG (GamerGirl) fan club on the Roblox site, consisting of 10,000 members (Roblox 2019). The fan club's message board wall includes several thousand messages to Karina and other fans, mostly praising Karina and requesting her to donate Robux (Roblox's official currency) to them, or to accept their friend requests, so they can play with her on the site. The fan club also features a page that allows fans to upload and purchase avatar upgrades featuring Karina. That is, a fan can use Robux to purchase a pink KarinaOMG jacket made by another Roblox player/designer as their avatar. The pink "jacket" includes a picture of Karina, enabling a player to display fandom "in game" by wearing the jacket. Karina has also had to negotiate with fans during online gameplay in instances where she has allowed them to play alongside her. In the episode "Building My Own Restaurant in Bloxburg" (GamerGirl 2017b), she has to block a number of fans who want her direct attention in the game rather than following the narrative she is constructing, which consists of her trying to sell food to customers.

One explanation for the lack of fan activity directed toward Karina is that other children identify with her more directly as a peer than as a celebrity. They are not so inclined to deify her through textual representations, but they want to hang out with her and receive her attention. In this sense, Karina is not a celebrity as defined by her representation in mainstream media or by representations in children's drawing and stories, as a text or sign, as Hollywood stars or television personalities are often framed in scholarship (Turner 2013). Rather, in Ferris's terms she "lives" celebrity as someone who is recognized by far more people than she can recognize back (Ferris 2011; Giles 2018). She is a more "local" celebrity than either Stampy or Stacy, even though she has a very large number of followers. While she lives in a large house in Spain and travels the world, the fact that she is primarily seen online playing games and hanging around with her family confirms her ordinariness. Her lack of appearances at conventions and in mainstream media seems to reinforce this perspective. From a material and discursive perspective (Giles 2018), Karina lives celebrity as a twelve-year-old who spends considerable time making videos that happen to have millions of followers online. Although she is not a household name as Stampy was for many families in the United Kingdom in 2014 and 2015 or a product that can be bought in department stores, her localized celebrity means that she will be recognized and pursued in the online spaces she frequents rather than in public or in traditional media.

GamerGirl's Authenticity

Karina's authenticity comes from being recognizable as a kid who could be a friend at school or living next door, and this is reinforced through her love for her family and the way she treats her brother with kindness. A significant threat to her authenticity is the risk of becoming unordinary as she and her family amass wealth and live an increasingly exclusive lifestyle. In addition, she has to contend with the complexities of navigating representational ideologies (Lange 2014) and the policing of gendered norms as she and her parents record video footage and images of her to post on her vlog channel and Instagram account.

As the kid next door, particularly when she is recording her gaming videos, Karina is recognizable as a fun preteen who enjoys Minecraft, Roblox, and The Sims—at least as a white, middle-class, North American preteen. Like Stampy and Stacy, she is safe to hang out with and is never angry, threatening, or dangerous. She avoids swearing in her videos, is largely constructive and positive, and does not speak in a controversial way about ideas or other people. She is always happy and fun to watch, and she passes the "parent test" in terms of being acceptable viewing for children. As is the case with Stampy and Stacy, Karina is fun to hang out with on a regular basis, especially for Roblox or Minecraft fans, and in this sense, she invites a parasocial relationship with fans. This opportunity for a "friendship" with Karina is perhaps even more pronounced than it is for Stampy and Stacy, given her closeness in age to her viewers. As Giles suggests, drawing on work by Perse and Rubin (1989), parasocial relationships function as "additional" friendships, sought out by media users because the celebrity they choose resembles the friends they already have (Giles 2018). In this sense, Karina's authenticity is attached to her ordinariness, although cutting across this is her affluence and privilege as a wealthy YouTuber.

In addition to being a fun and safe "kid next door," Karina also presents as a genuinely loving and supportive big sister and daughter. Across the 333 videos on the SIS vs Bro channel, Karina and Ronald consistently seem to get along and have fun together. This carries over into Karina's gameplay videos, which Ronald frequently joins. There is little evidence in any of the videos that the two annoy each other or resist presenting together. This does not come across as being staged or acted, but rather as a believable representation of their relationship. There is little sense, to use Tolson's (2001) framing, that Karina and Ronald are presenting "frontstage" or in a public way for their audience and that there is an alternative "backstage" or private version of their relationship. This is not to say that Karina and Ronald do not perform for the camera. However, their performance does not come across as being a cynical one that belies a hidden truth about the actual nature of their relationship. The regularity of the video recordings in a range of different scenarios would seem to make it difficult for them to fake their friendship for the camera. This includes recordings of what appear to be less presentational and more casual moments, for instance, while they are traveling together. In terms of authenticity and audience appeal, this consistency of sibling niceness seems to be an important part of their popularity. The idea that harmonious sibling relations would appeal to children is not surprising if research on what makes children happy is accurate. The children and young people in Chaplin's (2009) study report, for instance, that people and pets (including siblings) are much more important to their happiness than achievements, material things, hobbies, or sports. In this context, Karina and Ronald's modeling of sibling friendship is an important aspect of how social distance is reduced between the two YouTubers and their audience. They come across as an ordinary brother and sister who get along, and Karina represents as a caring big sister.

Despite the connection Karina has established with her viewers as a relatively ordinary preteen who gets along with her brother, there are significant threats to her authenticity, including her family's obvious wealth. A range of videos posted by Karina and Ronald show off their upscale lifestyle, including their expensive house, multiple overseas trips, and personal material possessions. A September 2017 video on the SIS vs BRO channel with 13.8 million views, for instance, features the two children touring palatial homes in Spain as the family tries to choose a new home to purchase (SIS vs BRO 2017a). Karina and Ronald take turns shooting footage of each other's excited reactions to each of the houses and their comments about the prospect of living in them. These are very large houses with grand staircases, infinity pools, and five or more bedrooms. A January, 2018 video (15.5 million views) shows Karina providing a tour of her newly decorated bedroom in the family's new house (SIS vs BRO 2018a). She shows the audience her oversized bedroom that would equate to a parents' master bedroom suite in most large middle-class suburban houses. It features a double bed, room for an art corner with an easel, a separate balcony with an expansive view, and a large bathroom for her personal use. She also shows off her Mac laptop computer for use on her bed and a separate iMac desktop computer, which she explains she mostly uses for watching YouTube videos. These computers are separate from the gaming computer on which she records her Let's Play videos. In a different video from August 2018 (SIS vs BRO 2018f), watched by 15.6 million viewers, Karina and Ronald discuss the most recent thing each of them watched on their iPhone Xs; it is unclear if this is a paid-for Apple sponsorship, but the video nonetheless displays the children's access to the latest smartphone technology. The pair are also featured in several videos traveling business class to different parts of the world, including their first business class trip to Dubai in February 2018 (29 million views; SIS vs BRO 2018b); a separate trip to Thailand a month later in March 2018 (22.9 million views; SIS vs BRO 2018c); and a trip to the United States a few months later in June 2018 (14.2 million views; SIS vs BRO 2018d). Each video shows the siblings enjoying the airport VIP lounges and the business class features of each plane as they complete the journey.

Some of these videos have attracted criticism from viewers, and at least one has been removed from the SIS vs BRO channel thumbnails and now appears as "unlisted" (SIS vs BRO 2017b). The video is a tour of the house in Spain that the family bought, and it attracted criticism in the comments section, mostly focused on Karina and Ronald's seeming lack of appreciation for how privileged they are. At one point, the children "jokingly" complain that their personal balconies are too small compared to the huge master bedroom balcony. In addition to the negative video comments, several YouTubers posted reaction videos criticizing the house tour video (Kane Thomas 2018; Ryan Franklin 2018; KeeperAction 2017; Tommy 2017). These videos all feature young male YouTubers who "roast" Karina and Ronald for their lack of perspective on their wealth and compare their own bedrooms and houses to Karina and Ronald's to put the pair's wealth into perspective.

Another significant threat to Karina's authenticity is the policing of gendered norms, particularly in relation to her Instagram posts and vlogging channel. In this representational space, Karina has to navigate a torrent of comments that range from supportive affirmations, to enthusiastic compliments about her appearance, to hateful, misogynistic, and demeaning put-downs. A dominant strand of criticism is that when she posts images of herself in fashion magazine–style poses featuring different outfits, she is acting in a role that is too grown up for her. A significant number of comments admonish her for trying too hard to look like an older teenager in these posts. This represents a threat to her authenticity because these comments criticize her decision to move beyond her image as the kid next door to compete with other Instagram microcelebrities. In part, Instagram authenticity for young women relies on what Retallack, Ringrose, and

Lawrence (2016) suggest is an alignment between postfeminism and neo-liberalism, where "self-perfection and success around appearance and desirability to men continues to represent one of the most important aspects of femininity in contemporary popular make-over culture." From this perspective, Karina's and her parents' representational practices risk exposing her to misogyny that she may not be equipped to deal with.

In her study of kids' participation on YouTube as both creators and viewers, Lange (2014, 159) refers to "tacit representational ideologies, which may be defined as sets of beliefs that creators, participants, and viewers use to interpret the ontology, structure, and meaning of human images, including their normative uses, appropriateness, moral basis, and consequences." The threat to Karina's authenticity in posting fashion-style images on Instagram is that there is a potential mismatch between her own and her parents' representational ideologies and those of her fans. If she is judged to be trying too hard to "grow up," she may risk the ire of her fans, who may prefer her to remain the safe "kid next door." A counterargument to this perspective, and an explanation for Karina's ongoing popularity, is Abidin's categorization of microcelebrities as being everyday, exotic, exceptional, and exclusive. It is highly plausible that Karina's fashion-style images, along with her exclusive lifestyle and travel videos, appeal to her audience as being exotic and exclusive, complementing her established everydayness. This has a range of implications for peer pedagogies that I return to in the chapter's final section. In the meantime, I turn my attention to Karina's modes of address, particularly within her Let's Play videos.

GamerGirl's Voice, Mode of Address, and Stylistic Features

For consistency across the chapters, I discuss one of Karina's Minecraft videos as a way to address her voice, commentary, mode of address, and stylistic features, even though she more frequently makes Roblox videos. "MY NEW FANCY HOUSE" (GamerGirl 2017a) uploaded on September 22, 2017, has 1 million views and is 22 minutes, 26 seconds long. The episode begins with Karina shout-talking: "Hey guys, it's Karina, and today we're back inside more Minecraft; today, we're back inside my realm." She begins in third-person perspective, with her avatar looking directly at the camera. The video differs from Stampy and Stacy's Let's Plays in that the top left-hand side of the screen shows a "picture in picture" image of Karina wearing a headset, and she looks into the camera and directly addresses her audience as she introduces the video.

Karina explains that she has been doing some work, chopping down trees and collecting cobblestone. She moves into first-person perspective and walks toward a half-built house, which she has started in the previous episode. She explains that there are no houses around, so she is going to make some that she can "sell" and that she is going to make one out of birch wood in this episode. She does not really introduce the episode or explain what she is doing; she just starts doing it and commentates as she goes. Meanwhile, another player, OMGitsUni, joins the space and tries to get Karina's attention. This is presumably someone Karina has allowed into her realm or a friend. Karina explains to the audience that her houses need to look good so people will want to buy them from her. She explains that the new house will be made exactly the same as the existing house, but from birch. She starts placing the blocks, counting as she goes to make the pattern she wants, but she does this in a slightly hesitant fashion and claims that she has forgotten how to make houses. After she makes a mistake and starts altering the house, OMGitsUni comes up and offers Karina an axe, which she takes, but only after bumping OMGitsUni out of the way because she is interfering with Karina's process. However, Karina thanks OMGitsUni for the axe. Darkness begins to fall in the game, so Karina uses a command to change to time from night to day. To do this she types "/ time set day" in the Minecraft chat window, a command that most regular Minecraft players know. She then continues building the house frame. She doesn't explain what she is doing as she goes—she just does it. A little way into the video, she starts to chop down a tree that has suddenly grown near the house and begins to mock-sing "Break it down, break it down . . ." Next, she uses dirt blocks as scaffolding to reach the higher parts of the building. She continues to follow the pattern of the building, following the model established in the previous episode.

Meanwhile, OMGitsUni logs back into the game—Karina did not realize that she had left—and the player makes a cryptic comment that confuses Karina. She keeps building, crafting new items as she goes. She quickly places a simple roof on the building and then jumps to the bottom to make a floor. She makes a comment about OMGitsUni leaving the game again (this time she notices). Next, another player, OliverOMG, joins, and Karina greets him. She makes a floor, but says it looks kind of ugly. She interacts with OliverOMG using the game's text messaging system, saying "yup" to the comment that she has built a new world. OliverOMG says the new world looks pretty. OMGitsUni joins again and says something cryptic again that Karina does not understand; she shakes her head and says, "You're confusing me." She continues to build and craft new items. As she removes dirt for the floor, she outlines her plans: she is going to add windows and so will need glass. OliverOMG and OMGitsUni continue to have a text-based chat in the background, seemingly about joining another world and about their friend who is on Roblox. Karina ignores this.

Next, Karina crafts some new items and then moves quickly to a mine next to her house. A new player joins the game, WolfProg, and Karina acknowledges this player by enthusiastically saying, "Wolf P.O.G joined the game!" and she types and sounds out HEELLOO in an over-the-top way a couple of times. She then uses a cartoonish voice to read out some of what her fellow players are saying in the background and to explain she is going to mine stone. Next, she makes a furnace and starts to smelt some materials for her build. In the background, the conversation continues in the chat window, with a debate about whether they should join a Roblox game that is going on. Now, GirlyCupcakeOMG joins the game, and Karina brings all their names up on the screen and counts on her fingers while saying, "We have 1, 2, 3, 4, 5 people on the game including me." She does this in an over-the-top way. Her friends are now fighting somewhere in the background, and the message <OMGitsUni was slain by Oliver OMG> comes up on the screen. Karina ignores all this and keeps building in the house she has worked on in the previous episode (she has left the new house without explaining why).

Karina now makes some glass, and in the background, we are alerted that OliverOMG has left the game. Karina makes some ladders to add to her home, then makes some glass panes and mock-sings, "Let's place these babies down." As she places the glass panes down, her friends are having a physical fight in the background (their avatars are whacking each other), which Karina ignores. Karina mines some more sand so she can make more glass. She then goes back to her house and smelts the sand to make glass while mock-singing, and she places the glass panes into the building. Girly-CupcakeOMG comes into Karina's house, and Karina whacks her and says, "Out of my house, out of my house." She adds a door to her house and says, "So people know it's my house." GirlyCupcakeOMG leaves a text comment asking "why u hit me," which Karina reads out. And then she adds her own message, "This is meh house," which she speaks out as she types. She then crafts more panes of glass and adds them to her house. She mock-sings and goes to collect more sand. Her friends continue to message each other in the background. Karina then abruptly ends the video and shout-talks while looking directly into the camera to address the audience: "Guys, I'm going to end the video right there. I hope you liked it. If you did, smash that like button. And I'll see you guys next time. Byeee."

It is immediately noticeable from the video that Karina's Let's Play video production style is less organized and more spontaneous than either Stacy's or Stampy's approaches. While she appears to have a loose plan, she does not seem to have spent much time preparing what will occur in the episode or what she will say. Her commentary is upbeat and energetic for the most part, although she pauses occasionally to think about what she is going to say. Her voice modulation might be described as somewhat chaotic, with a mixture of "shout talking," cartoonish exaggeration, and sing-talking among a more general presentational tone. Her approach resembles the kind of talk I have recorded in classrooms and home Minecraft gameplay sessions when multiple children are playing together, although her style is exaggerated because she is presenting for an audience. In this respect, her approach is perhaps more similar to children's actual gameplay than Stampy or Stacy's is. Karina's commentary is informative in the sense that she explains what she is doing in the game, although she does not outline her plan for the episode in any sort of detail and this reflects her casual approach to gameplay. Nevertheless, her commentary carefully steps the audience through what she is doing. In most cases, she clearly describes what she is doing and why. The appeal of the video for its 1 million viewers seems to be Karina's general personality, her ideas for what to do in the game, and how to complete straightforward tasks in the game.

The video's mode of address is very much an invitation for the audience to hang out while she and her friends spend some time in the game. While Stampy sets out to specifically entertain his audience and Stacy aims to build a narrative around her in-game pets and animals, Karina more or less plays Minecraft in the way that many other children play it. She creates a loose narrative around the idea that she is going to "sell" the houses she is building to her friends, but this doesn't make much sense because there is no currency in Minecraft, in contrast to Roblox. The storyline functions as a kind of speculative play scenario that might or might not lead to her friends' agreeing to purchase her houses by exchanging the house for other Minecraft resources. (It is worth noting that some Minecraft players have created very sophisticated bartering systems, but there is little evidence that Karina intends to organize her world in this way.) Karina's treatment of her friends also presents a significant contrast to how Stampy presents and treats the helpers and friends who appear in his videos. They hang out and interact with each other and occasionally with Karina, but they do not help with her build and she does not present exchanges with her friends as an opportunity to make a point about friendship and collaboration, as Stampy does. There is less explicit behavioral guidance and modeling from Karina than there is from the older two Let's Players.

In contrast with the title of the episode, there is nothing particularly unusual about the stylistic features of Karina's building style. Her "fancy new house" consists of a standard build, and her skills in making it are not exceptional or unusual. In this episode, she plays in a standard survival mode version of the game, without the addition of modifications, although in other episodes she sometimes plays in creative mode and introduces modifications to change the look of the world. Karina's main stylistic features are her voice, facial expressions, and hand gestures she introduces into the recording through the picture-in-picture image of her at the top left of the screen. The manner in which she includes dramatic gestures in her play no doubt appeals to many children. The audience is able to gain some insight into Karina's gamer personality through watching her play, and many would likely see this as a way of getting to know her a little more, as an addition to watching her SIS vs BRO videos and her vlogs and Instagram posts.

GamerGirl's Peer Pedagogies

KarinaOMG's peer pedagogies differ from Stampy's and Stacy's in some specific ways, particularly in terms of pedagogical classification and framing and in terms of the expectations she has for providing guidance to her audience. Her classification and framing of Minecraft knowledge is the loosest of the three Let's Players. She plays quite casually, and there is little indication that she sets out to teach her audience about Minecraft in an explicit way or that she presents her play as preferred, superior, or normative. Only the most novice players would find it difficult to replicate what she builds in the "fancy new house" episode. At the same time, the Minecraft knowledge she imparts is framed in a very casual and sometimes purposefully flip manner, punctuated with irreverent commentary and actions. Unlike Stampy, she does not seem as concerned to provide children with substantive content, and unlike Stacy, she does not seem motivated to build a cohesive narrative for her audience. This is not to say she does not impart information; at times, her commentary is cogent and would likely provide new insights for some players, particularly those who are new to the game. However, Karina's focus on Minecraft as she records is secondary to her focus on herself. In all likelihood, she understands her audience will be entertained by her personality rather than by the content of her videos.

Although Karina's Minecraft videos are not intentionally pedagogic in terms of how they teach about Minecraft, they might be described as casually pedagogic. By this, I mean the information imparted by the videos is secondary to the video's entertainment qualities. This approach is also evident in the challenge videos on the SIS vs BRO channel Karina shares with her brother, Ronald. Although the SIS vs BRO channel includes different kinds of videos, including vlogs and "routine" videos (where Karina and Ronald enact their daily routines in comedic ways), the backbone of the channel is challenge videos in which Karina and Ronald sit side by side as they undertake various kinds of challenges to see who can more effectively complete a task. "Slime" challenge videos are among the most popular on the channel. The pair's eighth most popular video is a slime challenge video, "Don't Choose the Wrong Soap Slime Challenge," that has attracted 63.8 million views (SIS vs BRO 2018h). Slime making is hugely popular on YouTube, with successful channels like the Tom Slime channel attracting 7.89 million subscribers. In addition, making slime has become an activity within classroom science and community-based STEM learning activities (Harris, Azevedo, and Pestrosino 2018; Harlow et al. 2018). Through these efforts, there is a definite pedagogization of slime making to bring it into line with formal science curriculum knowledge. There is a hint of this in the "Don't Choose the Wrong Soap Slime Challenge!!!" video. For instance, the episode explanation underneath the video says:

> Don't choose the wrong soap or hand lotion, and make sure you have activator!!! Without activator, you'll end up with goo instead of awesome slime :) We are sensing which mystery bottle has the best ingredients for our slime! Some

mystery bottles have glue, glitter, beads, activator, or other mystery ingredients. Ronald is lucky to find activator, but can Karina find it eventually? Let's make awesome slime with mystery soap bottles! Vote now who did the better slime :)

The reference to an activator in the explanation provides context for what might go wrong in the challenge, providing an opportunity to develop some scientific knowledge about the chemistry behind slime. The video, however, provides no explanation for why activator is necessary; it is simply implied in the challenge as an essential ingredient. In the video, Karina and Ronald choose different bottles of ingredients (they shake them to see if they can guess what is inside) and then combine the ingredients into large bowls and mix them. By the end of the video, each has a version of slime, although Ronald's is not very stretchy. While there is a loose pedagogic element to the video, it is not instructional or explanatory, and viewers who want to know more about slime would need to undertake their own research to better understand how slime works or how to make their own slime. As for classification and framing of chemistry knowledge, the video is pedagogically weak. As I have noted in the chapters on Stampy and Stacy, there is an element of this casual pedagogical approach in most Let's Play videos, but it is even more present in Karina's videos, across all of her content.

Karina is also less focused in her Minecraft videos than Stacy and Stampy on the purposeful development of everyday pedagogies for the moral and ethical development of her audience. Stampy's moral and ethical codes for positive and collaborative play and Stacy's guidance about pet and animal care are quite explicit pedagogical moves intended to teach their audiences particular values through intentionally constructed narratives and representational practices. There is little evidence that Karina sets out to teach her audience preferred attitudes or ways of being in the world in this way. In this context, Karina's pedagogical processes may be productively considered through the lens of performativity, which places as much emphasis on material performative acts as it does on language and representational practices—it is about "practices, doings and actions" (Barad 2007, 133). It does not really matter what Karina says about Minecraft as she plays, because her corporeality as a performer across various activities is what makes her authentic for her audience. And it does not matter if Karina sets out to teach values or attitudes because she enacts a pedagogical presence every time she records and uploads a video. In bringing GamerGirl/KarinaOMG into being, Karina repeats norms to make herself intelligible to her audience. Depending on the perspective of an outside observer, the performative designs she makes available may be considered both appropriately supportive or harmful, or both, for her viewers.

On one hand, Karina's positive demeanor and the care she shows toward her brother may be considered positively pedagogical because her actions provide a model for other children to follow in terms of appropriate online activity and sibling behavior. On the other hand, her embodiment of wealth and privilege as desirable goals might be seen as problematic, particularly from a critical pedagogies perspective (Giroux 1992, 187). Her house tours, travel vlogs, and Instagram posts promote a particular version of success based on the acquisition of material possessions and the celebration of access to exclusive experiences. Karina's online presence through gameplay on the GamerGirl channel, through challenge videos and vlogs on SIS vs BRO, and her presence on Instagram cannot be easily separated; her popularity and authenticity seem to accrue across these channels. Therefore, while she may not promote a particular pedagogical perspective within a single Minecraft video, it is likely that many children's relationships with Karina extend across these various aspects of her online activity.

This chapter has maintained that KarinaOMG differs in quite specific ways from Stampy and Stacy as a family-friendly Minecraft Let's Player. Although she can be included as part of the loosely defined family-friendly Minecraft Let's Play microindustry, her activity takes place in relative isolation. Her family's successful YouTube business seems to operate in isolation from the broader media industries, in a manner that differs from those of comparable YouTuber families. Apart from occasional paid sponsorships, the family's main income seems to come from AdSense revenue. There are no book deals or other media deals as exist for Stacy and Stampy and no extensive merchandise sales. Despite this, Karina and the Kurzawa family have built an immense YouTube subscriber base. Karina's authenticity also seems to derive from a different source than is the case for Stacy or Stampy. Although all three rely on everydayness as a key aspect of their authenticity, Stampy seems to rely more on the exceptionalness of his Minecraft play and entertainment abilities, Stacy on the exoticism of her modified Dogcraft server, and Karina on the exclusiveness of her lifestyle. Karina's authenticity also seems to rely on her activity across a range of activities, of which Minecraft is just one. For Stacy and Stampy, Minecraft play is central to their online personae, whereas for Karina, it is somewhat peripheral.

Finally, it seems clear that Karina's pedagogical practices are more casual than those of either Stampy or Stacy. For Karina, there is less focus on representational pedagogical practices than on material or embodied performative practices. Although both Stampy and Stacy also obviously embody pedagogical practices, as discussed in various ways in chapters 6 and 7, they also both engage in representational pedagogies, particularly in their more learning-based videos—the Wonder Quest and Field Trips series. In both series, knowledge is classified and framed through specific representational practices that align to formal institutional knowledge. Karina's more thoroughly casual pedagogical practices are embodied in the version of herself that appears in her videos. This means that the peer pedagogies made available to Karina's viewers are more directly invitations to connect to her and her activities than to the content of her videos.

9 What I Learned from Stampylonghead, StacyPlays, and KarinaOMG

In the three case studies outlined in chapters 6 through 8, I have aimed to illustrate how Let's Players create the conditions for intimate connections with fans, enabling peer pedagogies to emerge. I have provided examples of how peer pedagogies are relationships in which a flat structure between "teachers" and "learners" emerges through a creator's attempts to reduce social distance, connecting to viewers' needs for entertainment and knowledge. Along the way, I have shown how creating these conditions is a continuing challenge for Let's Players and that they do not always get it right. In this chapter, I tease out aspects of peer pedagogies on digital platforms by returning to the six questions that have informed my analysis. My aim is to draw together some of the commonalities and contradictions that arose across my consideration of the three Let's Players. In addition, I aim to identify further questions that might inform future research in the field.

My response to the six questions is necessarily limited by my focus on three particular Let's Players, and I acknowledge that a combination of three different YouTubers may have led to different conclusions. I also acknowledge that my focus on literacies, learning, and pedagogy has taken my work in a particular direction that might be blind to considerations that could arise using different analytical lenses. For instance, while I have drawn on aspects of media and communications studies in an attempt to understand peer pedagogies on digital platforms, I am aware that there are limits to how I have framed my analysis. I have not considered platform affordances that likely play a role in directing how Let's Play fans watch videos, such as the role of YouTube's algorithm. I am confident, however, that my discussion provides new insights into how children interact with and learn from Let's Players. A number of significant, novel, and surprising findings emerged from the analysis, as discussed in the sections below.

How Do Minecraft Let's Players Establish Authenticity in the Context of Social Media Entertainment?

The extent to which the notion of friendship plays an essential role in the relationships that develop between Let's Players and their fans is a significant finding in this study. The establishment of authenticity within these friendship relationships has ramifications for how we think about children's interactions on digital platforms. To date, a great deal of studies of children's social interactions with digital media have focused on the relationships they form with other children (Marsh 2004, 2011; Wohlwend and Kargin 2013), but this research draws attention to the relationships they form with microcelebrities. "Everyday people" become sources of entertainment for millions of children around the world, and authenticity has become a central ingredient of success for social media entertainment. Authenticity relies on audience members' emotional engagement with Let's Players' content, providing the opportunity for parasocial relationships to form (Marwick 2013), including the vicarious experience of friendship or companionship.

Stampy, Stacy, and Karina become a familiar presence in children's lives, often in a very material sense as their image and voice are regularly invited into the family home. As Buckingham (2000) noted, children's lives became less focused outwardly to the street and the neighborhood and more focused on the family home during the second half of the twentieth century, partly due to parental anxiety and perceptions of risk. At the same time, public forms of entertainment like movies and amusement parks have given way to domestic entertainment in the family home. In this context, children are as likely to answer the call to "let's play" from a Minecraft Let's Player as they are to play with a friend from their neighborhood. Putting aside some of the concern that has arisen within both the popular media and scholarship about the retreat from sociality (Turkle 2011; Putnam 2001), this offer of friendship and companionship from Let's Players has been taken up by large numbers of children. Family-friendly Let's Players offer regular and reliable companionship through sharing their play in fun and entertaining ways. Furthermore, Let's Players move from being strangers to peers as they mediate the familial and broader social world for children (Rojek 2015) in ways that are recognizable, trusted, and safe.

Let's Players attempt to establish authentic selves by reducing social distance between themselves and their fans and by being consistent and reliable over time. The analysis presented in the preceding chapters, however, shows significant differences in Let's Players' styles and approaches. That there is no one formula for Let's Player success is an important observation because children's digital media experiences as "consumers" are often explained away in overly generalized terms (Buckingham 2011). Stampy achieves an authentic self by being predictably fun and entertaining, but also through exceptional Minecraft play. Across the 649 videos in his Lovely World series and the hundreds of other Minecraft videos he has produced, he has been a consummate entertainer, continuously coming up with new ideas to have fun in the game. He has built a world containing wonderful buildings and fun minigames that he plays with his friends. He never gets angry or upset or becomes frightening, he never raises topics that would be likely to upset or concern a child, and he is kind and generous to his fans. In a similar way, over 345 episodes (and counting), Stacy has built an elaborate world for her Dogcraft series, which has become the setting for her to establish her credibility as an animal and pet lover. She has successfully established a persona as a caring and nurturing adult who can be trusted to be loyal to her animal companions. In contrast to Stampy, she sometimes seems exasperated with events in the game, but she is never angry or threatening. She is also very generous to fans and frequently acknowledges and rewards them. Her world is somewhat exotic because it employs several modifications that are not readily available to most children. Karina plays Minecraft in a casual manner that is immediately recognizable to children as being ordinary and familiar. In addition, her authenticity is established through her "kid next door" persona, her friendliness, and the love she shows toward her family, particularly her brother. Her appeal also relates to her success, including the exclusive lifestyle she leads and shares with her viewers as she travels the world.

Each Let's Player has struggled to maintain authenticity at various times. For Stampy, the struggle to remain authentic for child fans has centered on the disparity between his Peter Pan-esque child-like self and his self-perceived adult responsibilities. An aspect of this disparity has been Garrett's discomfort with being labeled a "YouTuber" and his desire to be taken seriously as a media producer. There is a sense in which he does not feel he is taken seriously despite his high level of success as a children's entertainer. He frames his turn toward making "educational" content as an opportunity to do something more profound for the large audience he has built.

However, the content is not as successful and does not have as much impact as his entertainment-based videos.

Stacy's struggle for authenticity has been over anthropomorphizing animals and the realities of interacting with animals or using them for entertainment, even when they are digital. Stacy's fans became upset with her when they perceived that she was being cruel and unfair to her dogs. Unlike Stampy's dilemma with making educational content, though, Stacy's Field Trips videos illustrate that it is possible to frame educational content in a way that maintains authenticity. By framing herself as learning alongside her viewers, Stacy manages to avoid the problem of placing herself in a more knowledgeable position about "official" knowledge.

The challenge facing Karina is twofold. She has to balance her ordinariness as a recognizable everyday kid with the exclusive lifestyle she wants to share with her viewers. This is risky, as she and her family found when Karina and Ronald seemed to display a lack of awareness about their level of privilege in one of their house tour videos. In addition, the fashion-style images Karina posts to Instagram have drawn some criticism as being inauthentic for showing Karina acting too old for her age.

What Kind of Microindustry Has Formed around Minecraft Let's Play Production?

The analysis outlined in chapters 6 through 8 provides important insights into why Let's Play videos are popular with children and why the genre has helped draw children away from set-top television consumption toward YouTube. Although a significant amount of research has established this trend internationally, there have been few academic studies about why children have migrated to YouTube in such large numbers. Furthermore, there have been few attempts to understand how family-friendly YouTubers have aimed to professionalize their practice or to take account of some of the challenges of YouTube culture.

YouTube's development as a platform for the distribution of social media entertainment has seen it evolve from being a distribution point for amateur video to being semi-industrialized and professionalized (Cunningham and Craig 2019). As YouTube became monetized through the Google AdSense system and created its YouTube "partnership agreements" approach to financially reward creators (Cunningham and Craig 2019), a plethora of ways for organizing creators and content emerged. This included the emergence of multichannel networks (MCNs), which a number of the family-friendly Minecraft Let's Players identified in this book have been associated with. I have described this group as a microindustry consisting of a loose association of creators who make similar Minecraft Let's Play content for children. In contrast to some popular media reports about the ease with which Let's Players generate income on YouTube, the analysis has shown the skill, hard work, dedication, and creativity that go into the production of successful Minecraft videos and channels. Through outlining Stampy's story, for instance, the analysis has emphasized Let's Players' vulnerability and how precarious their position is even when they have been financially successful.

While the family-friendly Minecraft Let's Play microindustry seems to be largely self-supporting and organic, YouTube's affordances play a role in helping to create more and less formal affiliations between creators. For instance, the "featured channels" section of each YouTuber's channel page points to other YouTubers audience members might enjoy watching, signaling elements of the microindustry. For instance, on her channel, StacyPlays features Stampy, Sqaishey Quack, iHasCupquake, LDShadowLady and Amy Lee; Stampy, in turn, features StacyPlays, Sqaishey, DanTDM, and iBallisticSquid. Gaining an understanding of the microindustry provides further insight into how its members support each other through collaboration and cross-promotional efforts.

A consideration of the microindustry has produced important insights, including an understanding of the size, scale, and impact of the audience for Let's Play videos and a way to understand each of the Let's Players in context. First, because of the size of the microindustry, it is possible to make some assumptions about the popularity of particular Let's Players by providing a sense of scale and reach. We know, for instance, that Minecraft is the most watched game on YouTube, having surpassed 200 billion total views in March 2019 (Let's Play Index 2019). Furthermore, we know that at various times, Minecraft Let's Players have been among the most subscribed YouTubers—with Stampy the fifth most subscribed YouTuber for a time in 2014 (Cohen 2014) and DanTDM the fourth highest paid YouTuber of 2018 (Robehmed and Berg 2018). Such metrics indicate that Let's Play videos have been among the most watched YouTube content and are part of the reason children have moved their attention away from traditional television toward video content on YouTube. Children in the United Kingdom, for example, spend more time online in a typical day than they do in front of a television set, and YouTube is children's primary online destination (Ofcom 2019a).

Second, exploring the microindustry has made it possible to place individual creators in context through tracing the relative size of their audience over time. Through this lens, each YouTuber's story of cultural production is laid bare. The shape of Stampy's career over six years from initial success to megasuccess and broader public recognition, to experiments with new formats, and, finally abruptly ceasing production, provides important insights into the limits and precarity of YouTube creator labor. Stampy's videos continue to attract 741,000 views per day, six months after posting his last video, which indicates the attractiveness of his videos to new viewers and loyal fans. However, his story has a similar arc to a number of other YouTubers who have found it difficult to maintain such an intense rate of production over time, working in relative isolation (Cunningham and Craig 2019). Although the microindustry provides opportunities for collaboration, Garrett suggests in his Let's Talk videos that the broader YouTube industry can be quite cruel, and his obvious disillusionment with YouTube culture comes through in these nongaming videos (stampylongnose 2017).

The microindustry analysis also provides interesting insights into Stacy Hinojosa's approach as a creator across different platforms, including traditional publishing. Although her videos attract relatively few views—6.8 million views over thirty days in 2020, compared to Stampy's 23.1 million and Karina's 47 million (on the GamerGirl channel alone)—Stacy continues to produce videos on a regular basis. It is likely she does this to maintain and build her fan base for her publishing activities; the first volume in her *Wild Rescuers* series was briefly a *New York Times* children's book best seller (StacyPlays 2018), and in 2019, the second book in the series was released (StacyPlays 2019).

As a member of the Kurzawa family, KarinaOMG is interesting from a microindustry perspective because the family's approach has been different from that of other Let's Players and YouTubers. Although the family's videos have been watched several billion times, their activity is quite localized, and they seem to operate independently. Their move to Spain physically separates them from a great deal of mainstream media activity, and in direct contrast to the families behind the highly successful Shaytards and Eh Bee Family channels, they have not appeared very often in public and have not featured in mainstream media stories. In addition, the case study outlined in chapter 8 provides important insights into the risks of being a child You-Tube creator within a family YouTube business, including the risk to reputation, the policing of gendered norms, and the risk of burnout. While there is no suggestion that Kuzawa's parents exploit their children in obvious ways as is the case on channels where children are purposely "punked" by their parents for laughs, clicks, and views (Leaver and Abidin 2017), there is an uneasy sense that Karina and her brother, Ronald, are in a precarious position in terms of their reputations, well-being, and transition into their teen years. The amount of content produced by Karina indicates that she works extremely hard for a twelve-year-old who also attends school every day. While it is beyond the scope of this book, the Karina case study raises vital questions about platform regulation, children's digital labor (Postigo 2016; Abidin 2017), and child autonomy and rights on digital platforms (Livingstone and Third 2017).

What Assumptions Do Let's Players Make about Their Viewers, and What Performative Practices Allow Them to Be Recognizable to Their Viewers?

One of the most surprising findings in this study is the extent to which fans' emotional investment seems to drive their desire to form relationships with Let's Players and to learn more about how to play Minecraft. Let's Players understand their fans' emotional attachment to Minecraft as a game and a platform. While this emotional connection is often perplexing to an older generation of gamers or to adults with a passing interest in contemporary gaming, successful Let's Players of all ages understand its appeal. A now clichéd response to Minecraft is that its graphics appear to be unsophis-ticated, and many non-fans see the game as blocky or ugly. Putting aside the obvious response from most Minecrafters that criticisms of the game's visuals are unfounded—see, for instance, James Delaney's book, *Beautiful Minecraft* (2016)—children's attachment to the game is far from superficial. Minecraft Let's Players not only recognize children's Minecraft fandom, they share a passion for Minecraft and celebrate the game as an important and worthwhile pastime. In contrast to official culture that often sees digital games as trivial at best or the cause of significant social problems at worst (Gee 2007b), Let's Players take Minecraft seriously. As I have demonstrated, Let's Players understand that Minecraft fans care about being able to design and build well, they care about the online worlds they create, they care about understanding modifications and hacks, and they care about the social currency afforded by acquiring Minecraft knowledge. As I argued in chapter 2, for many Minecraft players, the game forms a central aspect of what Deuze (2012) refers to as "media life," which recognizes the game's presence across online and offline lived experiences. The game is as much a part of their lives and identities as any other aspect of culture and society. Let's Players understand Minecraft's flexibility and sophistication as a platform that can be many different things to players, and they position themselves as particular kinds of Minecraft players. Karina, Stacy, and Stampy each play Minecraft differently, and this matters a great deal in terms of the fans they attract. As I have also suggested, the play scenarios that the three Let's Players developed, their commentaries, and their interactions with fans all suggest they make particular assumptions about their fans.

Analysis of Stampy, Stacy, and Karina's Let's Play videos and other creative outputs suggests that each of them makes somewhat different assumptions about their child fans, and this leads to a varied range of performative practices. This difference in approach by each of the Let's Players is informative because it challenges the notion that the children's audience is somehow monolithic or predictable or that there is a particular formula for targeting the children's audience. According to Buckingham (2011), contemporary marketing theory often describes children "in almost Pavlovian terms, as displaying programmed responses to particular marketing appeals or sensory signals, and in constant pursuit of instant gratification" (87). To the uninitiated, Minecraft Let's Plays might seem like a formula that simply works for children as long as the Let's Player is able to make his or her videos fun enough. It is clear from the analysis in the preceding chapters, though, that in addition to making their videos visually and aurally appealing, successful Let's Players attract children on a deeply emotional level. This is obviously an attraction to the Let's Players themselves, but it is also an attraction to Minecraft as a game.

Another assumption that Let's Players have about their viewers is that they want access to them on an emotional level, and Let's Players are generally willing to be as available as possible. As Cunningham and Craig point out (2019), it is difficult to scale up availability as Let's Players become more successful. While it may have been possible to respond to a reasonable proportion of fans in the early days of their production activity, this becomes far less possible when they have tens of thousands, and eventually millions, of subscribers. Making themselves available to their viewers requires ongoing relational labor that simply was not required of celebrities in the same way in the past. Let's Players cannot rely on the machinery of the star system associated with movie and television celebrity, supported by agents, publicists, and assistants. The social media presence of each of the Let's Players discussed in this book points to the additional work they undertake to be available to their fans. Within their Let's Play videos, Stacy rewards her fans through sharing their art in her "arf gallery" (stacyplays 2016a) and naming dogs after them in her Dalmatian Plantation, and Stampy rewards his fans by adding them to his Love Garden. These explicit tactics to reward fans help to consolidate the connection each Let's Player has already made to fans through the emotional appeal of their content.

An implied assumption that the three Let's Players have about their viewers is that they want to feel safe and at ease in their presence. Stampy spends a considerable amount of time modeling good play, being a "good sport" when playing minigames, and talking about the need for cooperation. Stacy overtly cares for animals and displays ongoing and explicit concern for her real-life and in-game pets. Karina is a caring big sister who likes spending time with her younger brother and other family members. In their own ways, each of the Let's Players displays what might be considered to be a social pedagogy (Cameron and Moss 2011) and level of care in terms of wanting to protect their audience from inappropriate or upsetting content. From a more cynical perspective, this might be read as being a smart, self-regulatory move to ensure children and their parents believe their content is safe and age appropriate. More generously, the approach might be seen to be a genuine response to audience expectations and a desire to be responsible. Stampy, for instance, has been very explicit about his desire to provide children with positive online experiences.

What Modes of Address Do Let's Players Establish through Their Use of Voice for Commentary, Including Intonation and Modulation, and through Use of Stylistic Features Such as Camera Shot, Editing, and Movement?

Let's Plays are among the new genres of YouTube videos that seem to confound some adults (Jenkins 2015). Along with unboxing videos, they draw the ire of adults who consider the videos to be overly commercialized and of little substance. In the case of Let's Plays, parents might ask why children bother watching other people play video games when they could be playing themselves (Vrabel 2017). The preceding chapters and the previous sections of this chapter have provided an answer to that question. However, throughout this book, I have also aimed to outline Let's Player's specific literacy practices in terms of how they construct their videos to appeal to children. I have aimed to build on the small amount of existing literature about the Let's Play genre to provide a comprehensive outline of the form's conventions, at least as they apply to family-friendly Minecraft Let's Plays.

Throughout the project, I have been interested in Let's Players' ability to make the blocky Minecraft avatar come to life for their fans. At the most fundamental level, a Let's Player shares his or her first-person point of view with the audience, placing them in the same position as the Let's Player. The audience sees exactly what the Let's Player sees. If the Let's Player is building, the audience is able to see exactly how the Let's Player builds, and they can pause and rewind the video at key moments to double-check the Let's Player's technique. If the Let's Player is fighting monsters, the audience is taken directly into combat, and if something unexpected occurs in the game, the audience experiences it with the Let's Player. If the Let's Player falls from a high place while undertaking construction, the audience essentially falls with the Let's Player, causing a visceral reaction (Keogh 2018). In essence, the Let's Player's point of view stands in for the camera in the production the videos. Therefore, as in all first-person gameplay, there is no reliance on camera shots to construct the audience's visual engagement. Having said this, Let's Players use their point of view in ways that might not be typical in unrecorded gameplay. They sometimes pause to show the audience particular items or scenery in a game, which would otherwise be unnecessary to gameplay.

Let's Players' commentary is essential to the meanings that are created for the audience. On one level, the sonic presence of a Minecraft Let's Player's voice is distinctive and continuous. Stacy's American accent, her use of uptalk with a regular rising inflection, and her use of "petese" as she addresses her animals is distinctive and recognizable. Stampy's British accent, his regular chuckle, and the excited pitch, pace, and tone of his voice are easily identifiable to fans. Karina's frequently shouty voice is also highly familiar to fans. The catchphrases they use are also highly familiar to fans. Stacy's regular concluding phrase "Paige and Molly love you, go rescue a dog"; Stampy's introduction "Hellooo and welcome to a Minecraft Let's Play"; and Karina's "Hey guys, it's Karina here . . ." signify a desire to be immediately recognizable. Despite the use of catchphrases, which mimics television presenter practices, these three are untrained, and it is likely that the amateurish quality of their voices seems more real and "everyday" to many fans. In addition, the loosely constructed nature of Let's Play content, which makes it slightly unpredictable and in the moment, also reinforces its familiarity and everydayness. While it is clear that most Let's Play episodes have a predetermined structure and planned events, they are primarily unscripted and ad-libbed. The commentary comes across as immediate, spontaneous, and genuine.

An important idea to emerge from this study is that Let's Players make a connection to their audience through the actions of their character and commentary, both in-world, and in real life. That is, StacyPlays is both an in-game avatar (StacyPlays) and the person behind the gameplay who is recording commentary—the YouTuber, StacyPlays. However, Stacy Hinojosa is not a star in the way that a Hollywood actor is, and the recognized author of Stacy's books is StacyPlays, not Stacy Hinojosa. There is a degree of irony that individuals who are trying to be authentic for their audience are known to the audience as constructed characters rather than as actual people. At the same time, Stampy's Let's Talk videos and the Stacy vlogs videos take the audience directly to the Let's Player as a person rather than a Minecraft character, even if they retain their Let's Player name. Karina's lifestyle videos do the same for her. In addition, there seems to be more loyalty to the Let's Player as a person than to the videos, as we saw with support for Stampy when he began to reduce the number of videos he was producing.

What Insights Can We Gain into Peer Pedagogies by Considering Fan Practices?

A key outcome of this study is that relational labor (Baym 2018) is not one-sided in the production and consumption of Let's Play videos. Fans participate in relational labor through commenting and other creative practices that are vital for the production of learning communities and for the creation of the conditions in which peer pedagogies potentially flourish. The most obvious way fans interact with Let's Play videos is through leaving comments or engaging with the commenting community. To date, much of the scholarly discussion about YouTube's comments function has focused on how YouTubers respond to "haters" (Lange 2014) or how the comments function works as an aspect of YouTube as a platform, for instance, as one of the metrics informing the platform's algorithm (Burgess and Green 2018). There has been less focus on how comments act as a space for community building and fan practices. Somewhat surprisingly, my analysis of the comments on family-friendly Let's Play videos suggests that in the best circumstances, comments are generally positive and viewers use the comments for expressing their fandom, connecting with other fans, and learning more about Minecraft. Many comments are also expressions of support for other fans in support of the comments they make about the Let's Player or about Minecraft. Madden, Ruthven, and McMenemy's (2013) scheme for classifying YouTube comments aligns with how fans commented on the Let's Play videos. They suggest that YouTube comments can be broken down into ten categories: information, advice, impression, opinion, responses, expressions of personal feeling, general conversation, site processes, video content description, and nonresponse comments. As noted in chapter 7, many comments on Stacy's videos are of children discussing their own pets, including stories about their pets' illnesses and treatment. Comments on Stampy's videos frequently express love for Stampy's Lovely World, and comments on Karina's videos have often been equally complimentary. Nevertheless, the relatively small number of hate comments on Stampy's videos have had a deleterious effect, with Stampy speaking out directly against online hate (stampylongnose 2016a).

Of interest to this book are comments that relate to learning. Within the thousands of comments on the three Let's Players' videos, I identified regular examples of fans seeking information and advice about Minecraft and how to achieve particular things in the game. Stacy is frequently asked about the modifications she uses in Dogcraft, including how to access the mods and add them to a world to modify the gameplay experience. Other commenters often answer these questions, providing details about the sites where the mods can be downloaded and whether they can be added to different Minecraft versions. In addition to seeking advice, fans often give advice and provide suggestions in their comments. For instance, Stampy fans frequently provide him with suggestions for what to build next or how to improve particular aspects of his builds. There is a distinct element of peer interrelatedness here in that fans seem to feel entitled to provide advice and that their ideas are likely to be as good as Stampy's.

Let's Play fans frequently create different kinds of art to make a connection to each of the three Let's Players. For instance, Stacy and Stampy promote fan art within their Let's Play videos to recognize fans' support. Most of this work acts as homage to the Let's Players and is potentially motivated by the opportunity to be recognized within the videos. Being added to Stampy's Love Garden, for example, garners recognition within the fan community. More generally, paying homage to Let's Players though creating fan art and posting it to online sites allows fans to publicly declare their support for the Let's Player. On another level, creating fan art allows fans to take ideas provided by the Let's Players to extend the story world for their own purposes (Jenkins 2013, 156). The thousands of stories on Wattpad about Stacy and Stampy are clear instances of fans creating stories for other fans, which often stretch the realities of the personal lives of the Let's Players. From the perspective of understanding peer relations, fan art allows fans to enter the world of the Let's Player in a more connected way than through watching the YouTuber's videos or commenting on their videos. Interacting with and extending a Let's Player's cultural artifacts in a way that is invited and celebrated by the Let's Player provides a unique opportunity to make a connection to the Let's Player. In addition, fan art that explores the emotional worlds of Let's Players—for example, in the form of Wattpad stories like the "adopted by StacyPlays" story discussed in chapter 7—provide insights into fans' emotional commitment to particular creators. Seen through the perspective of fans' extended stories, it is easy to appreciate the parasocial relationships that fans form with Let's Players. Fan art is often an outward expression of loyalty to a Let's Player, but it is also a disclosure of the fan's emotional attachment to the Let's Player.

How Are Minecraft Knowledge and Practice Classified and Framed in Various Ways by Let's Players, and What Is the Relationship of This to Peer Pedagogies?

A novel aspect of this book's approach is that it has aimed to treat children's Minecraft learning as important even if it does not "count" as legitimate knowledge according to institutionalized schooling. I have argued that children value learning how to play Minecraft effectively and how to take up subject positions around gameplay. The cultural capital (Bourdieu 1986) acquired through taking advantage of peer pedagogies has exchange value for children in both online and offline social interactions. Minecraft Let's Players' understanding of various aspects of Minecraft, what they do with Minecraft, and their actions and use of Minecraft knowledge and terminology establish their credibility and authenticity. As I have also noted throughout the book, Let's Players need to be accepted as authentic and everyday people, but if they do not have Minecraft credibility, they are unlikely to emerge as figureheads for specific Minecraft fan communities. In terms of pedagogy, what Let's Players say and do in their videos and beyond invites children to take up particular social-material practices and subject positions. As I argued in chapter 4, drawing on a performative conceptualization of pedagogy, learning is not merely a process of knowledge transfer between a teacher and student but an invitation to undertake discursive and material performative acts that repeat established disciplinary and social norms, with the potential to creatively vary them to establish new norms.

Each of the three Let's Players discussed in the book has his or her own strategies for inviting viewers to take up discursive and material performative acts and strategies for reducing social distance as they extend this invitation. Most fundamentally, their pedagogical strategies are generally intrinsic to successful Minecraft participation, where there are many options and opportunities for success. Stacy moves beyond Minecraft's immediate concerns to include knowledge and practice equating to ethical treatment of animals. For Stampy, appropriate and supportive Minecraft play and general good online behavior extend his in-game concerns. Both Let's Players also invite children to take up school-like knowledge in different ways, with different levels of success. Karina has the most casual pedagogical approach of the three; she places less emphasis on representational pedagogical practices and more on the embodied practices of being herself, which invites viewers to connect more directly to her than to her content.

I found it particularly useful to consider how Bernstein's theories of pedagogical classification and framing relate to Let's Player practices because stronger and weaker classification and framing relate to normativity and the options for performative practice. In Bernstein's terms, the "educational knowledge code" and the form it takes depend on social principles that regulate the classification and framing of knowledge made public in educational institutions (Bernstein 1973, 363). Bernstein suggests that "classification" refers to the degree of boundary maintenance between the contents of what is being learned (366), and "frame" refers to the degree of control "teacher and pupil possess over the selection, organization, and pacing of the knowledge transmitted and received in the pedagogical relationship" (366). Bernstein's concepts were intended to be applied in formal school settings to consider how subject knowledge is policed and the extent to which students have any form of control over their own learning. However, it is productive to apply the concepts to Minecraft Let's Plays.

Let's Players have the option to strongly or more loosely police what counts as official Minecraft knowledge. Of course, unlike school knowledge, Minecraft knowledge counts as being official in terms of its acceptance among the playing community. Nonetheless, given the social currency children often attach to Minecraft knowledge, the sanctioning of some forms of knowledge over others by community leaders like Let's Players has the potential to establish norms of practice. As I have discussed elsewhere (Dezuanni, 2019) the Minecraft Let's Player Grian has created a range of how-to Minecraft videos that quite strongly classify particular building practices as being more acceptable than others in the game. While none of the three Let's Players discussed in this book tends to strongly classify Minecraft knowledge, they make choices about what to focus on in their play, which draws attention to particular aspects of the game. Meanwhile, Minecraft knowledge is framed in various ways in general play by the three Let's Players, particularly according to how episodes are organized around narrative engagement. For instance, Stampy framed the building of a big barn through a combination of direct instruction as a how-to video, but also by introducing elements of fun through a minigame toward the end of the episode.

When Stacy and Stampy take up more teacher-like personae in, respectively, the Field Trips and Wonder Quest series, the two YouTubers risk their authenticity, arguably because the knowledge they share becomes more strongly classified and framed. Stampy's Wonder Quest series is the more strongly classified and framed of the two, as it aims to directly align to school-based curriculum concepts. At key points in the series, Stampy and his collaborators introduce official curriculum content, including mathematics and science concepts that are required to solve problems that arise in the story. The framing of these "schoolish" sequences is also strongly framed in terms of how they are presented to ensure that the educational concepts are clearly and precisely explained. In the flow of the episodes, they come across as being quite stilted as moments of adult-sanctioned learning. Stacy's Field Trips series is less strongly classified and framed, aided by their positioning as general explorations of the world that take place outside the classroom on a field trip. Although factual information is presented in the videos, Stacy is positioned not as the expert but as an interested student who is learning alongside her audience.

Peer Pedagogies

To complete this discussion, I revisit the definition of *peer pedagogies* outlined in chapter 4, in light of the discussion already presented in this chapter. The definition suggests that in relation to Let's Plays, peer pedagogies are relationships in which a flat structure emerges between teachers and learners, arranged through a creator's attempts to reduce social distance and their ability to meet a viewer's need for knowledge.

This chapter has argued that the flat structure existing between teachers and learners is premised on the idea that Let's Players make knowledge available in a manner that respects viewers' passions and their existing knowledge. There is little sense that Let's Players talk down to their audience or that they aim to come across as superior. Even when Stampy's exceptional Minecraft knowledge is on display, for instance, there is little sense of superiority in his tone or presentational style. I am not arguing that the flatness of the pedagogical relationship equates to equality between Let's Players and their viewers. Rather, I am suggesting that the work Let's Players put into reducing social distance between themselves and their fans results in viewers' feeling that they are on a similar level to the Let's Player, even if this is an illusion. Let's Play fans recognize Let's Players as gamers who share their passion for the game and as everyday individuals who spend considerable time producing entertainment for them. This perspective comes through as a strong theme in the comments fans leave on Let's Play videos.

A key attribute of successful Let's Players is the ability to reduce social distance in sustained and authentic ways. It is no small task to remain relatable and recognizable to fans when it is difficult to scale up personal connections to fans by responding to YouTube video comments and other social media messages. The process of maintaining a consistent approach to character development through narrative techniques and commentary is no doubt difficult. Stampy and Stacy have expressed in their vlog posts that it is stressful and tiring to make several videos each week over an extended period of time. As I have shown in the analysis, all three YouTubers have sometimes struggled to reduce social distance between themselves and their viewers.

Finally, the focus of this book has been on the learning that occurs as children engage with Let's Play content. My argument throughout has been that children have a strong desire to develop their own knowledge of Minecraft play and that watching Let's Play videos meets this need for knowledge. These videos provide ideas for how to play in Minecraft, including how to respond to the freedom the game provides as an open-world sandbox game. They also provide insight into how to design and build in new ways, how to solve technical challenges, and how to play with others in the game, including what to do together. Watching Let's Plays offers a model to children for making their own gameplay videos—either actually recorded videos or simply play-acted videos. Finally, Let's Plays provide insight into the various ways Minecraft is modified and repurposed by the gaming community. In all these ways, Minecraft Let's Players meet the needs of their viewers who have a passionate desire to know more about the game and its uses.

10 Conclusion: Media Literacy in the Age of Minecraft and YouTube

This book has been about the peer pedagogical relationships that are frequently central to children's interactions on digital platforms, fueled by fandom and impassioned learning. In this chapter, I turn my attention to the implications of these relationships for media literacy, which has received renewed interest in recent years as a result of concerns about the role of digital platforms in spreading misinformation (Polizzi 2018) and the misuse of user data (Pangrazio and Selwyn 2019). The existence of peer pedagogies on digital platforms requires a reconsideration of media literacy education's key concepts to include the relational work that occurs on digital platforms between microcelebrities and fans. At the most fundamental level, media literacy might be thought of as the ability to critically reflect on one's own and others' media consumption and production. Since at least the 1920s, parents, educators, concerned citizens, and scholars in numerous countries have argued in favor of education about various forms of media (Dezuanni and Goldsmith 2015). Such efforts have mostly aimed to protect young people from the media and have reacted to the perceived social, moral, and cultural consequences of young people's media consumption (Buckingham 2003).

There has been renewed interest in the objectives of media literacy as a means to address some of the social harms deriving from the rise of digital platforms. Concerns have been raised about the impact of so-called fake news on democratic processes (Mihailidis and Viotty 2017), and there has been increasing alarm over the realization that users' personal data are being shared and monetized by technology companies in unexpected ways or stolen through data breaches (Stoilova, Livingstone, and Nandagiri 2019; Livingstone 2018a). Meanwhile, children's access to and use of digital platforms has gained a great deal of attention, especially YouTube's initial refusal to acknowledge the vast children's audience present on its main service, as opposed to the YouTube Kids app (Romm and Bensinger 2019), and the consequent concerns related to advertising to children and children's access to inappropriate adult content (Koerber 2017). There have been calls for digital platforms to self-regulate and develop more transparent practices, and for governments to do more to rein in the companies. In parallel, media literacy has been promoted as a means to educate young people, and citizens more broadly, about the social consequences of digital media. A plethora of new and renewed media literacy initiatives have emerged, often funded by the technology companies themselves. For instance, in September 2019, Google hosted the Global Media Literacy Summit in London, bringing together numerous media literacy advocates, many of whom have been funded by Google to promote media literacy in different parts of the world. Not to be outdone, Facebook has developed media literacy initiatives globally, including the Digital Literacy Library (https://www.facebook.com/safety/educators).

Leading scholars have been quick to argue that media literacy is not a panacea for the problems of misinformation, privacy breaches, and other problems associated with digital platforms (boyd 2017; Livingstone 2018b). These perspectives have warned that while media literacy is an important element of responding to digital platform problems, it cannot be expected to take the place of more effective regulatory and policy responses. The debate over the relationship between media literacy and media regulation is not new. The so-called promote-and/or-protect dynamic has long been present within debates about how best to control the relationship between citizens and the media (von Feilitzen and Carlsson, 2003): Should society promote media literacy, or protect citizens through regulation, and what should be the appropriate combination of these approaches? The Internet has complicated these questions because of the difficulty of imposing regulations on radically decentralized media production and consumption.

While this chapter is informed by broader debates about the efficacy of regulation and education, I primarily discuss the consequences for media literacy of the findings outlined in the previous chapters of this book. YouTube, Let's Play culture, and peer pedagogies raise interesting questions about the role and form of media literacy education on and about digital platforms. They raise questions about the relational dynamics of digital platforms, an area of investigation that media literacy scholarship and initiatives focused on digital platforms have so far mostly ignored. Media literacy programs about digital platforms tend to focus on content analysis, representational practices, bias and fairness, information literacies, changing online behavior, safe practices, and reputation management. There has been much less focus on how individuals learn with and from other people online—for instance, through peer pedagogical practices. I am interested in how peer pedagogies may play a role as a means to promote media literacy but also as the focus of media literacy where peer pedagogies may be problematic or harmful. How can children and young people who watch, and make, Let's Play videos learn to critically reflect about digital platform content and the microcelebrities who produce Let's Play videos? Can successful Let's Players help to promote critical reflection?

To help answer these questions, I make a distinction between two broad approaches to media literacy education: the process model and the key concepts model. I find the key concepts model more helpful than the process model because of the potential for its approach to authentically align to the everyday conversations that take place in peer pedagogical relationships. This is because there is potential for the key concepts model to be less formally classified (Bernstein 1973) than the process model, as I argue below. The process model is inevitably more formally classified as pedagogical knowledge because it describes a set of educational goals, whereas the key concepts model describes aspects of a "circuit of culture" (du Gay et al. 1997). Of course, these key aspects may also be described in formal ways through media and communications theory, but they do not have to be.

The media literacy process model was developed by the National Leadership Conference on Media Literacy (Aufderheide and Firestone 1993), and subsequently expanded in the United States by the National Association for Media Literacy Education. This model defines media literacy as "the ability to access, analyze, evaluate, create, and act using all forms of communication" (NAMLE 2020). This definition has become widely used in efforts to respond to digital media. These processes are descriptors of action and effectively become media literacy goals—for instance, it is expected that a media literate person will learn to analyze media. Such processes are perfectly legitimate goals for media literacy, but they are less helpful in providing a sense of the textual and contextual components of the "circuits of culture" (du Gay et al. 1997) in which media are produced, circulated, and consumed. Thinking about Let's Play production and consumption and peer pedagogies through the process model has limitations because it is a highly classified set of processes for understanding media (Bernstein 1973). As I have demonstrated throughout this book, it is possible to analyze Let's Play culture, but unless attention is paid to the elements of production process and the dynamic interactions between producers and consumers, a great deal of nuance may be missed. Media production and consumption, especially on digital platforms, are much more than a linear process defined by discrete actions, and therefore media literacy requires a means to respond appropriately. The key concepts approach provides a convincing alternative, although it requires modification to remain relevant for digital contexts, especially to deal with the relational dynamics of digital platforms.

Drawing heavily on the British cultural studies approach to media and communications scholarship, the key concepts approach to media education was pioneered by Raymond Williams (1966) in *Communications* and Stuart Hall and Paddy Whannel (1964), in *The Popular Arts*. The model includes a focus on the textual and contextual elements of communication. The textual includes the language codes and conventions underpinning communication, and the ideologically infused representational practices that circulate cultural mythologies (Barthes 1957/1972). Consideration of contextual elements includes the study of audience, industries and institutions, and production practices and technologies. The British Film Institute produced an influential version of this model in its Key Aspects of Media Education publications in the late 1980s (Bazalgette 1992), and although different versions have been developed in the subsequent decades, the following concepts remain present in key concepts–inspired models: institution, technology, language, audience, and representation. Although these concepts are quite abstract when used in highly classified ways (Bernstein 1973) as a pedagogical model for media curriculum development, they may also be taken up in general conversation in everyday life and on digital platforms, as I illustrate in the following discussion of Stampy. In Buckingham's and Sefton-Green's (1994) terms and following Vygotsky (1986), media knowledge may be more or less spontaneous or scientific. As I argue below, the spontaneous knowledge developed and shared by Stampy may be considered a form of media literacy education.

Media Literacy with Stampy

Throughout this book, I have touched on how children may learn in critical and reflective ways as they interact with Let's Players. I have suggested, for instance, that Stampy's reflections on life as a Let's Player, his insights into video gaming, and some of the difficulties he has faced as a YouTuber may contribute to his authenticity. These reflections may also be thought of through a media literacy lens. A critical disposition often emerges in Stampy's videos that invites viewers to think about YouTube and Minecraft cultural practices. For instance, in an episode from his Let's Talk series, he answers a question he has received from a number of viewers: "How can I get more views on YouTube?" (MagicAnimalClub 2016c). In response to the question, he argues that in the past, he was more frequently asked about how to make effective videos, but that this has given way to the question about increasing views, which he argues reflects a change in YouTube creator attitudes and culture. In the video, Stampy shares an opinion that there has been a shift away from a focus on effective production practices to a focus on maximizing views and subscriptions at all cost, which he laments as a negative development for the platform. After suggesting that attracting views shouldn't be a creator's main priority, he explains some of the strategies YouTubers use to increase views, including manipulating video titles, the thumbnails that represent videos, following online trends, and collaborating with other YouTubers. He argues there are more and less positive ways of undertaking these strategies. He is critical of "clickbait" videos with misleading titles and thumbnails that deceive viewers. Stampy separates creators into two groups: one that places more emphasis on making "good" videos and another that is more focused on using YouTube tactics to increase views and subscriptions (he places himself in the first group). Through these reflections, Stampy raises questions about institutional and audience practices, and draws attention to some of the language codes YouTubers use to increase the number of views they receive. He does this in a casual and conversational manner, as a means to share his tacit YouTuber knowledge with his fans. This is a loosely classified process of knowledge sharing that nonetheless presents an opportunity for his viewers to raise questions about YouTube production and consumption.

Stampy also focuses on some of the nuances of audience practice in terms of gameplay preferences and Let's Player media production practice.

In a video in the Let's Talk series, Stampy explains why he plays Minecraft on a console system (MagicAnimalClub 2016b) where he talks about the affordances of the console versions of the game in comparison to playing Minecraft on a PC. He speaks about video game player preferences and the pros and cons of having access to endless modifications on the PC version. He points out that physical interaction with a game system controller differs from physical interaction with a PC. He also examines making movies within Minecraft as one of the ways people play the game, that he finds it easier to do this on a console system, and that this approach allows him to make better-looking videos. It is important to him that whatever he builds in Minecraft can be replicated by his viewers, and the console edition supports this. Other videos in the series include Stampy discussing fake versions of YouTube accounts and the implications for intellectual property (stampylongnose 2016d), audience behavior and how it affects the production of videos (stampylongnose 2016c), and a discussion about online safety (MagicAnimalClub 2016a), where he talks about how to deal with strangers online, the need to protect privacy, online scams, and data protection. These videos are more and less tightly classified and framed as teaching and learning. For instance, Stampy places more emphasis on direct instruction in the video about online safety than some of the other videos.

Overall, Stampy's concerns and advice in these videos constitute a form of media literacy education, usually in a loosely classified and framed manner. In his role as responsible adult, he aims to have a positive influence on his child fans by passing on his experience and wisdom in ways that reinforce a critical orientation toward both Minecraft and YouTube. A good example of Stampy's critical reflections on life as a YouTuber is his video "Let's Talk—It's Personal" (stampylongnose 2017c; 247,000 views) in which he discusses what it means to be "real" or "known" on YouTube, and how this relates to self-representational practices:

> I never really talk or tweet about my political views, or religious views, or, I think most importantly my emotions. . . . I think that there's a lot of YouTubers, or just viewers, or just people in the community in general, that really hold in high regard, like, "being real" on YouTube. You've got to be "real," you've got to be "genuine." You've got to talk about the stuff that other people are too scared to talk about, and, firstly, no one actually is. The second you are choosing what to edit in your videos, or even what to record . . . like everyone is kind of trying

to represent themselves in the best light possible. You know, it's normal, if you have five pictures of yourself and you are going to post one to Instagram, you're going to post the one where you think you look the best. I mean of course you are. And that goes to the same with YouTubers when they are uploading videos. You know, they're representing themselves in a way, no matter how real they are trying to be.

Aspects of the language and critical orientation that comes through in this reflection would not be out of place in a high school media literacy class. Stampy discusses one of the main concerns of this book: the question of what it means to be authentic as a YouTuber. His argument that no one is actually "real" because media representation involves processes of selection and construction incorporates one of the key concerns of most school media literacy or media studies courses. Media "representation" was identified by the British Film Institute as one of media education's "key aspects" in the late 1980s (Bazalgette 1992). There is also an echo in Stampy's comments of Len Masterman's (1980) argument for television studies in schools: *"Television education is therefore a demythologizing process which will reveal the selective practices by which images reach the television screen, emphasise the constructed nature of the representations projected, and make explicit their suppressed ideological function"* (9, original emphasis). In this sense, combined with his other discussions about industry, audience, and technology, there is an element to Stampy's reflective practice that accords with the kinds of goals and objectives of media literacy or media education advocates. I am not suggesting Stampy has set out to explicitly introduce media studies to his audience—his vlog is mostly too speculative and off-the-cuff for this. Rather, Stampy's perspectives can be considered as an aspect of his broader goal to be a responsible adult, who happens to know how things work on YouTube. Stampy aims to balance his success as a light-hearted children's entertainer and his desire to have a positive social and cultural impact on children. He is not content to merely entertain children, but has aimed to use his success to inform and educate his audience. He is particularly concerned to place his own practice in context, to explain why he produces videos in certain ways, and he is motivated to teach children about what he perceives to be problematic online practices. In some respects, Stampy's motivations are not very different from the motivations of several generations of media literacy educators who have sought to balance the entertainment children experience while consuming media, with an ability to think about the media. There is a difference, though, in the way Stampy approaches these topics as a high-profile YouTuber whose videos reach hundreds of thousands of fans. Stampy is able to use the relationship he has developed with his audience, including his authenticity and "peerness," to raise questions about the cultural practices that take place on the very platforms he communicates on. There is a constant tension between entertainment and education, and between Stampy as a fun "childlike" figure and a responsible adult. Nonetheless, Stampy's position has provided him with a unique opportunity to undertake a form of media literacy education.

Media Literacy for Digital Platforms

Media literacy education's history parallels concerns about the media's pedagogical functions at each stage of its evolution, which I briefly referred to in chapter 4. As concerned adults worried about the various ways media could "teach" children throughout the twentieth and into the twenty-first centuries, educational strategies emerged to counter the perceived influence of media. There is a comprehensive body of scholarship that traces this history that doesn't require repetition here (Alvarado and Boyd-Barrett 1992; Masterman 1980; Buckingham and Sefton-Green 1994; Hobbs 2009). It is worth noting, though, that with the emergence of YouTube and other social media platforms, we are in the midst of another media pedagogy moment that has caused concern, particularly with regard to children's access to YouTube. Although this book has focused on the practices of Let's Players whose content is generally regarded as safe and inoffensive within the confines of normative (white, middle-class, heteronormative) social expectations, a great deal of Minecraft and Let's Play content is far more controversial.

It is easy to find examples of not-so-family-friendly Minecraft content on YouTube, such as the channel XboxAddictionz (3.3 million subscribers) which uploads videos with titles like "Trolling the Strangest Kid Ever on Minecraft" (2017; 7 million views) or the channel Unstoppable-Luck (808,000 subscribers; 2019) which includes videos with titles such as "Super Bossy Girl Trolled on Minecraft" (5.6 million views) and "Weird Noob Trolled on Minecraft" (1.6 million views). On these channels and others like them, young, mostly male YouTubers set out to frighten or upset children and other young people, typically by destroying their Minecraft builds—generally without the victim knowing they are being trolled and recorded until the end of the video, if at all. There are distinct misogynistic and homophobic undertones in many of the videos in this genre.

More generally, controversies such as "Elsagate" in which popular children's content like the movie *Frozen* is combined with controversial adult content and then uploaded to YouTube have led to deep levels of adult concern about children's entertainment on YouTube (Bridle 2017; Maheshwari 2017). Despite the tendency for these controversies to become overblown in the popular media, these examples should not be dismissed, and there has been a call for YouTube as a company to regulate its content in appropriate ways (Rosney 2018). Furthermore, somewhat controversially, there is increasing momentum for governments to play a role in regulating YouTube and other social media content (Irvine 2018; Reality Check Team 2019). There is also increasing awareness that parents need to play a role in regulating their children's viewing habits on platforms like YouTube (Knorr 2019).

Perhaps the real task for media literacy, though, is not to address the extreme examples of egregious content that appear on YouTube under the guise of children's entertainment. An implication of the findings outlined in chapter 9 is that a significant focus for media literacy educators should be how children and young people can come to navigate appropriate parasocial relationships on YouTube and other digital platforms. Apart from passionate interest in the game Minecraft, it is friendship and companionship that motivates children to want to spend large amounts of time getting to know particular Let's Players. But how should adults help children choose who their microcelebrity "friends" should be? It might be argued that this is not really a question for media literacy advocates. After all, educators are not typically encouraged to become involved in advising children and their parents about who their friends should be. On the other hand, parasocial "friendship" with Internet celebrities is mediated and constructed and often motivated on the celebrity's part by the desire to generate financial reward. Let's Play production and consumption is part of the circuits of culture on digital platforms that raise many questions, including Let's Players' financial, social, and ideological motivations; the tactics they use to gain attention, including the ethics related to how they treat other people; the politics of how they represent themselves and others; the ways they use language features to communicate their ideas and to entertain; how they use platform features to advantage themselves; and how they leverage their relationship with their fans to achieve their objectives and goals. Children's relationships with Let's Players and other social media entertainers are not straightforward, and the particular knowledge that media literacy educators can apply to these relationships should be valued and harnessed.

Given the centrality of relationships to the circuits of culture that form on and around digital platforms, it is perhaps time to add a new media education aspect or concept to the list generated by the The British Film Institute in the late 1980s and 1990s, which has arguably not evolved to account for digital media. The concept of relationships should become core to media literacy education and there are already efforts along these lines. The Aspen Institute Task Force on Learning and the Internet (2014) argues that social and emotional learning, including relationship skills, needs to become central to media literacy and digital literacy efforts. Mediawijzer in the Netherlands, the Dutch Centre of Expertise for Media Literacy, presents relationships within social media settings as a media literacy competency, suggesting that "media-literate people know when other people are out of line and can put a stop to it effectively" (Mediawijzer 2019, 13). Meanwhile, in the United Kingdom, the London School of Economics' Parenting for a Digital Future project has argued that media studies should come together with the study of interpersonal communication in online contexts if scholars want to better understand how children participate on the Internet (Livingstone et al. 2015). In various ways, these and other international examples suggest that it is no longer enough to help children to think about the media using frameworks and models developed for predigital media. This is not to say new approaches cannot effectively use existing media literacy frameworks, as several scholars have argued (Buckingham 2010, 2019; Jolls and Wilson 2014). Rather, my suggestion is to effectively build on existing frameworks to account for interpersonal communication and relationships, which are so central to children's current media experiences.

Developing strategies for what a focus on relationships in media literacy should be is beyond the scope of this book. However, in relation to microcelebrities, it seems clear that questions related to parasocial friendships need to be central to the effort. This would necessarily focus on the ethical practices, values, motivations and behaviors of microcelebrities, and it is likely that media literacy interventions would be highly contested, given the recent history of debates over values education (Henderson 2011) and efforts to address racism, sexism, and homophobia in schools (Gillborn 1990; Meyer 2009; Rhodes 2018). Media literacy education, however, has always dealt with controversial topics and has been at the vanguard of efforts to address problematic media. Furthermore, in best practice, media literacy already provides pedagogical strategies for helping children and young people to have meaningful and critically reflective conversations about their media experiences. The real challenge for media literacy advocates will be how to have authentic and meaningful conversations with children about microcelebrities that ring true—indeed, that are authentic in ways that rival how parasocial relationships with microcelebrities are authentic to children and young people. This will require adults—parents, teachers, researchers, and other concerned citizens—to take YouTube and gaming culture seriously, not to criticize or judge it as trivial but to understand why it plays such an important role in children's lives. We can learn a great deal from social media entertainers like Stampy, StacyPlays, and KarinaOMG, not just about Minecraft and the Let's Play genre, but potentially about how to approach media literacy education in digital times.

References

Abidin, Crystal. 2017. "#familygoals: Family Influencers, Calibrated Amateurism, and Justifying Young Digital Labor." *Social Media + Society* 3 (2). https://doi.org/10.1177/2056305117707191

Abidin, Crystal. 2018. *Internet Celebrity: Understanding Fame Online*. Bingley: Emerald Publishing.

Adorno, Theodor. 1991. *The Culture Industry: Selected Essays on Mass Culture*. London: Routledge.

Alexander, Robin. 2001. *Culture and Pedagogy: International Comparisons in Primary Education*. London: Blackwell.

Alvarado, Manuel, and Oliver Boyd-Barrett, eds. 1992. *Media Education: An Introduction*. London: BFI Publishing.

AntVenom. 2019. "Wait . . . Mojang Is ACTUALLY Listening?!" YouTube video. https://www.youtube.com/watch?v=n0DjEF-N19w.

Arnroth, Thomas. 2014. *A Year with Minecraft: Behind the Scenes at Mojang*. Toronto: ECW Press.

Aspen Institute Task Force on Learning and the Internet. 2014. *Learning at the Centre of a Networked World*. Washington, DC: Aspen Institute.

Atkinson, Paul, Parlo Singh, and James Ladwig.1997. "Review Symposium." *British Journal of Sociology of Education* 18 (1): 115–128.

Aufderheide, Patricia, and Firestone, Charles. 1993. *Media Literacy: A Report of the National Leadership Conference on Media Literacy*. Washington, DC: Communications and Society Program, the Aspen Institute.

Banet-Wiser, Sarah. 2012. *Authentic: The Politics of Ambivalence in a Brand Culture*. New York: New York University Press.

Banks, John A. 2013. *Co-creating Videogames*. London: Bloomsbury Academic.

Barad, Karen. 2003. "Posthumanist Performativity: Toward an Understanding of How Matter Comes to Matter." *Signs: Journal of Women in Culture and Society* 28 (3): 801–831.

Barad, Karen. 2007. *Meeting the Universe Halfway: Quantum Physics and the Entanglement of Matter and Meaning*. Durham, NC: Duke University Press.

Barthes, Roland. 1957/1972. *Mythologies*. New York: Hill and Wang.

Baym, Nancy K. 2010. *Personal Connections in the Digital Age*. Cambridge: Polity Press.

Baym, Nancy K. 2018. *Playing to the Crowd: Musicians, Audiences, and the Intimate Work of Connection*. New York: New York University Press.

Bazalgette, Cary. 1992. "Key Aspects of Media Education." In *Media Education: An Introduction*, edited by Manuel Alvarado and Oliver Boyd-Barrett, 199–219. London: BFI Publishing.

BBC. 2014. "Stampy on Why His Minecraft Tutorials Have YouTubers Gripped." Uploaded March 7. YouTube video. https://www.youtube.com/watch?v=KAQidh25Lm0.

Beavis, Catherine, Michael L. Dezuanni, and Joanne O'Mara, eds. 2017. *Serious Play: Literacy, Learning, and Digital Games*. New York: Routledge.

Beers Fägersten, Kristy. 2017. "The Role of Swearing in Creating an Online Persona: The Case of YouTuber PewDiePie." *Discourse, Context and Media* 18:1–10.

Bennett, Jane. 2010. *Vibrant Matter: A Political Ecology of Things*. Durham, NC: Duke University Press.

Berg, Madeline. 2017. "The Highest-Paid YouTube Stars 2017: Gamer DanTDM Takes the Crown with $16.5 Million." *Forbes*, December 7. https://www.forbes.com/sites/maddieberg/2017/12/07/the-highest-paid-youtube-stars-2017-gamer-dantdm-takes-the-crown-with-16-5-million/.

Bernstein, Basil. 1973. "On the Classification and Framing of Educational Knowledge." In *Knowledge, Education and Cultural Change: Papers in the Sociology of Education*, edited by Richard Brown, 365–392. London: Routledge.

Bernstein, Basil. 2000. *Pedagogy, Symbolic Control and Identity*. Oxford: Rowman & Littlefield.

Bold, Melanie Ramdarshan. 2018. "The Return of the Social Author: Negotiating Authority and Influence on Wattpad." *Convergence: The International Journal of Research into New Media Technologies* 24 (2): 117–136.

Bourdieu, Pierre. 1986. "The Forms of Capital." In *Handbook of Theory and Research for the Sociology of Education*, edited by J. Richardson, 241–258. Westport, CT: Greenwood Press boyd, danah. 2017. Did "Media Literacy Backfire?" *Points—Data and Society*. January 6. Accessed October 13, 2019, at https://points.datasociety.net/did-media-literacy -backfire-7418c084d88d

Bridle, James. 2017. "Something Is Wrong on the Internet." *Medium*. Accessed October 14, 2019, at https://medium.com/@jamesbridle/something-is-wrong-on-the -internet-c39c471271d2.

Brown, Cheryl, and Laura Czerniewicz. 2010. "Debunking the 'Digital Native': Beyond Digital Apartheid, towards Digital Democracy." *Journal of Computer Assisted Learning* 26 (5): 357–369.

Buckingham, David. 1998. "Pedagogy, Parody and Political Correctness." In *Teaching Popular Culture: Beyond Radical Pedagogy*, edited by David Buckingham, 63–87. London: UCL Press.

Buckingham, David. 2000. *After the Death of Childhood: Growing Up in the Age of Electronic Media*. London: Polity Press.

Buckingham, David. 2002. "Introduction: The Child and the Screen." In *Small Screens: Television for Children*, edited by David Buckingham, 1–14. London: Leicester University Press.

Buckingham, David. 2003. *Media Education: Literacy, Learning and Contemporary Culture*. London: Polity Press.

Buckingham, David. 2010. "Do We Really Need Media Education 2.0?" In *Teaching in the Age of Participatory Media*, edited by Kirsten Drotner and Kim Christian Schroder, 287–300. New York: Peter Lang.

Buckingham, David. 2011. *The Material Child: Growing Up in Consumer Culture*. London: Polity Press.

Buckingham, David. 2019. *The Media Education Manifesto*. London: Wiley.

Buckingham, David, Jenny Graham, and Julian Sefton-Green. 1995. *Making Media: Practical Production in Media Education*. London: English and Media Centre.

Buckingham, David and Julian Sefton-Green. 1994. *Cultural Studies Goes to School: Reading and Teaching Popular Media*. London: Taylor and Francis.

Burgess, Jean, and Joshua Green. 2018. *YouTube—Online Video and Participatory Culture*, 2nd ed. Cambridge: Polity Press.

Burrell, Ian. 2015. "Stampy Cat: Joseph Garrett's Cartoon from Minecraft That Is Bigger Than Justin Bieber—and Has Just Been Linked to Disney." *Independent*, January 1. https://www.independent.co.uk/news/media/online/stampy-cat-cartoon-thats -bigger-than-bieber-earns-new-stamping-ground-9953225.html.

Burwell, Catherine. 2017. "Game Changers: Making New Meanings and New Media with Video Games." *English Journal* 106 (6): 41–47.

Burwell, Catherine, and Thomas Miller. 2016. "Let's Play: Exploring Literacy Practices in an Emerging Videogame Paratext." *E-Learning and Digital Media* 13 (3–4): 109–125.

Butler, Judith. 1990. *Gender Trouble*. New York: Routledge.

Butler, Judith. 1993. *Bodies That Matter: On the Discursive Limits of "Sex."* New York: Routledge.

Butler, Judith. 2004. *Undoing Gender*. New York: Routledge.

Cameron, Claire, and Peter Moss, ed. 2011. *Social Pedagogy and Working with Children and Young People: Where Care and Education Meet*. London: Jessica Kingsley.

Cambridge English Dictionary. 2020. "Peer." Accessed January 31, 2020, at https://dictionary.cambridge.org/dictionary/english/peer/.

CBBC. 2014. "Stampy in Real Life! Interview on Appsolute Genius—CBBC." YouTube video. Accessed November 19, 2014, at https://www.youtube.com/watch?v=jRDq7fBKHnk.

Chaplin, Lan Nguyen. 2009. "Please May I Have a Bike? Better Yet, May I Have a Hug? An Examination of Children's and Adolescents' Happiness." *Journal of Happiness Studies* 10 (5): 541–562.

Cisneros, Mike, and Sean Dikkers. 2015. "Starting up the Game: An Introduction to Minecraft." In *Teacher Craft: How Teachers Learn to Use Minecraft in Their Classrooms*, edited by Sean Dikkers, 35–47. Pittsburgh: ETC Press Carnegie Mellon University.

Clark, Travis. 2018. "The 11 Most Popular Gaming YouTube Stars—Some of Whom Made over $10 Million Last Year." *Business Insider*, February 15. https://www.businessinsider.com.au/most-popular-gaming-youtube-stars-ranked-2018-2.

Cohen, Joshua. 2014. "The 100 Most Viewed YouTube Channels Worldwide—December 2014." *Tubefilter*, January 15. https://www.tubefilter.com/2015/01/15/top-100-most-viewed-youtube-channels-worldwide-december-2014/.

Cohen, Ruth, and Jane Sampson. 2013. "Implementing and Managing Peer Learning." In *Peer Learning in Higher Education*, edited by David Boud, Ruth Cohen, and Jane Sampson, 50–66. New York: Routledge.

Collins, Allan, Diana Joseph, and Katerine Bielaczyc. 2004. "Design Research: Theoretical and Methodological Issues." *Journal of the Learning Sciences* 13(1): 15–42.

ConcernedApe. 2016. *Stardew Valley*. Android, Microsoft Windows, iOs, macOS, Linus, Xbox One, PS4, Nintendo Switch (video game).

Consalvo, Mia. 2003. "Zelda 64 and Video Game Fans: A Walkthrough of Games, Intertextuality, and Narrative." *Television and New Media* 4(3): 321–334.

Cunningham, Stuart, and David Craig. 2017. "Being 'Really Real' on YouTube: Authenticity, Community and Brand Culture in Social Media Entertainment." *Media International Australia* 164(1): 71–81.

Cunningham, Stuart, and David Craig. 2019. *Social Media Entertainment: The New Intersection of Hollywood and Silicon Valley*. New York: New York University Press.

Cunningham, Stuart, Michael L. Dezuanni, Ben Goldsmith, Maureen Burns, Prue Miles, Cathy Henkel, Mark Ryan, and Kayleigh Murphy. 2016. *Screen Content in Australian Education: Digital Promise and Pitfalls*. Brisbane: Digital Media Research Centre, Queensland University of Technology.

DanTDM. 2019. "This Is the New Minecraft!" YouTube video. Uploaded January 28. https://www.youtube.com/watch?v=h_od1N6oIgw.

de Rijk, Bram J. S. 2016. "Watching the Game: How We May Understand Let's Play Videos." Master's thesis, Utrecht University.

Delaney, James. 2016. *Beautiful Minecraft*. San Francisco: No Starch Press.

Deuze, Mark. 2012. *Media Life*. Cambridge: Polity Press.

Dezuanni, Michael L. 2015. "The Building Blocks of Digital Media Literacy: Socio-Material Participation and the Production of Media Knowledge." *Journal of Curriculum Studies* 47(3): 416–419.

Dezuanni, Michael L. 2018. "Minecraft and Children's Digital Making: Implications for Media Literacy Education." *Learning, Media and Technology* 43(3): 236–249.

Dezuanni, Michael L. 2019. "Children's Minecraft Multiliteracy Practices and Learning through Peer Pedagogies." In *Multiliteracies and Early Years Innovation: Perspectives from Finland and Beyond*, edited by Päivi Kristiina Kumpulainen and Julian Sefton-Green. London: Routledge.

Dezuanni, Michael L. 2020. "Minecraft 'Worldness' in Family Life: Children's Digital Play and Socio-Material Literacy Practices." In *The Routledge Handbook of Digital Literacies in Early Childhood*, edited by Ola Erstad, Rosie Flewitt, Bettina Kümmerling-Meibauer, and Íris Susana Pires Pereira, 366–375. London: Routledge.

Dezuanni, Michael L., Catherine Beavis, and Joanne O'Mara. 2015. "Redstone Is like Electricity": Children's Performative Representations in and around Minecraft." *E-Learning and Digital Media* 12 (2): 147–163.

Dezuanni, Michael L., and Joanne O'Mara. 2017. "Impassioned Learning with Minecraft." In *Serious Play: Literacy, Learning, and Digital Games*, edited by Catherine Beavis, Michael L. Dezuanni, and Joanne O'Mara, 36–48. New York: Routledge.

Dovey, John, and Helen W. Kennedy. 2006. *Game Cultures: Computer Games as New Media*. Berkshire: Open University Press.

Dredge, Stuart. 2014. "YouTube Star Stampylonghead Launching New Education Channel." *Guardian*, April 9. https://www.theguardian.com/technology/2014/apr/09/stampylonghead-youtube-education-minecraft-maker-studios.

Dredge, Stuart. 2015b. "Why YouTube Is the New Children's TV . . . and Why It Matters. *Guardian*," November 20. https://www.theguardian.com/technology/2015/nov/19/youtube-is-the-new-childrens-tv-heres-why-that-matters.

Dredge, Stuart. 2016a. "Your Kids Want to Make Minecraft YouTube Videos—But Should You Let Them?" *Guardian*, March 25. https://www.theguardian.com/technology/2016/mar/25/kids-minecraft-youtube-videos-stampy-diamond-minecart.

Dredge, Stuart. 2016b. "YouTube Backs Digital Star Stampy's New Minecraft Show Wonder Quest." *Guardian*, April 28. https://www.theguardian.com/technology/2015/apr/27/youtube-stampy-minecraft-education-wonder-quest.

Dredge, Stuart. 2016c. "Joseph Garrett, the Children's Presenter with 7.8 Million Subscribers." *Guardian*, August 28. https://www.theguardian.com/technology/2016/aug/28/stampy-joseph-garrett-youtube-childrens-presenter-millions-of-viewers.

du Gay, Paul. et al. 1997. *Doing Cultural Studies: The Story of the Sony Walkman*. London: Open University/Sage.

Durrant, Cal, and Bill Green. 2000. "Literacy and the New Technologies in School Reform: Meeting the L(IT)eracy Challenge." *Australian Journal of Language and Literacy* 23 (2): 89–108.

Eco, Umberto. 1979. "Can Television Teach? *Screen Education* 31 (12): 15–24.

Edwards, Susan. 2013. "Post-Industrial Play: Understanding the Relationship between Traditional and Converged Forms of Play in the Early Years." In *Children's Virtual Play Worlds: Culture, Learning and Participation*, edited by Anne Burke and Jackie Marsh, 10–25. New York: Peter Lang.

Egmont. 2019. "Minecraft: Official Magazine—Egmont UK." Accessed April 29, 2019, at https://www.egmont.co.uk/magazines/minecraft-official-magazine/.

Eh Bee Family. 2019a. Eh Bee Family (YouTube channel). Accessed April 24, 2019, at https://www.youtube.com/EhBeeFamily.

Eh Bee Family. 2019b. "EhBeeFamily—Family Friendly Online Content." Accessed April 25, 2019, at http://www.ehbeefamily.com/.

Ellsworth, Elizabeth. 1997. *Teaching Positions: Difference, Pedagogy, and the Power of Address*. New York: Teachers College Press.

Epic Games. 2017. *Fortnite*. Android, Microsoft Windows, iOS, macOS, Nintendo Switch, Xbox One, PS4 (video game). Poland: Epic Games.

Erstad, Ola. 2011. "The Learning Lives of Digital Youth—beyond the Formal and Informal." *Oxford Review of Education* 38 (1): 25–43.

Erstad, Ola, and Julian Sefton-Green, eds. 2013. *Identity, Community, and Learning Lives in the Digital Age*. Cambridge: Cambridge University Press.

Famous People. 2019. "Stacy Hinojosa (stacyplays)—Bio, Facts, Family Life of You-Tuber, Gamer." Accessed April 26, 2019, at https://www.thefamouspeople.com/profiles/stacy-hinojosa-32725.php.

Ferris, Kerry O. 2011. *Stargazing: Celebrity, Fame, and Social Interaction*. New York: Routledge.

Fiske, John. 1992. "The Cultural Economy of Fandom." In *The Adoring Audience: Fan Culture and Popular Media*, edited by Lisa A. Lewis, 30–49. London: Routledge.

Fjællingsdal, Kristoffer. 2014. "Let's Graduate—A Thematic Analysis of the Let's Play Phenomenon." Master's thesis, Norges teknisk-naturvitenskapelige universitet.

Foucault, Michel. 1988. *Technologies of the Self: A Seminar with Michel Foucault*. Amherst: University of Massachusetts Press.

Freire, Paulo. 1972. *Pedagogy of the Oppressed*. New York: Penguin Books.

Fun Kids. 2015. "Stampy (Joseph Garrett) Reveals His Minecraft Secrets!" Uploaded December 26. YouTube video. https://www.youtube.com/watch?v=H6W2Jo-1uD0.

Game Freak. 2016. *Pokémon Moon*. Nintendo 3DS (video game). Tokyo: The Pokémon Company, Nintendo.

Gameplay Publishing. 2017. *Stampy Cat Maths: Problems for Elementary School*. Scotts Valley, CA: CreateSpace.

GamerGirl. 2017a. "My New Fancy House!" Uploaded September 22. YouTube video. https://www.youtube.com/watch?v=XokDWNbxBqY.

GamerGirl. 2017b. "Building My Own Restaurant in Bloxburg." Uploaded November 23.YouTube video.https://www.youtube.com/watch?v=Nw2y2v_x5rA.

GamerGirl. 2020. GamerGirl (YouTube channel). Accessed February 1, 2020, at https://www.youtube.com/channel/UCije75lmV_7fVP7m4dJ7ZoQ.

Garrett, Joseph. 2016. *Stampy's Lovely Book*. New York: Random House.

Garrett, Joseph. 2017. *Stick with Stampy! Sticker Book*. London: Penguin Random House.

Gauntlett, David. 2015. *Making Media Studies: The Creativity Turn in Media and Communications Studies*. New York: Peter Lang.

Gee, James Paul. 2007a. *What Video Games Have to Teach Us about Learning and Literacy*, 2nd ed. New York: Palgrave Macmillan.

Gee, James Paul. 2007b. *Good Video Games + Good Learning: Collected Essays on Video Games, Learning and Literacy*. New York: Peter Lang.

Gee, James Paul. 2010. *New Digital Media and Learning as an Emerging Area and "Worked Examples" as One Way Forward*. Cambridge, MA: MIT Press.

Gee, James Paul, and Elizabeth Hayes. 2012. "Nurturing Affinity Spaces and Game-Based Learning." In *Games, Learning and Society: Learning and Meaning in the Digital Age*, edited by Constance Steinkuehler, Kurt Squire, and Sasha Barab, 129–153. Cambridge: Cambridge University Press.

Gilbert, Ben. 2019. "'Minecraft' Has Been Quietly Dominating for over 10 Years, and Now Has 112 Million Players Every Month." *Business Insider*, September 14, 2019. https://www.businessinsider.com.au/minecraft-monthly-player-number-microsoft-2019-9.

Giles, David. C. 2018. *Twenty-First Century Celebrity: Fame in Digital Culture*. Bingley: Emerald Publishing.

Gillbourne, David. 1990. *Race, Ethnicity and Education: Teaching and Learning in Multi-Ethnic Schools*. London: Routledge.

Gillespie, Tarleton. 2017. "Is 'Platform' the Right Metaphor for the Technology Companies That Dominate Digital Media?" *NiemanLab*, August 25. http://www.niemanlab.org/2017/08/is-platform-the-right-metaphor-for-the-technology-companies-that-dominate-digital-media/.

Gilman, Byron L. 2014. "Press Start to Play! Interactivity in the Video Game Medium." PhD diss., Creighton University.

Giroux, Henry. 1992. *Border Crossings: Cultural Workers and the Politics of Education*. New York: Routledge.

Giroux, Henry. 1994. *Disturbing Pleasures*. New York: Routledge.

Giroux, Henry. 1997. *Pedagogy and the Politics of Hope: Theory, Culture, and Schooling*. Boulder, CO: Westview Press.

Giroux, Henry. 2011. *On Critical Pedagogy*. London: Bloomsbury.

Glas, René. 2015. "Vicarious Play: Engaging the Viewer in Let's Play Videos." *Empedocles: European Journal for the Philosophy of Communication* 5 (1–2): 81–86.

Google. 2018. "Google Adsense—Make Money Online through Website Monetization." Accessed April 19, 2019, at https://www.google.com.au/adsense/start/.

Gore, Jennifer M. 1993. *The Struggle for Pedagogies: Critical and Feminist Discourses as Regimes of Truth.* New York: Routledge.

Grian. 2019. Grian (YouTube channel). Accessed April 28, 2019, at https://www.youtube.com/channel/UCR9Gcq0CMm6YgTzsDxAxjOQ.

Guinness World Records. (2017). *Guinness World Records: Gamer's Edition.* Vancouver, BC: Guinness World Records Ltd.

Hale, James Loke. 2018. "'Fortnite' Is Not YouTube's Most Popular Game." *Tubefilter.* September 19. https://www.tubefilter.com/2018/09/19/fortnite-is-not-youtubes-most-popular-game/.

Hall, Stuart, and Paddy Whannel. 1964. *The Popular Arts.* London: Hutchinson Educational.

Harlow, Danielle B., Alexandria K. Hanse, Jasmine K. McBeath, and Anne E. Leak. 2018. "Teacher Education for Maker Education: Helping Teachers Develop Appropriate PCK for Engaging Children in Educative Making." In *Pedagogical Content Knowledge in STEM,* edited by Stephen Miles Uzzo, Sherryl Browne Graves, Erin Shay, Marisa Harford, and Robert Thompson, 265–280. Singapore: Springer.

Harris, Sarah C., Flávio S. Azevedo, and Anthony J. Petrosino. 2018. "Curating Knowledge and Curating Fun: An Analysis of the Expanding Roles of Children's Museums." *Scientific Research* 9 (12): 1881–1896.

Harrison, Justin B. 2015. *Diary of a Wimpy Stampy Cat: Airplane Adventures.* Scotts Valley, CA: CreateSpace.

Hartley, John. 1999. *The Uses of Television.* London: Routledge.

Hartley, John. 2009. "Digital Literacy and the Growth of Knowledge." In *YouTube: Online Video and Participatory Culture,* edited by Jean Burgess and Joshua Green, 126–143. Cambridge: Polity Press.

Hartley, John. 2011. *The Uses of Digital Literacy.* New Brunswick, NJ: Transaction Publishers.

Hayes, Elizabeth R., and James Paul Gee. 2010. "Public Pedagogy through Video Games: Design, Resources and Affinity Spaces. In *Handbook of Public Pedagogy: Education and Learning beyond Schooling,"* edited by Jennifer A. Sandlin, Brian D. Schultz, and Jake Burdick, 185–193. London: Routledge.

Hayles, N. Katherine. 2003. "Translating Media: Why We Should Rethink Textuality." *Yale Journal of Criticism* 16 (2): 263–290.

Henderson, Deborah J. 2011. "Values, Controversial Issues and Interfaith Understanding." In *Teaching the Social Sciences and Humanities in an Australian Curriculum*, edited by Colin Marsh and Catherine Hart, 155–189. Sydney: Pearson Australia.

Hobbs, Renee. 2009. "The Past, Present, and Future of Media Literacy Education." *Journal of Media Literacy Education* 1(1): 1–11.

Hobbs, Renee, and Sandra McGee. 2014. "Teaching about Propaganda: An Examination of the Historical Roots of Media Literacy." *Journal of Media Literacy Education* 6 (2): 56–67.

Hogan, Diane M., and Jonathan R. H. Tudge. 1999. "Implications of Vygotsky's Theory for Peer Learning." In *The Rutgers Invitational Symposium on Education Series: Cognitive Perspectives on Peer Learning*, edited by Angela M. O'Donnell and Alison King, 39–65. Mahwah, NJ: Erlbaum.

Hoggart, Richard. 1957. *The Uses of Literacy*. London: Chatto & Windus.

Hung, Aaron Chia Yuan. 2011. *The Work of Play: Meaning Making in Video Games*. New York: Peter Lang.

Irvine, Amelia. 2018. "Don't Regulate Social Media Companies—Even If They Let Holocaust Deniers Speak." *USA Today*, July 19. https://www.usatoday.com/story/opinion/2018/07/19/dont-regulate-social-media-despite-bias-facebook-twitter-youtube-column/796471002/.

Ito, Mizuko. 2009. *Engineering Play: A Cultural History of Children's Software*. Cambridge, MA: MIT Press.

Ito, Mizuko. 2011. "Machinima in a Fanvid Ecology." *Journal of Visual Culture* 10 (1): 51–54.

Ito, Mizuko, Sonja Baumer, Matteo Bittanti, danah boyd, Rachel Cody, Becky Herr Stephenson, Heather A. Horst, et al. 2010. *Hanging Out, Messing Around, and Geeking Out: Kids Living and Learning with New Media*. Cambridge, MA: MIT Press.

Ito, Mizuko, Crystle Martin, Rachel Cody Pfister, Matthew H. Rafalow, Katie Salen, and Amanda Wortman. 2019. *Affinity Online: How Connection and Shared Interest Fuel Learning*. New York: New York University Press.

James, Carrie, Kate Davis, Andrea Flores, John M. Francis, Lindsay Pettingill, Margaret Rundle, and Howard Gardner. 2009. *Young People, Ethics, and the New Digital Media: A Synthesis from the GoodPlay Project*. Cambridge, MA: MIT Press.

Jenkins, Henry. 2006. *Convergence Culture: Where Old and New Media Collide*. New York: New York University Press.

Jenkins, Henry. 2013. *Textual Poachers: Television Fans and Participatory Culture*, twentieth anniversary ed. New York: Routledge.

Jenkins, Jolyon. 2015. "Should Parents Ever Worry about Minecraft?" *BBC News Magazine*, March 30. https://www.bbc.com/news/magazine-32051153.

Jolls, Tessa, and Carolyn Wilson. 2014. "The Core Concepts: Fundamental to Media Literacy Yesterday, Today and Tomorrow." *Journal of Media Literacy Education* 6 (2): 68–78.

Jowett, Garth S., Ian C. Jarvie, and Kathryn H. Fuller. 1996. *Children and the Movies: Media Influence and the Payne Fund Controversy*. Cambridge: Cambridge University Press.

Kane Thomas. 2018. "Sis vs Bro Are Bad Youtubers." Uploaded September 30. You-Tube video. https://www.youtube.com/watch?v=CkgFHZ51uYc.

Kantor, Emma. 2017. "Facts and Figures 2016: Children's Bestsellers Reflect Booming Backlists and Reinvigorated Franchises." *Publisher's Weekly,* March 23, 2017. https://www.publishersweekly.com/pw/by-topic/childrens/childrens-book-news/article/73159-facts-and-figures-2016-children-s-bestsellers-reflect-booming-backlists-and-reinvigorated-franchises.html.

Karina Kurzawa. 2020a. Karina Kurzawa (YouTube channel). Accessed February 1, 2020, at https://www.youtube.com/channel/UCNuC9twJI-mDg5TJQhy5RRQ.

Karina Kurzawa. 2020b. Karina Kurzawa (Instagram account). Accessed February 1, 2020, at https://www.instagram.com/kurzawa_karina/.

KeeperAction. 2017. "Sis vs Bro: Richest Kids of Youtube." Uploaded October 28. YouTube video. https://www.youtube.com/watch?v=vY7WeGLY66M.

Kelsey, Rick. 2017. "YouTube Star Dan TDM 'Not Prepared for Being a Role Model for a Young Audience.'" *BBC*, November 24. http://www.bbc.co.uk/newsbeat/article/42056879/youtube-star-dan-tdm-not-prepared-for-being-a-role-model-for-a-young-audience.

Keogh, Brendan. 2018. *A Play of Bodies: How We Perceive Videogames*. Cambridge, MA: MIT Press.

Kerttula, Tero. 2016. "'What an Eccentric Performance': Storytelling in Online Let's Plays." *Games and Culture* 14 (3): 236–255.

Kinder, Marsha. 1991. *Playing with Power in Movies, Television, and Video Games: From Muppet Babies to Teenage Mutant Ninja Turtles*. Berkeley: University of California Press.

King, Alison. 1999. "Discourse Patterns for Mediating Peer Learning." In *The Rutgers Invitational Symposium on Education Series: Cognitive Perspectives on Peer Learning*, edited by Angela M. O'Donnell and Alison King, 87–115. Mahwah, NJ: Erlbaum.

Klastrup, Lisbeth. 2009. "The Worldness of Everquest: Exploring a 21st Century Fiction." *Game Studies: The International Journal of Computer Game Research* 9 (1): http://gamestudies.org/0901/articles/klastrup.

Knorr, Caroline. 2019. "Parents' Ultimate Guide to YouTube." *Common Sense Media*, April 4. https://www.commonsensemedia.org/blog/parents-ultimate-guide-to-youtube.

Koerber, Brian. 2017. "Gaming the System: How Creepy YouTube Channels Trick Kids into Watching Violent Videos." *Mashable*, October 22. Accessed October 14, 2019, at https://mashable.com/2017/10/22/youtube-kids-app-violent-videos-seo-keywords/.

Kois, Dan. 2017. "Goop Therapy—How I Learned to Love My Kid's Obsession with Slime." *Slate*, May 12. https://slate.com/human-interest/2017/05/how-i-learned-to-love-my-kids-obsession-with-slime.html.

Kristi (@kalanthony2). 2019. *Wattpad*. Accessed April 19, 2019, at https://www.wattpad.com/user/kalanthony2.

Kumpulainen, Päivi Kristiina, and Julian Sefton-Green. 2014. "What Is Connected Learning and How to Research It?" *International Journal of Learning and Media* 4 (2): 7–18.

Kwebbelkop. 2019. "The Evolution of Minecraft! 2009–2019." Uploaded March 30. YouTube video. https://www.youtube.com/watch?v=f4hnJqGRTZ4.

Lange, Patricia G. 2014. *Kids on YouTube: Technical Identities and Digital Literacies*. London: Routledge.

Lankshear, Colin, and Michele Knobel. 2011. *New Literacies: Everyday Practices and Social Learning*, 3rd ed. Maidenhead: Open University Press.

Latour, Bruno. 2007. "Can We Get Our Materialism Back, Please?" *Isis: A Journal of the History of Science Society* 98 (1): 138–142.

Lave, Jean, and Etienne Wenger. 1991. *Situated Learning: Legitimate Peripheral Participation*. Cambridge: Cambridge University Press.

Leaver, Tama, and Crystal Abidin. 2017. "When Exploiting Kids for Cash Goes Wrong on YouTube: The Lessons of DaddyOFive." The Conversation. Accessed October 14, 2019, at https://theconversation.com/when-exploiting-kids-for-cash-goes-wrong-on-youtube-the-lessons-of-daddyofive-76932.

Leavis, F. R., and Denys Thompson. 1933. *Culture and Environment: The Training of Critical Awareness*. London: Chatto & Windus.

Lester, John. 2014. *99 Kids Jokes—Stampy Edition*. Scotts Valley, CA: CreateSpace.

Let's Play Index. 2019. "Minecraft—Let's Plays, Reviews, YouTube Channel Stats." Accessed April 16, 2019, at https://www.letsplayindex.com/games/minecraft-2011.

Livingstone, Sonia. 2002. *Young People and New Media: Childhood and the Changing Media Environment.* London: Sage.

Livingstone, Sonia. 2018a. "Children: A Special Case for Privacy?" *Intermedia* 46 (2): 18–23.

Livingstone, Sonia. 2018b. "Media Literacy—Everyone's Favourite Solution to the Problems of Regulation." Media Policy Project (blog), London School of Economics. Accessed October 13, 2019, at https://blogs.lse.ac.uk/mediapolicyproject/2018/05/08/media-literacy-everyones-favourite-solution-to-the-problems-of-regulation/.

Livingstone, Sonia, Giovanna Mascheroni, Michael Drier, Stephane Chaudron, and Kaat Lagae. 2015. *How Parents of Young Children Manage Digital Devices at Home: The Role of Income, Education and Parental Style.* London: EU Kids Online, LSE.

Livingstone, Sonia, and Julian Sefton-Green. 2016. *The Class: Living and Learning in the Digital Age.* New York: New York University Press.

Livingstone, Sonia, and Amanda Third. 2017. "Children and Young People's Rights in the Digital Age: An Emerging Agenda." *New Media and Society* 19 (5): 657–670.

Luke, Carmen. 1998. "Pedagogy and Authority: Lessons from Feminist and Cultural Studies, Postmodernism and Feminist Pedagogy." In *Teaching Popular Culture: Beyond Radical Pedagogy*, edited by David Buckingham, 18–41. London: UCL Press.

Luscombe, Belinda. 2017. "The YouTube Parents Who are Turning Family Moments into Big Bucks." *Time*, May 18. http://time.com/4783215/growing-up-in-public/.

Madden, Amy, Ian Ruthven, and David McMenemy. 2013. "A Classification Scheme for Content Analyses of YouTube Video Comments." *Journal of Documentation* 69 (5): 693–714.

MagicAnimalClub. 2013. "Stampy—Gaming Setup." Uploaded July 17. YouTube video. https://www.youtube.com/watch?v=ochfhGeiE3A.

MagicAnimalClub. 2015. "MineCon 2015—Day 1." Uploaded July 7. YouTube video. https://www.youtube.com/watch?v=PIq9o75vNYo.

MagicAnimalClub. 2016a. "Let's Talk—Online Safety." Uploaded January 11. YouTube video. https://www.youtube.com/watch?v=5VUsxQulYrg.

MagicAnimalClub. 2016b. "Let's Talk—Why I Play Minecraft on Console." Uploaded January 20. YouTube video. https://www.youtube.com/watch?v=ppIdwWCNjWw.

MagicAnimalClub. 2016c. "Let's Talk—How Can I get More Views On YouTube?" Uploaded February 17. YouTube video. https://www.youtube.com/watch?v=HcVyQ_qfRVs.

Maheshwari, Sapna. 2017. "On YouTube Kids, Startling Videos Slip Past Filters." *New York Times*, November 4, 2017. https://nyti.ms/2hGScmo.

Major, Nathaniel Lloyd. 2015. "Online Stars and the New Audience: How YouTube Creators Curate and Maintain Communities." Master's thesis, University of California, Irvine.

Marcuse, Herbert. 1964. *One-Dimensional Man*. Boston: Beacon Press.

Marsh, Jackie. 2004. "The Techno-Literacy Practices of Young Children." *Journal of Early Childhood Research* 2 (1): 51–66.

Marsh, Jackie. 2011. "Young Children's Literacy Practices in a Virtual World: Establishing an Online Interaction Order." *Reading Research Quarterly* 46 (2): 101–118.

Marshall, P. David. 2010. "The Promotion and Presentation of the Self: Celebrity as Marker of Presentational Media." *Celebrity Studies* 1 (1): 35–48.

Marwick, Alice. 2013. *Status Update: Celebrity, Publicity, and Branding in the Social Media Age*. New Haven, CT: Yale University Press.

Masterman, Len. 1980. *Teaching about Television*. London: Macmillan Education.

Mediawijzer. 2019. "10 Media Literacy Competences." Accessed April 30, 2019, at https://cdn.mediawijzer.net/wp-content/uploads/sites/6/2013/09/ENG-10-media-literacy-competences.pdf.

Meehan, Frank. 2014. "StampyLongHead Is the Future of Kids' Creative Education: How Minecraft YouTuber StampyLongHead Inspires My 8 Year Old and His Friends to Code, Create and Build." *Medium*. December 9. https://medium.com/@frank_meehan/i-just-want-to-watch-stampylonghead-how-minecraft-youtuber-stampylonghead-inspired-my-8-year-old-9b4bc3b64704.

Melson, Gail F. 2009. *Why the Wild Things Are: Animals in the Lives of Children*. Cambridge, MA: Harvard University Press.

Merz, Theo. 2014. "Stampylongnose: The Youtube Star You've Never Heard Of." *Telegraph*, July 23. http://www.telegraph.co.uk/men/the-filter/10980512/Stampylongnose-the-Youtube-star-youve-never-heard-of.html.

Meyer, Elizabeth. 2009. *Gender, Bullying, and Harassment: Strategies to End Sexism and Homophobia in Schools*. New York: Teachers College Press.

MicroProse. 1991. *Civilisation*. MS-DOS, Microsoft Windows, macOS, PlayStation, Sega Saturn, Super NES.

Mihailidis, Paul, and Samantha Viotty. 2017. "Spreadable Spectacle in Digital Culture: Civic Expression, Fake News, and the Role of Media Literacies in 'Post-Fact' Society." *American Behavioral Scientist* 61 (4): 441–454.

MINECON. 2019. "MINECON 2018, Minecraft." Accessed April 29, 2019, at https://www.minecraft.net/en-us/minecon/.

Minecraft. 2011. "The Evolution of Minecraft." Uploaded December 6. YouTube video. https://www.youtube.com/watch?v=t0eqSgkDuW0.

Minecraft. 2019a. "Official Minecraft Books!" Accessed April 29, 2019, at https://www.minecraft.net/en-us/article/official-minecraft-books.

Minecraft. 2019b. "The Minecraft Movie Is Just Around the corner." Accessed April 29, 2019, at https://www.minecraft.net/en-us/article/the-minecraft-movie-is-just-around-the-corner.

Minecraft Dungeons. 2019. "Minecraft: Dungeons." Accessed April 29, 2019, at https://www.minecraft.net/en-us/dungeons/.

Minecraft Shop. 2020. "Official Minecraft Store—Powered by J!NX." Accessed January 30, 2020, at https://www.minecraftshop.com/.

Minecraft Skins. 2020. "Minecraft Skins—The Skindex." Accessed January 30, 2020, at https://www.minecraftskins.com/.

Minecraft Wiki. "Programs and editors/Mod Coder Pack." Accessed April 29, 2019, at https://minecraft.gamepedia.com/Programs_and_editors/Mod_Coder_Pack.

Mojang. 2020. *Minecraft.* Microsoft Windows, Android, iOs, macOS, Linus, Xbox 360, Xbox One, PlayStation Vita, PS3, PS4, Wii U, Nintendo Switch, Kindle Fire, Gear VR, Apple TV, Fire TV (video game). Sweden: Mojang.

Mojang. 2019. *Minecraft Annual 2019.* London: Egmont Books.

Montfort, Nick, and Ian Bogost. 2009. *Racing the Beam: The Atari Video Computer System.* Cambridge, MA: MIT Press.

Mosley, Griffin. 2015a. *Stampy Cat's Strange New World.* Scotts Valley, CA: CreateSpace.

Mosley, Griffin. 2015b. *The Crazy Adventures of a Mining Maniac ft. Stampy Cat.* Scotts Valley, CA: CreateSpace.

Mosley, Griffin. 2015c. *Stampy's Love Affair: A Novel ft. StampyLongHead.* Scotts Valley, CA: CreateSpace.

Murphy, Patricia F. 1996. "Defining Pedagogy." In *Equity in the Classroom: Towards Effective Pedagogy for Girls and Boys,* edited by Patricia F. Murphy and Caroline V. Gipps, 9–22. Paris: UNESCO.

NAMLE. 2020. *Media Literacy Defined.* National Association for Media Literacy Education. Accessed January 31, 2020, at https://namle.net/publications/media-literacy-definitions/.

New London Group. 1996. "A Pedagogy of Multiliteracies: Designing Social Futures." *Harvard Education Review* 66 (1): 60–92.

Newman, James. 2016. "Stampylongnose and the Rise of the Celebrity Videogame Player." *Celebrity Studies* 7 (2): 285–288.

Nguyen, Josef. 2016. "Performing as Video Game Players in Let's Plays." *Transformative Works and Cultures* 22. Accessed April 19, 2019, at https://journal.transformativeworks .org/index.php/twc/article/view/698.

Nieborg, David B., and Thomas Poell. 2018. "The Platformization of Cultural Production: Theorising the Contingent Cultural Commodity." *New Media and Society* 20 (11): 4275–4292.

Niemeyer, Dodie J., and Hannah R. Gerber. 2015. "Maker Culture and 'Minecraft': Implications for the Future of Learning." *Educational Media International* 52 (3): 216–226.

Nintendo EPD. 2017. *The Legend of Zelda: Breath of the Wild.* Wii U, Nintendo Switch (video game). Tokyo: Nintendo.

Novy, Marianne. 2004. *Imagining Adoption: Essays on Literature and Culture.* Ann Arbor: University of Michigan Press.

Ofcom. 2019a. "Children and Parents: Media Use and Attitudes Report 2018." Accessed April 19, 2019, at https://www.ofcom.org.uk/__data/assets/pdf_file/0024/ 134907/Children-and-Parents-Media-Use-and-Attitudes-2018.pdf.

Ofcom. 2019b. "Why Children Spend Time Online." *Ofcom,* January 29. https:// www.ofcom.org.uk/about-ofcom/latest/media/media-releases/2019/why-children -spend-time-online.

Oosterloo, Eline. 2017. "A Let's Player's Playful Attitude in a YouTube Community." Master's thesis, Utrecht University.

Oxford Living Dictionaries. 2019. "Pedagogy." Accessed April 29, 2019, at https:// en.oxforddictionaries.com/definition/pedagogy.

Pangrazio, Luci, and Selwyn, Neil. 2019. "'Personal Data Literacies': A Critical Literacies Approach to Enhancing Understandings of Personal Digital Data." *New Media and Society* 21 (2): 419–437.

Papacharissi Zizi. 2015. *Affective Publics: Sentiment, Technology, and Politics.* Oxford: Oxford University Press.

Papacharissi, Zizi. 2018. *A Networked Self and Love.* New York: Routledge.

Papert, Seymour. 1980. *Mindstorms: Children, Computers, and Powerful Ideas.* New York: Basic Books.

Papert, Seymour. 1993. *The Children's Machine: Rethinking School in the Age of the Computer.* New York: Basic Books.

Papert, Seymour. 2002. "Hard Fun. *Bangor Daily News*. June 24. http://www.papert.org/articles/HardFun.html.

Perse, Elizabeth M., and Rebecca B. Rubin. 1989. "Attribution in Social and Parasocial Relationships." *Communication Research* 16 (1): 59–77.

Persson, Markus. 2012. "Gender in Minecraft." *World of Notch*, July 28. https://notch.tumblr.com/post/28188312756/gender-in-minecraft.

Phelan, Peggy. 1993. *Unmasked: The Politics of Performance*. London: Routledge.

Planet Minecraft. 2019. "Discussion." Accessed April 23, 2019, at https://www.planetminecraft.com/forums/minecraft/discussion/.

Polizzi, Gianfranco. 2018. "Misinformation and Critical Digital Literacy: To Trust or Not to Trust?" Media Policy Project (blog), London School of Economics. Accessed October 13, 2019, at https://blogs.lse.ac.uk/mediapolicyproject/2018/12/03/misinformation-and-critical-digital-literacy-to-trust-or-not-to-trust/.

Postigo, Hector. 2016 "The Socio-Technical Architecture of Digital Labour: Converting Play into YouTube Money." *New Media and Society* 18 (2): 332–349.

Precey, Matt. 2014. "Minecraft Gamer's YouTube Hit 'More Popular than Bieber.'" BBC News, March 7. https://www.bbc.com/news/uk-england-hampshire-26327661.

Provenzo, Eugene F., Jr. 1991. *Video Kids: Making Sense of Nintendo*. Cambridge, MA: Harvard University Press.

Publisher's Weekly. 2017. "The On-Sale Calendar: January 2017 Children's Books." *Publisher's Weekly*, November 6. https://www.publishersweekly.com/pw/by-topic/new-titles/on-sale-calendar/article/72122-the-on-sale-calendar-january-2017-children-s-books.html.

Putnam, Robert. 2001. *Bowling Alone: The Collapse and Revival of American Community*. New York: Simon and Schuster.

Ranking the Brands. 2018. "Kids Most Loved Brands." Accessed April 25, 2019, at https://www.rankingthebrands.com/The-Brand-Rankings.aspx?rankingID=214&year=1241.

Reality Check Team. 2019. "Social Media: How Can Governments Regulate It?" *BBC News*, April 8. https://www.bbc.com/news/technology-47135058.

Recktenwald, Daniel. 2014. "Interactional Practices in Let's Play Videos." Master's thesis, Saarland University.

Re-Logic. 2011. *Terraria*. Android, Microsoft Windows, iOs, macOS, Linus, Xbox One, PS4.

Resnick, Mitchel. 2017. *Lifelong Kindergarten: Cultivating Creativity through Projects, Passion, Peers, and Play*. Cambridge, MA: MIT Press.

Retallack, Hanna, Jessica Ringrose, and Emilie Lawrence. 2016. "'Fuck Your Body Image': Teen Girls' Twitter and Instagram Feminism in and around School." In *Learning Bodies: Perspectives on Children and Young People* edited by Julia Coffey, Shelley Budgeon, and Helen Cahill, 2:85–103. Singapore: Springer.

Rhodes, David. 2018. "Australian Sex Education Isn't Diverse Enough. Here's Why We Should Follow England's Lead." *Conversation*, August 7. https://theconversation.com/australian-sex-education-isnt-diverse-enough-heres-why-we-should-follow-englands-lead-100596.

Robehmed, Natalie, and Madeline Berg. 2018. "Highest-Paid YouTube Stars 2018: Markiplier, Jake Paul, PewDiePie and More." *Forbes*, December 3. https://www.forbes.com/sites/natalierobehmed/2018/12/03/highest-paid-youtube-stars-2018-markiplier-jake-paul-pewdiepie-and-more/#7a6256a909ac.

Roblox. 2020. "karinaOMG(GamerGirl) fanclub." Accessed January30, 2020, at https://www.roblox.com/groups/3234527/karinaOMG-GamerGirl-fanclub#!/about.

Roblox Corporation. 2005. *Roblox*. Android, Microsoft Windows, iOS, macOS, Xbox One, Macintosh Operating Systems, Fire OS.

Rojek, Chris. 2015. *Presumed Intimacy: Parasocial Interaction in Media, Society and Celebrity Culture*. Cambridge: Polity Press, 2015.

Romm, Tony, and Greg Bensinger. 2019. "Google Fined $US170m for Tracking Data on Kids as Young as 6." *Financial Review*, September 5. Accessed October 14, 2019, at https://www.afr.com/technology/google-fined-us170m-for-tracking-data-on-kids-as-young-as-6-20190905-p52o4z.

Rosney, Daniel. 2018. "After Logan Paul Scandal, YouTube Says It Shouldn't Be Regulated like TV." *BBC*, January 22. http://www.bbc.co.uk/newsbeat/article/42766079/after-logan-paul-scandal-youtube-says-it-shouldnt-be-regulated-like-tv.

Royal Society Edinburgh. 2015. "2015 RSE Christmas Lecture: Stampy's Christmas Cake Caper Clip 1." Uploaded December 8. YouTube video. https://www.youtube.com/watch?v=lqf8PTqn8ag.

RubRubaaduubdub. 2020. *Adopted . . . By StacyPlays?!* Accessed January 31, 2020, at https://www.wattpad.com/story/118027495-adopted-by-stacyplays.

Ryan Franklin. 2018. "Spoiled Rich Kids of YouTube [SIS vs BRO]." Uploaded March 23. YouTube video. https://www.youtube.com/watch?v=3CmbF6iBDoc.

Schön, Donald. 1987. *Educating the Reflective Practitioner*. San Francisco: Jossey-Bass.

Scully-Blaker, Rainforest, Jason Begy, Mia Consalvo, and Sarah Christina Ganzon. 2017. "Playing Along and Playing for on Twitch: Livestreaming from Tandem Play to Performance." In *Proceedings of the 50th Hawaii International Conference on System Sciences*, 2026–2035.

Sefton-Green, Julian. 2013. *Learning at Not-School: A Review of Study, Theory, and Advocacy for Education in Non-Formal Settings.* Cambridge, MA: MIT Press.

Selwyn, Neil. 2009. "The Digital Native—Myth and Reality." *Aslib Proceedings: New Information Perspectives* 61 (4): 364–379.

Senft, Theresa M. 2008. *Camgirls: Celebrity and Community in the Age of Social Networks.* New York: Peter Lang.

Shaytards. 2019. The Shaytards (YouTube channel). Accessed April 25, 2019, at https://www.youtube.com/user/SHAYTARDS.

Sheridan, Mary, and Jennifer Rowsell. 2010. *Design Literacies: Learning and Innovation in the Digital Age.* New York: Routledge.

Shulman, Lee. 1987. "Knowledge and Teaching: Foundations of the New Reform." *Harvard Educational Review* 57 (1): 1–21.

Silcoff, Mireille. 2014. "A Mother's Journey through the Unnerving Universe of 'Unboxing' Videos." *New York Times Magazine*, August 15. https://www.nytimes.com/2014/08/17/magazine/a-mothers-journey-through-the-unnerving-universe-of-unboxing-videos.html.

Simon, Brian. 1983. "The Study of Education as a University Subject in Britain." *Studies in Higher Education* 8 (1): 1–13.

SIS vs BRO. 2017a. "SHOPPING FOR A NEW HOUSE!!!!" Uploaded September 2. YouTube video. https://www.youtube.com/watch?v=ZgrxU4aFO0I&t=1350s.

SIS vs BRO. 2017b. "HOUSE TOUR!!!!!" Uploaded October 3. YouTube video. https://www.youtube.com/watch?v=Q4kx8p1u5rA.

SIS vs BRO. 2018a. "Karina's Room Tour." Uploaded January 6. YouTube video. https://www.youtube.com/watch?v=ERfbbgWLT14&t=1s.

SIS vs BRO. 2018b. "Going to DUBAI." Uploaded February 28. YouTube video. https://www.youtube.com/watch?v=hmel4cPP0Xk.

SIS vs BRO. 2018c. "Going Vacation in Business Class!!!" Uploaded March 30. YouTube video. https://www.youtube.com/watch?v=Je_j83Tfyhc.

SIS vs BRO. 2018d. "Going To USA!!!!" Uploaded June 20. YouTube video. https://www.youtube.com/watch?v=qZFuRyqoSlw.

SIS vs BRO. 2018e. "MEETING YOUTUBERS!!! WHATREALLY HAPPENED AT VIDCON!!!" Uploaded June 23.YouTube video. https://www.youtube.com/watch?v=SKBa3zhvVMw.

SIS vs BRO. 2018f. "Last Thing on Our iPhone X!!!" Uploaded August 1. YouTube video. https://www.youtube.com/watch?v=ZZ6cXilL9ms.

SIS vs BRO. 2018g. "25 Things You Didn't Know About SIS vs BRO!!!" Uploaded October 10. YouTube video. https://www.youtube.com/watch?v=pfGhXLS9iXI.

SIS vs BRO. 2018h. "Don't Choose the Wrong Soap Slime Challenge!!!" Uploaded November 10. YouTube video. https://www.youtube.com/watch?v=8haEgpm9zX0.

SIS vs BRO. 2020. *SIS vs BRO* (YouTube channel). Accessed February 1, 2020, at https://www.youtube.com/channel/UChLN0bJgq6d15OK2HVB4YTg.

Smith, Aaron, Skye Toor, and Patrick van Kessel. 2018. "Many Turn to YouTube for Children's Content, News, How-To Lessons." PEW Research Centre, November 7. https://www.pewinternet.org/2018/11/07/many-turn-to-youtube-for-childrens-content-news-how-to-lessons/.

Smith, Thomas, Marianna Obrist, and Peter Wright. 2013. "Live-Streaming Changes the (Video) Game." In *Proceedings of the 11th European Conference on Interactive TV and Video*, 131–138.

Snubmansters. 2015. "Copious Dogs Mod." Accessed January 31, 2020, at http://ww1.snubmansters.com/.

Social Blade. 2020a. "thediamondcart YouTube Stats, Channel Statistics." Accessed January 30, 2020, at https://socialblade.com/youtube/user/thediamondminecart.

Social Blade. 2020b. "PopularMMOs YouTube Stats, Channel Statistics." Accessed January 30, 2020, at https://socialblade.com/youtube/user/popularmmos.

Social Blade. 2020c. "GamerGirl YouTube Stats, Channel Statistics." Accessed January 30, 2020, at https://socialblade.com/youtube/channel/UCije75lmV_7fVP7m4dJ7ZoQ.

Social Blade. 2020d. "YouTube Statistical History for Stampylonghead." Accessed January 30, 2020, at https://socialblade.com/youtube/user/stampylonghead/monthly.

Social Blade. 2020e. "Analytics Made Easy." Accessed January 31, 2020, at https://socialblade.com/.

Social Blade. 2020f. "Stacyplays YouTube Stats, Channel Statistics." Accessed January 31, 2020, at https://socialblade.com/youtube/user/stacyplays.

Social Blade. 2020g. "Karina Kurzawa YouTube Stats, Channel Statistics. Accessed February 1, 2020, at https://socialblade.com/youtube/channel/UCNuC9twJI-mDg 5TJQhy5RRQ.

Social Blade. 2020h. "RonaldOMG YouTube Stats, Channel Statistics. Accessed February 1, 2020, at https://socialblade.com/youtube/channel/UCfjLwqL4XSPUD T7hVnViCmw.

Social Blade. 2020j. "SIS vs Bro YouTube Stats, Channel Statistics. Accessed February 1, 2020, at https://socialblade.com/youtube/channel/UChLN0bJgq6d15OK2HVB4YTg.

Social Blade. 2020j. "Freddy YouTube Stats, Channel Statistics. Accessed February 1, 2020, at https://socialblade.com/youtube/channel/UCtJe4NoCrHVFiLxcIi4gPvg.

Squire, Kurt. 2011. *Video Games and Learning: Teaching and Participatory Culture in the Digital Age*. New York: Teachers College Press.

Squire, Kurt. 2012. "Designed Cultures." In *Games, Learning, and Society: Learning and Meaning in the Digital Age*, edited by Constance Steinkuehler, Kurt Squire, and Sash Barab, 10–31. Cambridge: Cambridge University Press.

Stacy Hinojosa. 2019. "Stacy Hinojosa—YouTube Creator—StacyPlays YouTube Channel, LinkedIn." Accessed April 28, 2019, at https://www.linkedin.com/in/stacyhinojosa.

Stacy Plays Wiki. 2019. "Stacy Hinojosa: StacyPlays Wiki, FANDOM Powered by Wikia." Accessed April 28, 2019, at https://stacyplays.fandom.com/wiki/Stacy_Hinojosa.

stacyplays. 2014. "Slime and Drool: Dogcraft (Ep.20). Uploaded June 14. YouTube video. https://www.youtube.com/watch?v=r2mrkneg3Ko.

stacyplays. 2015. "The Creeper Simulator: Dogcraft (Ep.89)." Uploaded February 7. YouTube video. https://www.youtube.com/watch?v=rfL5NtHkOao.

stacyplays. 2016a. "The Arf Gallery: Dogcraft (Ep.229)." Uploaded June 8. YouTube video. https://www.youtube.com/watch?v=CrS32vYbO_0.

stacyplays. 2016b. "ON STAGE IN FRONT OF 14,000 PEOPLE!—MINECON 2016 DAY 1." Uploaded September 27. YouTube video. https://www.youtube.com/watch?v=3AY5B98xlVM.

stacyplays. 2017a. "MY NEW SERIES—MINECRAFT FIELD TRIPS (TRAILER)." Uploaded January 16. YouTube video. https://www.youtube.com/watch?v=UGGHcdRBWdM.

stacyplays. 2017b. "Minecraft IRL! THE MEGA TAIGA." Uploaded January 20. YouTube video. https://www.youtube.com/watch?v=m3Eo5StoMAo&t=227s.

StacyPlays. 2018. *Wild Rescuers: Guardians of the Taiga*. New York: HarperCollins.

stacyplays. 2018. *StacyPlays* (YouTube channel). Accessed June 28, 2019, at https://www.youtube.com/user/stacyplays/about.

stacyplays. 2019. "About." Accessed March 28, 2019, at https://www.youtube.com/user/stacyplays/about.

StacyPlays. 2019. *Wild Rescuers: Escape to the Mesa*. New York: HarperCollins.

stacyvlogs. 2017a. "Page Gets Surgery! (Warning: Graphic)." Uploaded July 4. YouTube video. https://www.youtube.com/watch?v=02F_HGR0UfQ.

stacyvlogs. 2017b. "My Mom Has Cancer." Uploaded October 14. YouTube video. https://www.youtube.com/watch?v=x1VSKy4KkDQ.

stacyvlogs. 2019. StacyVlogs (YouTube channel). Accessed March 28, 2019, at https://www.youtube.com/user/stacyvlogs.

stampylonghead. 2015. "Minecraft Xbox—Big Barn [348]." Uploaded October 21. YouTube video. https://www.youtube.com/watch?v=86suYf8eAqk.

stampylonghead. 2017. "My Lovely Problem." YouTube video. Uploaded August 26. YouTube video. https://www.youtube.com/watch?v=a04kzHAmgQo.

stampylonghead. 2019. Wonder Quest (YouTube channel). Accessed March 28, 2019, at https://www.youtube.com/channel/UC7O_8zNcaWMEj4Kc844Cieg.

stampylongnose. 2016a. "Let's Talk—Hate Comments." Uploaded March 13, 2016. YouTube video. https://www.youtube.com/watch?v=KOumeKDMddo&t=1s.

stampylongnose. 2016b. "Let's Talk—Family Friendly Youtuber." Uploaded March 24. YouTube video. https://www.youtube.com/watch?v=a2rOiSZ0agc.

stampylongnose. 2016c. "Let's Talk—You Can't Please Everyone." Uploaded April 11. YouTube video. https://www.youtube.com/watch?v=0BtVmQfWsEg.

stampylongnose. 2016d. "Let's Talk—Fake Stamps." Uploaded May 4. YouTube video. https://www.youtube.com/watch?v=XTibbJhPIsI.

stampylongnose. 2017a. "Let's Talk—Is My Channel Dying?" Uploaded March 11. YouTube video. https://www.youtube.com/watch?v=N9DTw12rqgM.

stampylongnose. 2017b. "Let's Talk—The Future of My Channel." Uploaded May 9. YouTube video. https://www.youtube.com/watch?v=D7Re4Ztp6ok.

stampylongnose. 2017c. "Let's Talk—It's Personal." Uploaded November 15. YouTube video. https://www.youtube.com/watch?v=29A7xIpqftI.

stampylongnose. 2018a. "Let's Talk—Questions and Answers—Episode 4." Uploaded on June 6. YouTube video. https://www.youtube.com/watch?v=gy_YwRodlyk.

stampylongnose. 2018b. "Let's Talk—How Minecraft Is Changing." Uploaded June 12. YouTube video. https://www.youtube.com/watch?v=nL6JiqnAvVI.

stampylongnose. 2018c. "Let's Talk—Good and Bad News." Uploaded August 6. YouTube video. https://www.youtube.com/watch?v=jL_p8iRo0jg.

stampylongnose. 2019. Stampylongnose (YouTube channel). Accessed March 29, 2019, at https://www.youtube.com/user/stampylongnose.

Steinkuehler, Constance, and Yoonsin Oh. 2012. "Apprenticeship in Massively Multiplayer Online Games." In *Games, Learning, and Society: Learning and Meaning in the Digital Age,* edited by Constance Steinkuehler, Kurt Squire, and Sasha Barab, 154–184. Cambridge: Cambridge University Press.

Stoilova, Mariya, Sonia Livingstone, and Rishita Nandagiri. 2019. *Children's Data and Privacy Online: Growing Up in a Digital Age.* Research findings. London: London School of Economics and Political Science. Accessed January 31, 2020, at http://www.lse.ac.uk/my-privacy-uk/Assets/Documents/Childrens-data-and-privacy-online-report-for-web.pdf.

Stone, Tom. 2018. "Official Minecraft Books! A Beginner's Guide to the Library of Minecraft!" *Mojang,* December 12. Accessed April 22, 2019, at https://www.minecraft.net/en-us/article/official-minecraft-books.

Suggitt, Connie. 2018. "YouTube Star Stampy Cat Sets New Minecraft Record for Gamer's Edition 2019." *Guinness World Record,* September 7. http://www.guinnessworldrecords.com/news/2018/9/youtube-star-stampy-cat-sets-new-minecraft-record-for-gamers-edition-2019-539361.

Sutton-Smith, Brian. 2001. *The Ambiguity of Play.* Cambridge, MA: Harvard University Press.

Telltale. 2019. "Minecraft: Story Mode—Telltale." Accessed April 29, 2019, at https://telltale.com/series/minecraft-story-mode/.

Tolson, Andrew. 2001. "'Being Ourself': The Pursuit of Authentic Celebrity." *Discourse Studies* 3 (4): 443–457.

Tom Slime. 2019. Tom Slime (YouTube channel). Accessed April 25, 2019, at https://www.youtube.com/channel/UCOs8VELPB5GC_eKibH9e-CQ.

Tommy. 2017. "10 Year Old Buys $1,000,000 Mansion . . . [Sis vs Bro]." Uploaded October 8. YouTube video. https://www.youtube.com/watch?v=mW2C_2juJmU.

Top Tens. 2018. "Top Ten Child Friendly Minecraft Youtubers." Accessed April 26, 2019, at https://www.thetoptens.com/child-friendly-minecraft-youtubers/.

Topping, Keith. 2005. "Trends in Peer Learning." *Educational Psychology* 25 (6): 631-645.

Turkle, Sherry. 2011. *Alone Together: Why We Expect More from Technology and Less from Each Other.* New York: Basic Books.

Turner, Graeme. 2013. *Understanding Celebrity.* London: Sage.

UnstoppableLuck. 2019. *Unstoppable Luck* (YouTube channel). Accessed April 30, 2019, at https://www.youtube.com/user/UnstoppableLuck/videos.

Verant Interactive 989 Studios. 1999. *Everquest.* San Diego: Sony Online Entertainment.

VidCon. 2019. "About—VidCon US." Accessed April 29, 2019, at http://vidcon.com/about/.

Von Feilitzen, Cecilia, and Carlsson, Ulla. 2003. *Promote or Protect? Perspectives on Media Literacy and Media Regulations.* Göteborg University: Nordicom UNESCO International Clearinghouse on Children, Youth and Media.

Vrabel, Jeff. 2017. "Why Do My Kids Waste Hours Watching Millennials Play Video Games on YouTube?" *Washington Post*, October 12, 2017. https://www.washingtonpost.com/news/parenting/wp/2017/10/12/why-do-my-kids-waste-hours-watching-millennials-play-video-games-on-youtube/.

Vygotsky, L. S. 1986. *Thought and Language.* Translated by A. Kozulin. Cambridge, MA: MIT Press.

Walkerdine, Valarie. 2006. "Playing the Game: Young Girls Performing Femininity in Video Game Play." *Feminist Media Studies* 6 (4): 519–537.

Wattpad. 2019. "Wattpad—Where Stories Live." Accessed April 26, 2019, at https://www.wattpad.com/.

Wenger, Etienne. 1998. *Communities of Practice: Learning, Meaning, and Identity.* Cambridge: Cambridge University Press.

Whitton, Nicola. 2014. *Digital Games and Learning: Research and Theory.* New York: Routledge.

Willett, Rebekah. 2018. "*Microsoft* Bought *Minecraft* . . . Who Knows What's Going to Happen?! A Sociocultural Analysis of 8–9-Year Olds' Understanding of Commercial Online Gaming Industries." *Learning, Media, Technology* 43 (1): 101–116.

Willett, Rebekah, Chris Richards, Jackie Marsh, Andrew Burn, and Julia Bishop. 2013. *Children and Media Playground Cultures.* New York: Palgrave Macmillan.

Williams, Raymond. 1958. *Culture and Society.* London: Chatto and Windus.

Williams, Raymond. 1968. *Communications (second edition).* London: Penguin.

Wingfield, Nick. 2015. "Minecraft Stars on YouTube Share Secrets to Their Celebrity." *New York Times*, May 20. https://nyti.ms/1EY9SLR.

Wohlwend, Karen E., and Tolga Kargin. 2013. "'Cause I Know How to Get Friends—Plus They Like My Dancing': (L)earning the Nexus of Practice in Club Penguin." In *Children's Virtual Play Worlds: Culture, Learning and Participation,* edited by Anne Burke and Jackie Marsh, 10–25. New York: Peter Lang.

Wonder Quest. 2015. Wonder Quest—Episode 1:| Stampylonghead aka Stampy Cat." Uploaded April 25. YouTube video. https://www.youtube.com/watch?v=_AuP6eQjV8Q.

Woollaston, Victoria. 2014. "Making Money out of MINECRAFT: Barman Gives Up Job to Upload Tips on the Game—and Now His YouTube Channel Gets More Hits Than One Direction and Justin Bieber." *Daily Mail Australia*, March 6. http://www.dailymail.co.uk/sciencetech/article-2573860/Making-money-MINECRAFT-Barman-gives-job-play-game-professionally-Youtube-channel-gets-hits-One-Direction-Justin-Bieber.html.

XboxAddictionz. 2017. "?TROLLING THE STRANGEST KID EVER ON MINECRAFT! (MINECRAFT TROLLING)." Uploaded September 26. YouTube video. https://www.youtube.com/watch?v=Xlroa9HMM7Q.

YouTube. 2014. "Minecraft's Stampy Longnose and Squid on Good Morning Britain Interview 26/5/2014." Accessed January 31, 2020, at https://www.youtube.com/watch?v=8M-xel5ZQds.

YouTube. 2019. "More Updates on Our Actions Related to the Safety of Minors on YouTube." Creator (blog). Accessed October 14, 2019, at https://youtube-creators.googleblog.com/2019/02/more-updates-on-our-actions-related-to.html

Zariko, Zhia. 2016. "Screening Embodiment: Let's Play Videos and Observable Play Experiences." Master's thesis, RMIT University.

Index